Y0-BZF-774

No Shoes in Summer

The material for this book was initially compiled
by students at Grange Community College,
Donaghmede, Dublin 13

No Shoes in Summer

Compiled and edited by
MARY RYAN,
SEÁN BROWNE & KEVIN GILMOUR

GARDEN CITY PUBLIC LIBRARY

GARDEN CITY
NEW YORK

WOLFHOUND PRESS

Reprinted 1995

First published 1995 by
WOLFHOUND PRESS Ltd
68 Mountjoy Square
Dublin 1

and Wolfhound Press (UK)
18 Coleswood Rd
Harpenden
Herts AL5 1EQ

© 1995 Texts: Individual contributors
Compilation and editing © 1995 The editors

All rights reserved. No part of this book may be reproduced or utilised in any form or by
any means electronic or mechanical including photography, filming, recording, video
recording, photocopying, or by any information storage and retrieval system or shall not,
by way of trade or otherwise, be lent, resold or otherwise circulated in any form of binding
or cover other than that in which it is published without prior permission in writing from
the publisher. The moral rights of the author have been asserted.

Wolfhound Press receives financial assistance from the Arts Council/An
Chomhairle Ealaíon, Dublin.

British Library Cataloguing in Publication Data
A catalogue record for this book is available from the British Library.

ISBN 0 86327 487 0

2 4 5 3

Typesetting: Wolfhound Press
Cover design: Daire Ní Bhréartúin
Cover painting: 'The Swing' by George Russell (AE). Courtesy of The Gorry Gallery
Printed in Ireland by Colour Books Ltd

CONTENTS

CHAPTER I: AN SAOL FADÓ IN DEV'S IRELAND
Sketches of Ireland 1920s to 1940s

CHAPTER II: BEFORE THE SCHOOL BUS

First Communion and Confirmation

CHAPTER III: GOD BLESS THIS WORK! Rural Ireland as it was

CHAPTER IV: EMERGENCIES AND OTHER TROUBLED TIMES

CHAPTER V: STRANGERS IN BALLYMUN: Dublin and Environs

CHAPTER VI: LOVE'S SWEET LULLABY

CHAPTER VII: REMEMBERED LIVES
Reminiscences and Autobiographical Fragments

CHAPTER VIII: THE RAMBLING HOUSE
With some pishogues and other sayings

CHAPTER IX: THE HOLLY BOUGH
Memories of Christmases long ago

CHAPTER X: TIMES OF SORROW, TIMES OF JOY

CHAPTER XI: IN STORY AND IN VERSE

CHAPTER XII: THE FOUR SEASONS

FOREWORD
Eilís Dillon

The mixed culture in which we live, often a great advantage in the matter of understanding our fellow-man, makes us all uneasy lest we are endangering our own invaluable native culture, underrating it to the point where it may feel that it has nothing further to contribute to our lives. This anthology can relieve our feelings from that apprehension. The danger remains, of course, but the essential vitality that produced the absorbing interest in humanity, which is the basis of the newly-admitted culture, is very evident.

Reading through these contributions to our living cultural heritage, I was struck by the general optimism and pleasure in natural beauty of all kinds, which they celebrate. Summers are always sunny, drinking fathers and uncles are forgiven or at least understood, mothers are appreciated though sometimes laughed at, much as in A CHILD'S CHRISTMAS IN WALES, with the same beady-eyed, dispassionate, understanding stare.

The idea of the anthology is a splendid one. When I became a grandmother, I didn't appreciate the 'Welcome to the club' attitude that came from the generation that had already arrived there, somewhat older than I was, perhaps. I soon found out that grandparents are highly valued in our society, because of the national interest in storytelling and by extension in history. As a nation, we are sometimes criticised for our interest in history but I believe that a country that doesn't know its own history is a worthless one. Living in many countries I have observed that the most successful societies exist when there is no conflict between the generations, when communication exists between the different ages and each one constantly learns from the other.

This anthology differs from one that I remember in the thirties, when school-children were asked to note stories and folklore recited by their elders. Alas, the children were not proof against the opportunities this invitation offered for invention, and they delightedly supplied many pieces of folklore which will confuse future scholars if they are taken for gospel.

One of the most striking things about this collection is the flexibility of the contributors, who, moving through so many life stages, always take with them a clear impression of free, open minds full of human kindness and understanding. There is one woman who describes an experience of five life stages from office cleaner to world traveller in Africa. I know few people who could write so well and so clearly and with such literary certainty.

I hope there will be more of these pieces and that this collection will reach the audience it deserves.

Eilís Dillon

ACKNOWLEDGEMENTS

The editors can never thank enough:

Marcella McNally, Robert P. Savage, Gay Byrne and Eithne Hand, Jeremiah Cronin & the Co. Dublin V.E.C., and the following in alphabetical order:

Bridie Beale, Valerie Caughlin, Mary Coll and John Battler, Colleagues at Grange Community College, Frank Costello, Tony Dodd, Merseyside Radio; P.J. Downey, Etty Drumm, Very Rev. Cecil A. Faull, Susan Gamble, Gardai in Ballina, Dunlaoghaire, Drogheda, Ferrybank, Kiltimagh, Manorhamilton, Mitchelstown, Limerick; Tom Johnston, Nan Joyce, Dellemar Keane, Libraries in Downpatrick, Enniskillen, Newry, Warrenpoint; Beatrice Lennon, Nell McCafferty, Nuala McCafferty, Jean McKeown, Finín Máirtín, Gertrude Meehan, Gerry Miller, Rosemary Moriarty, Siobhan & Brendan Mulvey, Pat O'Donovan, Radio Sport, RTE; Dáithí Ó Máirtín, Stephen O'Hare, Breege and Martin Joe O'Toole, Parents' Association at Grange Community College, Past and present students at Grange Community College, Lisa Pollard, Post Office at Kiltimagh and Pontoon; Roxboro Community Guards, Secretarial Class Grange Community College, Stafford Police, Mary Teefy, Margaret Tobin, Albert Walsh, Wolfhound Press' long-suffering and patient staff. A special appreciation for Méabh Browne who helped select the title and assisted in proof-reading, etc.

The following are the Transition Year students (1993/'94) at Grange Community College who organised the initial collection and collation of this anthology:

Michelle Birney, Seamus Carberry, Barry Deegan, Noel Dowling, Carol Duffy, John Hughes, Claire Kelly, Terence Kelly, Marie Magee, Neville Magee, Derek McMahon, Kelley O'Brien, Lisa O'Brien, Paul O'Brien, Robert Phillips, Brian Pitt, Karen Rowan, Aidan Scully, Trevor Towell, Joanne Whelan.

GRANGE COMMUNITY COLLEGE GOLDEN WRITING FUND

A substantial portion of any royalties earned from the sale of this book will be used to help fund the new 'Grange Community College Golden Writing Award'. This award will consist of financial prizes for people over 60 years of age who wish to record their memories or engage in creative writing.

The following people are trustees of the fund: Eamonn de Buitlear, Robert Carrickford, Breda Dunlea, Lola Heffernan, Hugh Leonard, David Lord, Mary Ryan, Andree Sheehy-Skeffington, Hilda Tweedy.

It is hoped that the fund will become a permanent feature of Irish life.

INTRODUCTION

This book is a unique and exciting anthology of memories, folklore, creative writing, poetry and pishrogues — the extraordinary voices of women and men born between the 1890s and the 1930s.

The history you will find in these pages is not to be found so readily in conventional history books. Here are the voices of a cross-section of the people of Ireland, from all four provinces, from every county, and beyond. All share one common purpose — to relate their experiences in their own words and to tell us something about their lives. While reflecting their differences of experience, the book celebrates being Irish, in many and diverse ways.

No Shoes in Summer grew out of a Transition Year project in a County Dublin V.E.C. school. In an attempt to foster better communication between the generations, Mary Ryan's class in Grange Community College, Donaghmede was encouraged to collect memories, writings, folklore, tales etc. from their grandparents and other older people of their acquaintance. The project bore first fruits in a number of booklets issued by the students, and this encouraged a more ambitious effort, contributions being invited on a national scale through the Gay Byrne Show on radio.

The result was a veritable avalanche of over a million words in autobiographies, stories, poems, etc. What appears in this volume is a selection from this material, a selection sometimes achieved only after the most painful decisions on what to leave out. All of those who submitted material are represented in this volume — on the basis that each person's experience, each person's memory has something to offer.

The book is divided into twelve chapters covering various themes. A word of caution however — contributors range naturally over many topics, places and times; so for example, nuggets of folklore appear in several sections, and dramatic stories of the 'Troubles' can be found in other chapters. The first chapter was used to collect a number of longer contributions and to serve as a kind of introduction to the era and to the book as a whole.

In response to the huge array of talent evident in these contributions, an independent trust fund called 'Grange Community

Golden Writing Fund' has been established to promote and support writing by Older People. Part of the profits from this book go to finance this fund. It is hoped that writing competitions for older people who create fiction, non-fiction and poetry will be the legacy of this publication.

This is the contributors' book. It is their lives, their work, their thoughts and memories which are presented here, and as editors we are grateful to them for being prepared to record for the present and for the future generations their life experiences. In particular, these Third-Agers offer to the young readers today an invaluable and entertaining portrait of life in pre-sixties Ireland. We have been privileged as editors to have worked on their book. We hope that it offers as much pleasure and enrichment to you, the reader as we have experienced during our involvement with the anthology.

The Editors.

I

AN SAOL FADÓ IN DEV'S IRELAND
Sketches of Ireland 1920s to 1940s

The ideal Ireland that we would have, the Ireland that we dreamed of, would be the home of a people who valued material wealth only as a basis for right living, of a people who, satisfied with frugal comfort, devoted their leisure to things of the spirit, a land whose countryside would be bright with cosy homesteads, whose fields and villages would be joyous with the sounds of industry, with the romping of happy children, the contests of athletic youth and the laughter of happy maidens, whose firesides would be forums for the wisdom of serene old age ... .

Eamon de Valera (Address broadcast on Radio Éireann)
St Patrick's Day, 1943

CHILDHOOD AND OTHER MEMORIES
Dersie Leonard (b 1918)

(Extracts from an autobiography) Burren, County Clare, 1920s

I arrived in this world on a dark February day. It was raining in the hopeless manner it does at that time of the year, when the atmosphere is laden with vapour and the shrubs and evergreens glisten and shine in blackness against the dull sky. I grew up in the lower end of the Burren, a remote area of County Clare. It was very beautiful and historic with lakes and rivers, good land and bad, bog and rocks, not to mention fairy rings and forts — in fact everything a person could wish for.

I started school at six years of age. It was a small mixed school and life was fairly pleasant there. There were just two rooms and two female teachers. The toilet was outside; it wasn't very hygienic and had no door to it.

I walked the three miles there and back with my brothers and sisters. On our way we used call for the classmates and friends

whose houses we happened to pass. Age difference wasn't important in those days; neither did it matter whether our friends were
male or female.

The journey to school was a nice walk on a sunny day but in
bad weather was another story. There was very little shelter on
the road; there were no walls and ditches were few and far between, so we had to brave the elements. Very often in winter we
got soaked to the skin.

All the pupils had to, in turn, pick sticks on their way to school.
These sticks were used to start the school fire. If they were wet
this was an almost impossible task and we all had to sit around in
our wet clothes waiting. Some pupils were asked to bring a horse
load of turf to keep the fire burning for the year so there was
never any shortage of fuel once the fire got going.

The teachers were not much better off than the pupils. Both of
them lived a few miles from the school and had to cycle there and
back. We were very lucky in that our Headmistress made cocoa in
the lunch hour. This was much appreciated by everyone. Then,
when school was over, we had to trudge the long road home
again in the evenings. More often than not we wet our clothes,
stockings and boots (which had more than likely just about dried
out by then) a second time.

In bad weather we were always cold and miserable on the long
walk home. Often we used have to take a short cut through
water-logged fields to avoid Mrs. Connor, one of our odd neighbours, but more about her later on. We never delayed but hurried
home to a hot dinner of bacon, cabbage and lovely floury potatoes.

In the country, in the Twenties, there were few distractions for
children in the evening. We didn't have our classmates knocking
on the door with, 'Are you coming out to play?' In the winter
there were always plenty of jobs to be done around the house after the dinner. A can of spring water might have to be got, or turf
to be carried in for the fire, not to mention the washing up and
tidying.

When the chores were done it was time to do our school exercise. This generally took about three hours. Each night we had to
learn a few questions from the Catechism and the Bible had to be
learned from cover to cover. Inspectors called regularly to the
school and no-one escaped their questions. If a child didn't have
the correct answer then God help him or her — on the Inspector's
departure the ruler or switch was taken out without hesitation.

Banks of turf were rented to people who had no bog of their
own and to people from the village three miles away. On the

day appointed to cut the turf these people would arrive at about seven o'clock in the morning. They would be seen jogging along in their pony and cart, heading for the bank apportioned to them where they would spend twelve hours back-breaking work to keep their families warm and cosy for the winter.

As children we loved this day of days. A turf fire was set and lit and a kettle placed over it. The tea always tasted of heather and was slightly smoky. When the tea had been made the fire was put out because if it spread, hundreds of acres of bog and turf would be in danger. Then we set off to our picnic spot in the nearby forest where we set up a shop under some trees. By this I mean a make-believe shop. We picked wild violets, heather and primroses and sold them for old broken delft which we called 'chanies'. To this day I can remember that spot and know exactly where it is, although I haven't visited it for forty or more years.

When the turf was cut it had to be saved. This involved leaving it flat to dry. After some days each sod had to be turned over and then put into little heaps raised off the ground. When saved and dried the sods were thrown into clamps weighing about two hundredweight and another several days were spent drawing these home.

Although cutting, saving and drawing home the turf was a long, tedious job, it seemed much easier in those long hot summer days. Today very few people cut turf in this manner. With modern equipment there is no longer any need for this very physical work. Besides, I doubt present generations would have the muscle and bone of their forefathers.

Many years later, after my father's death, the bog on his home place was reclaimed. Now it is clear fertile land yielding wheat and other crops. In my youth the road leading up to it was what one would describe as the 'old bog road'. Now it is a beautiful new road, about two miles long. I wish my parents and their neighbours could see it now. Perhaps they can.

My mother was born in 1876. Not only was she a very beautiful woman and a pillar of strength and courage, but she was also what would now be called an all-rounder. You name it, she did it. She had a spinning wheel and she used spin wool from the sheep's fleece and then knit beautiful warm clothes for us. For years afterwards that old spinning wheel stood in an attic room. In the Thirties there was no interest in something that was no longer in use. Perhaps this was because there wasn't enough time to pursue interests and hobbies or perhaps because we were too concerned with the business of survival. Either way this spinning wheel was forgotten about and fell to pieces. In those days, beautiful antique furniture, which could be bought for little or nothing, suffered the same fate. With spiralling prices nowadays only the well-off can afford to furnish their homes with this type of furniture.

My mother was also a great cook. I shall never forget her beautiful baking or cooking. She used to make apple tarts regularly, and rhubarb, when in season. Apple tarts were made from flour, a pinch of salt and thick cream poured from the crock in which it was kept. These were mixed together, kneaded and rolled out on a white scrubbed table.

Apples were then prepared and added to the pastry on a large 'Dunville's' tray. Dunville's was a whiskey and these trays were used in public houses for carrying drinks to the snug. The top pastry was then added and a few slits put in to let out the steam. Some egg was then brushed over the tart and a sprinkling of brown sugar added. The tart was then baked in a pot oven with plenty of red coals on top and bottom. This took about one hour. When the lid was removed the aroma that filled the kitchen was such that it remained for the rest of the day. The tart had so much juice in it, that when cooled the filling became jelly.

1927 saw the advent of electricity. I remember seeing the electric light being switched on in a large town around about that time. Everyone came out of their houses and shops and stood on the street waiting for the 'magic' to happen. There was such an uproar and wonder that some thought the end of the world was near.

In the country we had oil lamps — one to hang on a wall in the kitchen and a fancy one with red coloured glass for the parlour. Candles were used otherwise. At that time the open fire was a tradition in every farmhouse. There were two hobs, one at each side of the fire. It was a cosy warm place on a cold frosty night. Sometimes the heat was scorching and anyone who stayed long enough in front of the fire got nasty fire marks. Consequently these marks were associated with people who sat there all day burning their shins.

Every kitchen boasted a settle bed, in case of necessity. This bed was about six foot long and made entirely from wood. When closed it contained a feather tick, pillow and bedclothes. When needed, the hinges were opened and the front dropped down, leaving the bed flat on the floor. When made up, the occupant could lie there and watch the turf fire smouldering.

Christmas in the country at that time was magic. Preparations took place a while in advance of the celebrations. Every place was white-washed and sometimes dyes were used to get different colours, i.e. yellow, pink or maybe a nice green. Fancy oil cloth was bought to put over the fireplace. This enhanced it no end. Velvet was used in the parlour.

About a month beforehand people set off in their traps or sidecars for what we called 'Christmas'. We used say 'Mama and Dad have gone for the "Christmas"'. By that we meant that they had gone for the goodies. Raisins, sultanas, spices, golden syrup, treacle, jams, stout, claret and the bottle of Buckfast Tonic Wine were purchased. One thing was certain — this Christmas didn't last too long. About two weeks later my parents would have to purchase these items all over again.

On Christmas Eve the youngest member of the household would light the first candle. I can remember my father lifting my youngest sister one particular Christmas Eve. Then, when all the candles were lit the room was like magic. Afterwards we were all sent to bed to give my poor mother a chance to prepare for the following day but we were so excited we couldn't lie down. Sleep was out of the question: Santa was coming.

For hours we kept annoying my poor mother. One minute she'd think we were asleep, the next minute we'd be standing there trying her patience. Her main worry was how she was going to fill the stockings hanging over the fireplace. Eventually she crept in to see if we were asleep. We closed our eyes and remained motionless. 'Fine! I can now fill the stockings', she said to herself.

Even though she was a very tall woman, for some strange reason, my mother stepped up on a stool and began to fill our stockings. She put a jumping jack — a wooden toy that jumped — into mine. There was also a Jack in the Box which popped up when the box was opened. Anyhow, this particular Christmas Eve, my poor mother turned around and found us all standing there behind her. That was the end of poor Santa.

When horses or ponies had their manes or tails cut or trimmed the hair was always put safely away. My uncle usually hung it neatly from the rafter in an outhouse. When he had a supply it was brought down for filling upholstery, horses' saddles and collars. One day when my cousin was housekeeping a traveller called to the door enquiring as to whether she had any feathers or horsehair for sale. My cousin replied that she had and sold whatever horsehair was in the outhouse for two shillings and six pence, or twelve and a half new pence. She was delighted with herself as she now had enough money to go to a dance. All was

3 1507 00290 5385

well until her father went into the outhouse to add to his collection of horsehair. He looked up at the ceiling and, to his amazement, the horsehair had vanished.

On our farm, and on the neighbouring farms, all the fields were named. The reason for this was probably because the farms were not very compact. When we had to round up the cows, or other animals, we would be told to go to such and such a field. The following are some of the names:

An Túirín — field to the house; Páirc an Tobair — field at the well

Mothar an Riascach — marshy field; Tochar — causeway

Páirc in Áirde — the high field; Páirc Mhór — the big field

Gort an t-Sagairt — the field of the priest;

Seachtar Cuid — the seventh part; Páirc Bhui — the yellow field

Mothar Garbh — the area of brushwood

There were two other families in our little village or hamlet. Both of these were farming families also and led very hard working lives as was the wont in those hard times. There was no specialisation as there is now and we and our neighbours tried to be self-sufficient. Every member of the family lent a hand and we produced all that was required for the year.

Today the farm where I grew up and my mother's home farm are still being farmed by my cousins and the family name is being carried on. The house where I was born is now a thriving guesthouse.

In my youth almost all the farmers got their working boots made. These were beautifully constructed with plenty of nails in the soles. They were very heavy and extremely sturdy and were worn constantly, perhaps sixteen hours a day. Each pair was expected to last twelve months. Then and only then did the wearer get a new pair.

I well remember goose fat (goose greasing) being rubbed into these boots. This was to keep them waterproof. The grease had to be applied near an open fire. With the heat and a warm pair of hands the fat disappeared into the leather. If applied cold, greasy white spots appeared all over the boots.

If these boots could talk they would have some tales to tell — up dale, down hollow, meeting Tom, Dick and Harry, having a chat about local affairs, about what price their owner got at the last fair. This would be exaggerated, of course, with each farmer trying to outdo the other.

Sunday footwear was always bought ready-made. These boots were made with a lighter, softer leather and were always polished on Saturday night for Sunday Mass, or for going to town visiting, or to funerals, etc.

The tailor had to be visited also. First of all a suit length for a lady or gent had to be bought in the local drapery or outfitters. This cost about £2 5s 0d which included the trimmings, lining and buttons. It was then brought to the local tailor who took about two weeks to make a ready-to-wear suit.

In the early part of my youth, flour was purchased by the farming community in cotton sacks of eight or ten stone. It was then stored in a warm part of the kitchen, usually in a flour bin. This bin was a press with a sloping front. A hinge divided the top half from the bottom and gave easy access. When the lid was turned back the flour could be effortlessly removed. Other meals or grain were stored in the same way. It was very clean and kept out mice.

When emptied, the cotton sack was taken outdoors where it was well shaken and steeped in cold water to remove the flour. It was then treated with Sunlight or carbolic soap to remove the printing which read: such and such a brand 'Sunrise Flour'. The stitching was then ripped and the cotton boiled in washing soda for a long time until the brand name was completely removed. When rinsed it was spread on the grass to bleach. At the end of the day what had once been a flour sack had become a beautiful piece of snow white cotton. This could then be used to make several items — pillowcases with handmade lace added, embroidered tablecloths and even vests.

One time a young man, by the name of Burns, from the local village got a new bicycle. It was a sports Raleigh model. Every morning he cycled the three miles out our road, perhaps to enjoy the countryside or perhaps because he had an eye for some young girl.

A local farmer commented thus: 'Did you see Burns, with his head down and his arse up on a silver bicycle, with the "sunrise" on his chest and the "sunset" on his behind!' He meant, of course, that Burns was wearing a flour bag vest.

Tom and Bidsy, brother and sister, were an uncle and aunt on my mother's side. As a child, when I knew them, they were in their nineties and were very quaint and a bit strange, or at least I thought so. They had some land and every two weeks Tom would tackle the donkey and they'd set out for Ennis which was about five miles on. The poor donkey walked more often than he trotted — he was very old as well.

Their mission to town, as far as Tom was concerned, was a simple one, to get their provisions. But Bidsy, on one occasion, had other ideas. She wanted to go to Confession and Communion the following morning so she stayed overnight in my Aunt's house. I was there at the time.

Before going to bed Bidsy got a naggin of whiskey, put it under her pillow, called me and said: 'You'll watch me while I sleep in case I die'. Both of them died a short time afterwards. They were lovely old people.

Tom was very generous and every time he'd come to town he'd give me two shillings and sixpence which, may I say, was no sooner calved than licked. Two and six was a lot of money in 1929 and I'd spend it right away, usually on chocolate macaroons. They were delicious and, more than likely, I'd get a full box for my money. On one occasion, much to my disgust, I was told to return them to the shop.

Once as a small child I went visiting Tom and Bidsy with my parents. As they lived some distance from where I was born, we didn't see them too often. Right in front of their door was an apple tree laden with rosy apples. Tea time arrived and the old lady took down a 'Railway' cake, a currant at every station, and wet some tea.

I made a disappearance because I didn't want to drink the tea or eat the cake, thinking that, because Bidsy was old, neither of these could be clean. Children are sometimes like that. Anyhow, when all was ready, I was called in and so I sat down and pretended to eat and drink, but what I in fact did was this; I emptied a cup of tea with no milk in it under the table and where do you think it went — right into Bidsy's boots! Some of it landed on the poor dog as well and he ran out with his tail between his legs. Bidsy exclaimed: 'My God, what's that! Oh, sorry! An accident!' I dropped the slice of 'Railway' cake and the second dog ran out the door with that!.

In and around 1936 there was an extremely bad outbreak of fevers — rheumatic fever, scarlet fever and diphtheria. This outbreak has haunted me for over fifty years, the reason being that I contracted rheumatic fever when I was eighteen years of age.

What happened was this. A young girl who lived next door had the fever and I was advised to stay away from her. I didn't heed what I was told and went to visit her instead. In a short time I became ill. My temperature was very high and I was admitted by Ambulance to the County Fever Hospital.

It was a terrible experience but I was so ill that I didn't fully understand what was happening to me. After about four weeks I began to improve but worse was to befall me. After six weeks I contracted scarlet fever. The priest was called to anoint me and I overheard a discussion at the end of my bed. They said I was dying but I was too sick to care.

It was an experience that has remained with me all my life. After sixteen long weeks I came out a very different teenager to the one that went in. There was only one other patient in my ward — a baby. On and off the only nursing care that was available was a middle-aged lady who was in and out of the Mental Hospital. I remember one night in particular when the baby cried she lifted it up and flung it as far as she could. Such was the care in those times! There was however one nurse who was an angel of mercy but God help the patients when she was off duty!

On St Patrick's Day I was allowed home and I returned to my parent's house in the country. I couldn't walk and I looked like a skeleton. My mother nursed me back to health but then my hair fell out. After a matter of weeks, however, I was nearly my own self again. I say 'nearly' because these diseases leave a scar for life.

After about four or six weeks I was sent to Lisdoonvarna with my friend for the Sulphur Baths in the hope that I would be cured or that the sulphur would take the rheumatism out of my system. There was a great belief in Sulphur Baths in those days.

By this time I was on top of the world and I wasn't too interested in either Sulphur water or baths. My friend and I went to the baths all right but not to bathe. I wasn't going to waste my money on such nonsense. We drank plenty of the water though because that cost only a penny a glass.

We used go to the Royal Spa Hotel at Glenbourne where we danced the night away. There was no charge at that time. Nor was there any drinking at those dances either. Perhaps the men had a drink or two but I never saw a young girl with drink taken.

RECOLLECTIONS OF A VILLAGE

Áine Aherne (b 1912)

Nohoba, Kinsale, County Cork, 1920s

I come from a village in South Cork. I had one brother, six years older than I. As there were no other children of my age in the village, it was decided that I should be sent to school at the age of three-and-a-half. That was unusual, as six was the age at which most children started.

The school, a very old building, did not look like a school at all; it was just one room, 40ft by 20ft.

There were two large windows inset with diamond panes of glass in front and a long narrow window in the gable. A wooden porch with four steps led down to the school yard in front. This porch acted as our cloakroom.

The room had one large fireplace, the grate being high off the ground. The fire was lit by tearing up old school copies and lighting them on the ground under the grate until the sticks caught fire. Two big boys would be sent off to gather the sticks when they were needed. Each child brought in about two shillings to pay for coal. There were two teachers in the school, Mr. Summers, the principal, and Miss O'Reilly, his assistant.

A short time after I started school a terrible tragedy took place in the village. Mr. Summers the teacher was shot dead in the street at about 2 a.m. He was not a popular man. I remember him in the pub which my mother had, standing against a pillar with his legs crossed and in a loud voice laying down the law. He always stood in the same place. My only memory of him in school was hearing him bellow at the children while taking a singing class. The song they were trying to sing was 'The Last Rose of Summer'.

It seems there was a motive for the murder. About three women living in the neighbourhood whose husbands were working away from home would invite him in at nighttime to chat by the fire and maybe have a cup of cocoa. I think he was a lonely man who liked to talk and enjoy the comfort of the fire. He lived in one room in a cottage near the school.

The husbands and brothers of these women took a different view of his visits. About six months before the murder he got a warning by way of a beating-up late one night. This was the way husbands who strayed from the straight and narrow were punished in that part of the country. For example, I remember being alone in the kitchen one night when the back door opened and this face appeared covered in blood. I got a terrible fright. He said, 'It's all right, it's me, John Doyle. I fell off my bicycle. Get your mother'. Afterwards I heard his brothers-in-law beat him up.

There was never anybody arrested for Mr. Summers' murder. It happened about the time our Free State was formed, and the law was not rigorously enforced. As his successor we got a young man — a native of the parish — who was an excellent teacher.

A new school replaced the old one some years ago. I passed by the old one recently. It was freshly painted; I believe it is now used as a parish hall.

There were only about thirty people living in our village so there were no secrets, everyone knew everything about each other. The land surrounding the village was good and it was thickly populated. The people were always very curious. Often out for a walk we would see one or two people in the distance; we then had fun guessing who they were. When they came near, and after the first greeting, the next question was, 'Where are you going?'

There were no motor cars except the odd one passing on its way from the nearest town and it was a mystery as to where that was going. Very soon though they would have found out that it might have been the solicitor from town going to visit some person to make his will; then of course, to the locals, he was just as good as dead. The priest and the doctor had a motorbike each and when they passed late at night people were in panic as to who was bad. I remember I knew by the sound of the bikes as to whether it was priest or doctor; that was a help.

Most people had a pony or donkey and trap but we young people walked. It was no trouble to walk seven miles to the nearest town or four miles to a hurling match on a Sunday afternoon.

Harvest time was great. I remember hearing the whistle of the steam engine early in the morning before going to school and it was magical; and mornings always seemed crisp, bright and very frosty. The engine passed through the village going from one farm to the next. It was huge. It had a mighty big wheel in the centre of its front and a funnel over that; then two smaller wheels at the back. Over that was a platform for two men who always had black faces, from smoke I suppose. That great engine pulled the thresher, which was a flimsy affair to my eyes. It was long, high, and made of wood, but to me it just seemed like bits and pieces.

At the threshing there were crowds of men; each farmer would send a man to help and there was no pay involved. There was a barrel of porter inside the kitchen door as it was very thirsty work, and stacks of bowls; the men coming in to dinner each got a bowl of porter — otherwise as they felt the need they helped themselves. The neighbouring women came to help prepare the dinner in the kitchen and brought delft or anything else that was needed. I think the usual menu was bacon, cabbage and potatoes. The potatoes were always heaped in the middle of the table. In some houses a dance would take place in the kitchen after the threshing was over; that was a real treat.

After the harvest was over all was quiet until Christmas.

The excitement started when the cleaning began in early December. In those days most houses were white, so on the first fine day the white-washing got underway; the outside first — the walls of the house, outhouses, pillars, etc. When dry it was a dazzling blue-white, thanks to the 'blue-bag' which was generously applied to the wash.

Then indoors to the kitchen, very large rooms, where the walls always got discoloured quickly owing to the huge fireplace where the fire was going all day boiling mighty big pots — food for the animals. Every inch of wall, ceiling, and in some houses, about a foot or maybe more, of the floor all around the walls got a thick coat. In the farmhouses the women of the house usually had a bucket of lime at hand and every Saturday she would give the wall around the fireplace a rub.

Then, when the walls were fresh and white, new pictures were put up — not so much in the farmhouses — but I have seen cottage walls where not a space was left without a picture. They were mostly calendars; it did not matter if they were out of date, I believe they always were anyway. Sometimes it would be a coloured picture from a magazine which would have come wrapped around something. A cottage I knew had a wall covered with tin lids. At that time the boiled sweets came to the shops in tins, something like the paint cans now. These were used for keeping milk, etc. in, but this girl used the lids to decorate her wall and she kept them shining like we would keep brass or copper today.

In these large farmhouse kitchens the furniture was always the same. A huge dresser which often formed a partition between room and kitchen; a settle, which was a wide wooden bench with back and arms and closed in all round. The seat could be removed and the inside was like a box; this was meant to be used as a bed — they were known as settle-beds. A rough table usually stood against the wall inside the door to hold a couple of buckets of spring water. Then a large wooden table against another wall, this was pulled out when the men were called in from the fields and a good meal provided. They all sat round on benches. The fourth wall of the room was taken up with an enormous fireplace. There were two doors leading to front and back yards.

The housewife was always very concerned with her flock of turkeys during the time coming up to Christmas. She would have worked very hard all year rearing them. Turkeys are very delicate birds when young and need great care and attention. When they are grown they are inclined to ramble and if not watched closely the cry would go up that turkeys were missing, and immediately everyone in the house would run in all directions. They were usually found fields away.

In those days the housewife had a yard full of fowl of all kinds. They provided her with money for the house. Vanmen called round each week. My first memory was of horse vans but later they were motor vans or trucks. The vans were stocked with grocery of all kinds. They took the eggs and butter from the housewife. The butter was home-made and in return they supplied groceries or anything else required.

The turkeys provided the money for Christmas as well as clothes for the children and household needs. Turkey fairs were held in the towns coming up to Christmas and the boss and his wife took their birds in. They were sold live and travelled in horse and cars hemmed in by high creels. There was great excitement in the town on fair days as the shops did good business, and also the pubs.

The women did not drink and often had a rough time on the way home; most of the men would call to their local and the wives would be left sitting outside, often in the freezing cold. If they got a good price for the birds all were in good spirits. As far as I can remember they were satisfied with one shilling and six pence per pound — about seven pence in today's money. Sometimes great rumours would go around that turkeys were going at two and six per pound — a fortune — but it seldom materialised.

I recall one Christmas in particular; it was early 1930s, the turkeys were brought to the fair and the price offered was only six pence per pound. First the women would not sell at that price. The day wore on and towards the evening they had to sell; all they got then was fourpence hal'penny per pound. I heard that it was terrible to see the women crying — there was no money for Christmas. These were very hard years for everybody.

For Christmas the local shops were stocked up. What we liked to see was the barm bracks arriving, mountains of them it seemed. There would be no room in the shop and they would be piled high on the sitting room table and even on the sofa.

The shopkeepers had to look after their customers; everybody got some gift. Good ones got a brack and a red 1lb. candle, others got just a brack, another just a red candle, and so on. The men who got tobacco were taken very quietly down to the parlour for a glass of whiskey. It all added to the excitement.

In our own shop during the year a big stack of weekly papers came every Thursday, but the thrill when the 'Holly Bough' arrived, with its red cover and Christmas design, was something else. Reading matter was very scarce; we had 'The Messenger' every month but got through that very quickly. Occasionally we had the 'Ireland's Own' or the 'Our Boys'.

The last job before Christmas was to decorate the house with holly and ivy. A lot of time was spent on the Christmas candle. First to the out-house where the mangolds were kept; they were like turnips and were fed to the horses. A nice large round one was selected, the bottom pared to make a flat base for sitting on the table. Then a hole was bored in the top and the large llb. candle, usually red, was set into it and packed around with paper to keep it steady. Next, crêpe paper was cut into strips and fringed, then laid around the mangold. Halfway up the candle another decoration was arranged with a frill of crêpe paper and red berry holly. Holly was also put at the base of the candle. It was very important to have *red* berries for the candle.

All the family had to be present on the evening of the 24th December, Christmas Eve, for the ceremony of lighting the candle. This was a very solemn and emotional moment. Sometimes the youngest of the family lit it, other times the eldest; it depended on the custom of the district.

Christmas Eve was a fast day, no meat allowed. It was a tradition to have an evening meal of saltling fish (hake), with potatoes, white sauce and butter, followed with tea and Christmas cake. It was marvellous, the only time we got shop fruit cake. Soon afterwards the children would be ready for bed, stockings put hanging up of course. Santa was rather stingy, perhaps an orange, a few little books, a packet of crayons and sweets. But the children were thrilled with little gifts, the important thing was that Santa had come to them. On Christmas morning there were three masses in the village church, all the rest of the year there were just two. But for two of the Christmas masses the priest, as he finished one, started the next without leaving the altar, so it seemed like one long mass.

Then home for breakfast and the long wait for dinner. The custom where I lived was that everybody stayed in their own homes on Christmas Day. I always thought that it was a very long, lonely day.

CEANN TRÁ INS NA FICHIDÍ AGUS NA TRIOCADAÍ

le Jonathan Moriarty (b 1912)

Kerry, 1920s

I dtosach na fichidí bhí daoine a thaistil an domhan agus a tháinig chun cónaithe i gCeann Trá. Seana máirnéalaigh Shasana abea iad siúd go raibh pinsean acu o rialtas Shasana de bharr seirbhís sa chabhlach. Orthu san bhí Seán O Cíomhán — an Cléireach a thugtaí air mar bhí sé in a chléireach sa séipéal i gCeann Trá in a óige; Séamus Ó Conchubhair nó Craig mar b'fhearr aithne air — seoideoir abea é; Vancouver, Bill Rooney — deirtear gur throid Bill sa Boer War — agus Claus agus Henry Browne. Gan Vancouver a chur san áireamh ba ó Cheann Trá gach éinne acu.

B'é Craig an t-aon seoideoir a bhí taobh thiar de Thráilí agus tháinig cloig chuige ó Annascáil anoir. Ní fhaca uaireadóir riamh á dheisiú ag Craig; ní dóigh liom go raibh uaireadóir ag éinne sa pharóiste ach ag an máistir scoile ach cloisfeá tic-toc na gclog thíos ag an gCrosaire. Bhí clár mór buí os cionn siopa Craig agus scríte air i litreacha móra dubha bhí — 'Dublin 212 ½ miles'.

Thuas i mbarr an bhaile bhí Mary agus seana Mary — beirt pinsinéir, máthair agus iníon. Cailleadh seana Mary nuair a bhí sí nach mór céad bliain.

Bíodh gur baile beag é Ceann Trá ba iontach an méid ceardaithe a bhí ann — siúinéir, seoideoir, cúipéir, maintín, dhá ghabhain, táilliúir agus gréasaí.

NA RINNCÍ

Do thagagh na sluaite chun na rinncí a bhíodh dhá uair sa tseachtain i Halla Mikie Martin. Tiustiún (4p) ar an gCéadaoin agus 6p ar an nDomhnach an táille dul isteach a bhí ann. An banna ceoil a bhí ann na Mossaí Martin ar an mbosca ceoil agus an Balbhán Bán ar an drum. B'é Muiris Crain an dóirseoir agus an pá a bhí aige ná leath-choróin do gach oíche. Tar éis an rinnce do thabharfadh sé an leath-choróin do Chraig chun é a chur i dtaisce dó i mála a bhí aige sa tsiopa.

Ar ócáidí áirithe bhíodh rinncí móra san Halla agus leath-choróin an táille dul isteach. Bhí an t-airgead gann an uair úd — éinne go raibh an leath-choróin aige bhí sé istigh sa rinnce agus an duine nach raibh sé aige bhí sé amuigh ag caitheamh bullán cloch ar díon an Halla.

Nuair a bhíodh na mná go leadaránach ag teacht amach ar an urlár an rinnce deireanach do sheasadh Mikie ar an stáitse agus screadadh sé amach 'Now Ladies you have ten minutes to make it'. Nuair a dúnadh an Halla chuaigh Muiris ar imirce go Sasana agus deirtear gur thug sé an mála leath-choróin leis.

AN PUB

Bhí an pub i lár an bhaile agus thagaidís ó chian agus ó chomhngar ag trial ar táirne Morgan agus Nora. Ní mór an meas a bhí ag Morgan ar hygiene agus an buicéad uisce a fhaigheadh sé ón gcaidéal go luath ar maidin, is leis sin a glanadh sé na gloinní go léir go dtí meán-oíche. Dá dtagadh éinne isteach chuige ag lorg leithris déarfadh Morgan leis go raibh 100 acra taobh thiar den chúl doras. Do thabhradh sé réamháis na h-aimsire leis. Déarfadh sé le stróinséar dá bhféachfadh sé amach an fhuinneog agus dá bhfeicfeadh sé Cuan go raibh báisteach ag teacht. Dá bhféachfadh sé amach agus ná feicfeadh sé Cuan — déarfadh Morgan go raibh sé ag báistigh. Sé tigh táirne Páid Quinn anois é.

SCOIL CARTAÍ

Bhí tarrac mór ar an scoil cartaí a bhíodh i dtig Thaigh Uí Cíomháin ins na fichidí agus na triochadaí. '31' a n'imrídís de ghnáth agus 'Solo' níos déanaí i dtig Jack Slattery. Bailíodh daoine isteach ins na tithe seo go rialta don cuideachta.

PEIL

Sna Fichidí bhí foireann peile Ceann Trá páirteach sa West Kerry League — níor bhuadar an craobh riamh ach bhí fóirne maithe acu agus peileadóirí maithe. Orthu san bhí Seán agus Gearóid Sayers, Micheál Ó Sé, Briain Ó Luing (uncail do Seán, Tomás agus Mikeen Pádraigh).

Ins na triocadaí i league na Gaeltachta bhí foireann ana mhaith acu agus bhuadar craobh na Gaeltachta go minic. I dtosach b'iad Mike Aindí Ó Sé, Sean Léan Ó Muircheartaigh, Micheál Ó Fiannachta agus Máirtín Séars na peileadóirí ba mhó cáil orthu agaus níos deanaí bhí Tomás Ó Luing, Bartaí Garvey agus Mícheál Ó Murchú, a bhuaidh craobh comórtas na h-Éireann le Ciarraí, ag cabhrú leo.

Sa chluiche ceannais theigheadh na sluaite ón bparóiste siar thar Mám Na Gaoithe go Baile An Fheiritéaraigh — cuid acu ar rothair agus cuid maith acu ar siúl mar bhí an t-airgead gann agus ní raibh na rothaí acu. Sa tráthnóna bhí na tithe táirne go léir i mBaile An Fheiritéaraigh ag cur thar maoil agus an tigh táirne i gCeann Trá lán go doras san oíche sin.

Nuair a bhíodh deireadh leis an gcluiche théimís go dtí tigh Dónailín Keane. Bhí clós laistiar den bpub agus nuair a bhí taoscán maith ólta ag Tom Connor, sheasadh sé in airde ar an gclaí agus in árd a ghutha thugadh sé ainmneacha na stáisiún traenacha trasna na Stáit Aontaithe. Más buan mo chuimhne mar seo a bhí — New York, Buffalo, Cleveland, Chicago, Lincoln, Denver, Salt Lake City agus San Francisco. Ba mhór an sult a bhaineamar as.

Ainm amháin a luadhas anseo — Mike Aindí Ó Sé. Bhí stíl agus ealaíon aige nach raibh ag éinne eile sa pháirc agus thagadh daoine amach ón nDaingean agus ós na paróistí maguaird ag féachaint air ag imirt. Bhuaileas le Mike Aindí i gCeanntrá — tamall roimhe sin bhí sé ag imirt mar lán chúl do Chiarraí Thiar ar Charlie Sullivan — peileadóir go raibh aithne air go foirleathan timpeall na hÉireann. Fuair Charlie poinnte amháin ar Mhike. Do dheineas cómhgháirdeas leis. Dúirt Mike liom dá bhfaigheadh sé braon té don bhricfeasta ar maidin ná faigheadh Charlie an poinnte sin féin.

I dtosach na dtriochadaí a bhí ann. Bhí an cogadh eacnamaíochta ar siúl — bhí beithíoch bliana á dhíol ar thrí phúint agus gamhain á dhíol ar leath-sovereign. Ba dheacair don bhfeirmeoir beag clann a thógaint nó a oiliúint. Bhí prátaí acu do gach aon bhéile sa ló. Sin a bhí i gceist ag Mike Aindí.

TURAS GO BLEÁ CLIATH GO CRAOBH COMÓRTAS NA H-ÉIREANN 1924

Chualas go raibh Paddy Kevane ón gCaisleán agus John Griffin, Cahirbuilg ag taisteal chun an chluiche. Timpeall ar a thrí a chlog ar maidin d'éiríos agus chuireas mo bhalcaisí nua orm. Bhí mo bhróga éadroma istigh i seomra mo mháthar agus níor bhachas leo ach chuireas mo bhróga táirní orm. Bhí eagla orm go gcloisfí mé nó go bhfeicfí mé ag dul isteach sa t-seomra. Do léimeas ar mo rothar beag agus as go brách liom síos go stáisiún traenach sa Daingean. Bhí sé timpeall a cheathair a chlog ar maidin nuair a shroiseas an stáisiún. Bhí timpeall scór duine ar

ardán na traenach. D'fhéachas timcheall — thuit an lug ar an lag
orm — ní raibh tásc na tuairisc ar Paddy Kevane ná ar John Griffin. D'aithníos 'Tom the Gabha' agus an 'Kerryman' agus cúpla
duine eile. Do chuas go oifig na dticéad agus cheannaíos ticéad
fillte leath luach go Bleá Cliath ar dhá scillínge déag.

Thosnaíomar ar an dturas ar an 'Tralee and Dingle Railway' go
Tráilí. Bhí timcheall leath dosaen stáisiúin ann agus bhí paisinéirí
ag fanacht ag gach aon cheann acu agus bhí slua maith bailithe sa
traen nuair a shroiseamar Tráilí.

Do thuirlingeamar agus leanas an slua — níorbh fhada gur
thángamar go séipéil eile, an 'Kerryman' i dtosach agus gach
éinne á leanúint. Do shúileamar isteach — bhí an aifreann á léamh
— do leanamar ár treoraí. Suas go barr an tSéipéil agus amach
linn tré dhoras bheag a bhí taobh thiar den altóir. Níorbh fhada
gur shroiseamar stáisiún eile 'The Great Southern Railway'.
Chuamar isteach sa charáiste agus as go brách linn go Bleá Cliath.

Nuair a thángamar amach as Droichead an Rí (an stáisiún) bhí
eagla agus scanradh orm — gluaisteán ag imeacht in gach aon treo.
Chuir na tramanna iontas agus abhaltacht orm. Bhí na bróga tairní
ag sleamhnú fúm ar an sráid. Rugas greim an fhir bháite ar Tom the
Gabha agus sa deire léimeamar isteach sa tram. Tar éis tamaill do
thuirlingeamar den tram agus chuamar isteach i teach Ósta
'O'Briens Hotel' i Parnell Street. Bhí ispíní, slisíní bagún agus putóga
agam — b'é an chéad béile agam ón oíche roimhe sin. Níl fhios
agam cé dhíol as — ní raibh faic agam.

Sa deire shroiseamar Páirc an Chrócaigh. Rug duine éigin ar
mo lámh agus scaoileadh isteach saor mé. Chuir fear eile in airde
ar an bhfalla a bhí taobh thiar de Ardán Ógáin go mbeadh radharc
maith agam ar an gcluiche. Cill Dara ins na geannsaithe bána
agus Ciarraí ins na geansaithe uaine agus órga. D'aithníos cuid
mhaith des na peileadeoirí — Joe Barrett, Jack Walsh, Con Bros-
nan, Bob Stack, John Joe Sheehy agus Paul Russell i bhfoireann
Ciarraí agus Frank Malone, Matt Gough, Larry Stanley, Paul
Doyle agus Jack Higgins i bhfoireann Cill Dara. Do bhuaigh Ciarraí an cluiche le dhá pointe.

Nuair a shroiseamar Stáisiún an Daingin, tháinig garda
chugam agus dúirt se liom go rabhadar am chuardach i rith an lae
timpeall an pharóiste agus istigh sa Daingean. Do léimeas ar mo
bhicycle agus nuair a shroiseas Ceann Trá ni dhéarfad faic ar an
fáilte a chuireadh romham. Do chuas isteach sa leaba ar a
cheathair a chlog ar maidin agus tarraingeadh amach mé ar leath
uair tar éis a h-ocht agus ar an mbicycle arís liom síos go Scoil na
mBráthar sa Daingean. Nuair a chuas isteach sa rang tugadh
'Bualadh Bos' mór dom. Níor mar a chéile an fáilte a chuireadh

romham i gCeann Trá agus a fuaireas sa scoil.

Do scóráil Paul Russell a bhí ag imirt ar leath chúl ar dheis an poinnte deireannach sa chluiche sin. Nuair a chuas isteach i dtig Tady Kevane oíche Dé Luain thugas cúntas an chluiche dóibh. Do thagadh dhá pháipéir sa tseachtain go Ceann Trá an uair úd — an Weekly Independent ar an Aoine agus An Kerryman ar an Satharn. Ar an Independent dúbhradh go bhfuair Eamonn Fitzgerald an poinnte deireannach agus nuair a chuala an dream sa chistin é sin chaith cuid mhaith acu amhras orm an rabhas ag an gcluiche in aon chor. Do tháinigh An Kerryman tráthnóna Dé Satharn agus i nótaí P.F. bhí pictiúr Paul Russell an fear a fuair an poinnte deireannach. B'éigin dos na 'Doubting Thomases' a chreidiúint go rabhas ag an gcluiche.

Sa bhlian 1934 i gCraobh Comórtas Laighin, Loch Garman v Cill Dara i gCill Coinnigh bhíos ag imirt ar an dachad slat ar fhoireann Loch Garman. Do chaitheadh an liathróid isteach i lár an ghoirt agus ritheas siar chun na toisigh dom áit féin. Baineadh geit asam. Cé bhí romham am mharcáil ach Jack Higgins féin. Is ar éigin a d'aithníos é mar bhí aois mhaith aige agus mheasas nach raibh aon toirt ann. Ba mhór an deifríocht a bhí idir an fear a bhí am mharcáil an lá sin agus an gaiscíoch a bhí ag imirt i bPáirc an Chrócaigh deich mbliana roimhe sin.

NA TRIOBLÓIDÍ

Bhíos thíos ar an gcrosaire lá agus chonacas triúr fear ag theacht amach ó thig táirne Jonaí — beirt píléir agus fear go raibh handcuffs air gafa acu. B'é an Seabhac an príosúnach a bhí gafa acu.

Rud eile atá im chuimhne ná lorraí lán 'Tans' ag gabháil siar thar an crosaire agus gunna ag gach duine acu ina láimh. Fear amháin go raibh cuma an diabhail air a chuireadh scanradh ort le féachaint air a bhí thiar i ndeire an lorraí agus machine gun in a lámha aige agus an bairrle dírithe amach uaidh aige. B'é siúd Balbriggan. Do chuireadh leath an bhaile mhóir sin tré thine agus dúradh go raibh baint aige leis — sin é an fáth gur tugadh Balbriggan air.

Domhnach amháin agus daoine ag teacht abhaile ón Aifreann do stop lorraí Tans ag Ó Rahilly's. Do léim beirt amach agus rugadh ar Mike Fitzgerald, Ballintrasna agus cuireadh isteach sa lorraí é agus d'imíodar leis. Timcheall a sé a chlog sa tráthnóna tháinigh an lorraí thar nais. Do stop sé san áit céanna agus ligeadh Mike amach saor. Ón lá sin go dtí an lá gur chuaigh Mike ar imirce go dtí na Stáit Aontaithe níor tugadh aon ainm eile air ach 'Bal' — do gabhadh Mike mar giall.

Táim ag dul siar anois go aimsir an Civil War. Bhí baile an Daingin i seilbh na Republicans an tráth seo. Duine de na Árd Oifig abea 'Sean a Chóta' (deartháir Kruger) i gharsún an Daingin. Do tháinigh arm na Staters gan coinne lá agus ghabhadar an baile. Más buan mo chuimhne d'éalaigh na Republicans as an mbaile.

Rugadh ar Seán a Chóta i dtigh táirne sa Daingean agus cuireadh 'na príosúnach é ar bhórd loinge ar bharr an ché. Nuair a bhí sé ag siúl isteach sa long do scread sé amach in árd a ghutha 'Goodbye Old Ireland I am going to Cork'.

CUAIRT LOINGE

Bhíos sa leaba im chodhladh go déanach san oíche agus dhúisigh fothram amuigh ar an mbóthar mé. Bhí daoine amuigh agus gach éinne acu ag féachaint amach ar gcuan. Nuair d'fhéachas amach baineadh geit asam — bhí an cuan lán de shoilse. Níos iontaí fós bhí na soilse ag preabadh. Mheasas gur radharc diaga a bhí ann agus nach den saol seo é.

Longa cogaidh Shasana a bhí ann a tháinig isteach i bhfothain sa chuan go maolódhadh an ghaoth. Bhí an fharraige suaite mar bhí gaoth agus tarrac ann a chuir na soilse ag preabadh sna longa. Fanfaidh áilleacht na radhairce sin im aigne go deo.

Cuimhne eile tráth an ama seo. Bhíos istigh sa leaba go moch ar maidin. D'fhéachas amach an fhuinneog agus cad a chífinn ach crainn loinge taobh amuigh den bhfhuinneoig. Chuireas mo chuid éadaigh orm go tapaidh agus amach liom síos go dtí an slip cómh tapaidh is a bhéarfadh na cosa mé. Nuair a shroiseas an slip chonaic me long mhór i ngreim ins na carraigreacha idir Céin Amháin agus an slip. Chaitheas an lá thícs ar an gcarraig mhór i gCéin Amháin ar thaobh na loinge. 'George Zandra' an t-ainm a bhí uirthi. I rith an lae bhailigh na sluaite timpeall na loinge. Bhíodar thuas ar bharr na haille agus thíos ar na carraigreacha. Go déanach sa tráthnóna tháinigh tug ó Queenstown agus d'éirigh léi an long a tharrac de na carraigreacha agus í chur ag snámh arís. Ba mhór an díomá a bhí ormsa ag féachaint uirthi ag dul amach béal an chuain.

NA H-OILEÁNAIGH

Is minic a chonacas na h-Oileánaigh ag siúl duine i ndiadh duine in aon líne amháin suas go Tigh Táirne Jonaí. Bhíos ana óg an uair úd agus mheasas go raibh gach aon duine acu ag caint agus nach raibh éinne ag éisteacht.

BUALADH AN CHLOIG

Béas eile a bhí againn ná bualadh an chloig (Bell a thugaimís air) Oíche Chinn Bhliana. Bhailíodh scór againn ag an gcrosaire timpeall meán oíche agus siar linn go léir agus an clog á bhualadh againn agus sinn ag béicigh in ard ár gcinn agus ár ngutha — 'Old Year Out — New Year In' . Théimis siar go Árd A Bhóthair agus tríd na mbailte go léir sa pharóiste. Ní thagaimis abhaile go timpeall a cheathair a chlog ar maidin. Chaitheas fiche bliain ag leanúint an chloig timpeall an pharóiste agus níor dhein éinne aon ghearán riamh orainn, bíodh gur cuireadh oíche codalta amú orthu go minic. Níor deineadh aon díobháil maillíosach riamh agus anois féachaint siar ar bhóithrín na smaointe cuireann simplíocht agus macántacht na ngéagóirí iontas orm.

Is mór an t-athrú atá tagtha sa pharóiste anois. Tá fearas agus treallamh de gach aon t-saghas ins na tithe agus áiseanna aibhléise agus seomraí fleaidh. Is fada a bhíodar 'na ghátair.

Leath céad blian ó shin ní raibh i gCeann Trá ach tithe tréigthe. Anois tá sliocht sleachta na sean daoine ag teacht thar nais arís chun conaithe ins na tithe agus tá beocht agus anamúlacht tagtha thar nais arís don bhaile a bhí gan anam uair.

PORTRAIT OF AN EPOCH

Patricia Kelly (b 1916)

Oxmanstown Road, North Circular Road, Dublin, 1920s – 30s

School children are often asked to write essays on 'The Good Old Days' or 'The Best Age to Live in'. Reams can be written on either. But there is no denying that the place and society in which one spends one's childhood and the developing years are the two main experiences which create the most lasting impression. No age is perfect and while one age will not correct all of the faults of a previous one, it will surely create its own.

I am the product of an Irish society of the Nineteen Twenties and Thirties. To give you my experience is to present you with a microcosmic view of Irish life as it was at that period. You will see that it was an inward-looking society founded on fear, superstition, narrow-mindedness, and ignorance promoted mainly by the church and ably supported by the last remnants of Victorian conventions.

I am a Dubliner and the Dublin of that time was a very small city and a very different one to the one we know today. There are some who would say that it was a better Dublin. But what is good, better, best? All relativities are opinions. I was born and reared close to the Phoenix Park; gas-lit North-West Dublin was then bounded by the North Circular, the Park, River Liffey, Smithfield, Church Street, Stanhope Street and Grangegorman Asylum. You could say that it was exactly like a small country town with all a small town's fears and phobias — fear of prose-lytisation, fear of diseases, post-rebellion and civil war fears, suspicion of neighbours, fears of the military who searched our fathers when they had us out for our Sunday walks. A general narrow-mindedness made the inhabitants of our township look on the townships of Ballsbridge and Donnybrook as existing only in outer space. But one didn't cross the Liffey anyway, certainly not for exploratory or investigatory reasons, because our town-ship had all the necessary institutions — the Roman Catholic Church, Church of Ireland, Methodist, we could even boast of a famous friary. There were the Christian Brothers, and the Con-vent, a hospital and the Asylum and the abattoir which brought the country to the town on Wednesday and Thursday nights with fearful moans and cries which made us all restless in our beds. But our greatest boast was that one of the ancient five Royal roads to Tara — Stoneybatter, Manor Street, Prussia Street, Navan Road — ran right through our township.

Close to this Royal Road lay our Parish Church, and not far from it stood the Convent, an institution of marked repute follow-ing in the traditions of the great founder of the Irish Sisters of Charity — Mother Mary Aikenhead. At that time the Parish Priest was a typical example of the cleric of the time, conservative, authoritarian, who believed in inculcating the tenets of religion by fear, the fear of God, of Hell, damnation, ostracisation, ridicule, you name it, he used it as a weapon in the promotion of sanctity and right living. He knew what was right for each and every one of his parishioners in their daily lives. From the pulpit he told them for whom to vote, and he wasn't slow to denounce the party he did not favour, and woe-betide those who did not follow his direction, though under a system of secret ballot it was amazing that he should know the defaulters, but he knew, that was for cer-tain. Women were a particular irritation to him, we knew from the regular spates of torrential invective aimed at these imbecilic irrational, and none of them knew how to treat their Lords and Masters whom the Good God had deemed fit to provide them with, their husbands.

Nuns, of course, were women — habits and coifs didn't change that and this brings me to the hub of the story. Our school had the usual cross-section of nuns — good, bad and indifferent. You could count among the bad ones, the one who would put brown paper skirts around the end of the children's dresses if she decided that they were too short. She might, at the same time, feel like adorning a child with a dunce's hat to go with the skirt if she were in the mood, which was frequent. But there was one little nun there, Sister Angelica, who captured the hearts of all who knew her. She radiated kindness, joyousness, humour and courage — the courage of directness in the ambivalent atmosphere of the time. It was she who countered the fears engendered in us by the restrictive mores of our society. She would try to change our negative feelings into positive thinking, and encouraged those who kept their heads down in conditioned degradation to see the light at the end of the tunnel. It wasn't that she was in any way against the establishment, but that she had a love of life and people, and especially children which swept her along with a lilt of laughter which affected all who met her.

Came the time when she was put in charge of the Children of Mary, who were having their meetings in the newly-built hall attached to the Convent. Being only seven years of age then I was too young to join, though I did look forward to the future when I could sport the blue cape and look grand. At that stage, I had a yearning for uniforms. In the meantime, of course, we had our regular May and June processions dressed in our best, when the long crocodile of children would wind its way all around the grounds of the convent singing 'Oh wrap your nose up'[*Ora Pro Nobis*] and 'Cows in Australia laytisia' [*Causa Nostra Laetitia*]. Such indeed was our understanding of the compulsory Latin of our religion at that time. Sister Angelica was very much in evidence, and always made sure to congratulate us on our clothes, our singing and our good behaviour.

Among the adults, news of events in the new hall went the rounds. There were Whist-drives, sales-of-work, dancing lessons, and there was talk that even a pantomime might be undertaken, with an all-female cast of course. All these functions were to eliminate the debt on the hall. Indeed, everything seemed to be going well, until the blow struck.

The neighbourhood was shaken by the news that an apparition had occurred at the grotto of the Parish Church. The Parish Priest and the Church Clerk were the selected two to whom Our Lady of the Grotto expressed herself. It was reported that her statue was seen to shed tears, the head turned and looked towards the Convent, and said, 'Seven Years' — 'Seven Years'. Those of an older generation will, of course, remember the electrifying omen the number seven was in those days, with its potential for either

good or evil. They will remember the seven years and seven quar-
antines in connection with limbo and purgatory, and the seven
years bad luck anticipated if one broke a mirror. On the good side
I can recall that a well-known bone-setter of our neighbourhood
attributed success in his profession to the fact that he was the seventh son of a seventh son.

But to get back to my story. No sooner had the news of the
apparition been digested by the neighbourhood than the next bul-
letin was issued and that let it be known that the Parish Priest
with a very determined clerical retinue had invaded the Convent,
and denounced the nuns, and in particular Sister Angelica, the
nun in charge of the Children of Mary, and in charge of functions
in the hall. It was announced that in view of the fact that the
statue had said 'Seven Years' — 'Seven Years' the Children of
Mary would not be allowed to wear their cloaks for seven years
and that the hall was not to be used for any further functions. We
children were completely baffled by the significance of all this,
and the reasons for it. Of course no amount of understanding
could be gleaned by us from the few disjointed references made
by our parents and adults in general. It seemed to me that women
preserved an ostentatious silence as a defence against the barely-
concealed air of amusement exhibited by their menfolk. It was
something which would not be discussed before children. Indeed,
precious little was discussed before children in those days. The
only sustained reference which I personally heard, I heard by accident when I was out of sight, but within earshot of my father
one day when he was communicating with our next door neighbour over the garden wall.

'Well Mick', said my father, 'what do you think of it all?' 'I'd
say that it was the froth on a pint of stout your man the clerk
saw', said Mick the neighbour. 'Aye indeed. But what could have
happened in that hall that brought all this on?' 'Maybe a fellow
kissed a girl at a Whist-drive', said my father. 'But shure I didn't
think fellows were allowed into the hall at all', said Mick. 'Well,
now you have me, but I know one thing', said my father, 'that
Parish Priest is a great man for making a mountain out of a
molehill.'

That was the only fragment of information which I had to trade
with my class-mates for their equally confusing scraps gleaned
from their sources. We tried to pool our knowledge to come to a
coherent explanation. Most of us knew what a mountain was, but
none of us knew what a molehill was. Indeed, if the Department of
Education of the period had not removed Nature Study from our
curriculum as an unbefitting subject for *city* children, I feel sure we

should have been much further along the road to discovery. So confusion continued to reign supreme. If we asked any question of adults we were told fearfully that it was a *miracle* and that we would be *wise* to accept it. But in the acceptance of this wisdom based on fear and lack of knowledge and indeed a faith indoctrinated by fear, it was no wonder that the faith itself was always in danger of slipping or vanishing altogether, as soon as one learned to question it. Ah, but then, one was not supposed to question it, even if one had the gift of brains bestowed on one, we were told, by a benevolent God. There were of course areas of which the Church held that the gift of brains was intended to lie fallow. Perhaps the only true wisdom was doubt, a *secret* doubt which undermined instinct, that instinct by which we should have been able to understand our fellow-beings, our adults, our parents and our Church.

The most terrifying part of it was that we were all so guilt-ridden that each one of us was sure that inexplicably she had some part in this deep and dark event, and the number of children's confessions increased enormously. Not that this alleviated the general distress, in fact for those who already entertained scruples it only intensified them and made the condition worse. A sister of a class-mate of mine would be no sooner stepping out of the confession box, but she would feel she was committing a mortal sin, and she would promptly dive back in again to the other side of the box or into a nearby box.

But worse was yet to come. To my dying day I shall never forget the terror we felt at the funeral three months later of our beloved nun, Sister Angelica, for indeed she lasted but three months after her denunciation. She had taken to her bed, and we never saw her again. We were all lined up along the avenue to watch the cortege slowly wend its way towards the main gate and off to its final resting place. Among the hundreds of children there was not a dry eye. Their beloved Sister Angelica had been taken in the flower of her youth from all she loved and from all who loved her. Our parents lined the route too and even in the vast sea of funeral silence whispers were audible — 'She died of a broken heart' — 'He lacerated her with that tongue of his' — 'You know the kind he is' — 'He has banned the wearing of cloaks for seven years' — 'What next, I wonder?'

Seven years later I was admitted into the Children of Mary when the ban had been lifted on the wearing of cloaks and a new Parish Priest presided over the parish. I cannot say I was overjoyed. Acceptance after the penitential *seven years* seemed to me to have nightmarish overtones. Besides that the pleasure of wearing a uniform had been satisfied for me in the interim by my membership of the local guides, and the St. John's Ambulance Cadets. Through my training in the latter I learned that no-one *'died of a broken heart'*, so now I was prepared to seek a scientific or medical reason for the death in *so short a time* of our beloved nun. With the limited acumen of an adolescent of the period (well-heeled, over-educated teenagers had yet to be invented) my thoughts would go around and around and invariably would become riveted at the same point — could it have been rapid T.B. to which she succumbed, because indeed we were all too well aware of its high incidence at the time, and for many decades to come, and it was a disease which created its own aura of mystery, shame, fear and consequently secrecy. Whether or not I was right in my deduction I cannot tell, but I feel sure that whatever the cause, her death must have been accelerated by the harshness of the denunciation to which she was subjected at the time.

Did I ever hear what happened in the Hall? You might well ask. Never. I grew into adulthood, entered the labour market and my family did an unheard-of thing for those days — *they crossed the Liffey* and came to live in outer space in Ballsbridge. Only now do I look back with the telescopic memory of old age and what I see tells me that I really did live in that world, and indeed it must have become part of the person I am, which astonishes me. I lost touch with my classmates, many of whom emigrated, others entered the Convent, and I have never come across anyone who knew the whole story, so now I have become the bemused custodian of an incredible unsolved mystery.

DOWN MEMORY LANE

Margaret Duffy (b 1920)

(Extract from full length autobiography) Little Mary St., Ormond Sq., Cabra, Dublin City, 1920s – 30s

Mammy opened a little grocery shop to try and make a decent living. My aunt came to help Mammy with the shop and help with the family as she had no children of her own, but things did not work out as expected so Mammy gave up the shop.

Tilly sold the house up on Hollybank Road. By this time her husband had died. She was getting on in years and decided to come back into the city and live in the rooms over the clothes shop. By this time we children were all growing up and getting bigger. We got a flat not too far away and we still kept in touch with Tilly. Things were changing and time was moving on and we were all going to school. We were all very sad when Tilly died. I cannot recall how long it was after we had left before it happened. It was the end of a long friendship.

Mammy only got 12s 6d from the Relieving Officer at the dispensary but we never experienced any hardship. We got no help from any charitable organisation. This is why we all grew up with a lot of independence.

Food was very cheap in those days. You could go up to Boland's Bakery in Meeting House Lane and get a load of bread for one shilling; also you could ask for a 6d worth of fancy. It consisted of rejects from the shops or the bakery. I remember the man's name was Simon.

When I was young most women did not carry shopping bags. All the messages or shopping would be carried in a big apron tied around their waist. The apron was made from fine sacking or flour bags which people often made into sheets for the beds. My own Mammy often spent days boiling the flour bags to get rid of the big large stamp of the mills that was printed on each flour bag. They lasted for years. Now we have shopping made a lot easier for us with all the supermarkets.

I have many happy memories of going down to Woolworths around Easter and Christmas time. They had lovely displays of beautiful chocolate Easter eggs with all the children's names and beautiful little flowers, also lovely coloured sugar eggs that could be bought for 3d or 6d. Because this store was very well known, it never sold anything that cost any more. You could buy glasses, wedding rings, all class of fashion jewellery for 6d. I am sure that some of the items bought in Woolworths are now classed as antiques. It was always well stocked and plenty of shoppers were to be seen there everyday. Many a home was made brighter with all the ornaments and knick-knacks that were bought in Woolworths.

Potatoes and eggs were very cheap, milk a penny a pint. If you went down to Moore Street late on Saturday night you would get plenty of bargains in the vegetables and meat as the shops did not close until 10 o'clock at night, sometimes later. You could buy one dozen herrings for 6d. Fresh rabbits cost two for 1/-(one shilling).

Around where we lived many of the women sold fish and fruit in the markets. They were very decent, generous and friendly people in those days. Some days if they did not sell all the fish or the vegetables they would give them to the neighbours. All the people seemed to live from day to day. I can remember the coal man came around with a little donkey and cart and people would buy the coal for 3d a stone, they never bought it in bulk. Also you could buy coal blocks for 1d each.

We children were a healthy lot, we never seemed to suffer with all the problems parents of today have rearing their children. There was never much medication kept in our house. Mammy's favourite treatment for most ailments was a little dab of iodine, roasted salt in a silk stocking, tied around your throat and the famous 2d bottle of Syrup of Figs, or camphorated oil, which was rubbed on the chest.

I was the only one of the family to have my tonsils removed as a child. I think I was about six years old. I can remember the day quite well. I was brought up to the Richmond Hospital in North Brunswick Street. I was admitted at 8 o'clock in the morning on one Thursday. I did not have any idea what was to happen to me. When we arrived Mammy and I went up to one of the big wards. There were other children having the same treatment, but it did not take very long to get everyone organised and put to bed. When Mammy undressed me the nurse told her to collect me at three o'clock the same day. Mammy just said don't cry or worry, I will bring you home at three o'clock.

Shortly afterwards the doctor came into the ward. I remember his name was Dr. Johnston. He had a wide band around his head with a big light at the front of his forehead. He was a big man and was very jolly and smiled at all the children. The next thing I can recall is being carried down the corridor by another man, in his arms and he was wearing a green coat. I was put on a table and a mask was put over my face from behind. I can remember kicking madly. When I woke up some time later I was crying, Mammy was sitting at the side of the bed. After a while the nurse cleaned me up and carried me down the stairs, where Mammy had a baby's pram to take me home, as we lived a distance away from the hospital. Some of the roads were made of cobblestones and were very shaky and with the rocking of the pram, I got very sick before I reached home. I was terrified.

I was put to bed feeling very sorry for myself. My brother and sister came into the bedroom and they both fell asleep from the effect of the anaesthetic. It was a very quiet day in our house as the three of us slept until the next morning. After a few days I was right as rain. The children of today are better cared for, as there is better opportunity and very good medical attention given to them.

Mammy had to make a new start in her life to provide for us, so she went out to work cleaning other people's houses in Rathgar and Palmerston Park and made very good friends there. I do remember her telling us she had to walk a good distance as there was only trams in those days, but as she was working three days a week and was paid 2s 6d per day it made it worthwhile. She would get all the left-over food from the cook.

I can remember going out to see some of the big houses that Mammy worked in. As we lived in a small flat, I was always interested when she would talk about all the different rooms she had to clean. So one fine day she brought us up to show us one of the houses. We went in by the servant's entrance and the cook gave us lovely tea, biscuits and cakes.

We travelled from South Great George's Street and we were all very excited. We got a tram car which took us to Palmerston Park. We went for a walk after leaving the house and we came to where there was a small river and plenty of green trees and bushes. It was the first time I saw a real bird's nest. It had three blue eggs with brown speckles on them. We were not allowed to touch them. We also spent a lot of time in St. Stephen's Green. Mammy would always pick up small feathers the birds would shed. The big feathers were kept for blessing the house with holy water before she would go to bed at night. The small brightly coloured ones she would keep to restyle her hats and use them for decorations. She was always very tidy and neat about the way she looked. She took great care of her clothes.

She was very fond of hats and I can remember watching her restyling them. She would steam them over a pot of boiling water and then she would put them on a large pudding bowl and reshape them and finish them off with a new ribbon or a fancy piece of veil. She had a lovely selection of the hat pins women wore in their hats in those years.

In one of the houses there were children around our own age. We always got their cast-off clothing, which was always in very good condition. People often wondered how we were so well dressed while some of the children we played with did not even have shoes to wear. I can tell about a lovely dress I wore for my Holy Communion. It was white jap silk and it was very pretty with little flowers embroidered in silk thread. It was a party dress that belonged to one of the little girls where Mammy worked.

It was a very happy day for me as all the children were invited back to the school and we had a party. We received Communion in the convent chapel and afterwards walked around the convent gardens singing hymns. The name of my school was George's

Hill Presentation Convent, considered to be one of the best schools in Dublin and one of the oldest. It was opened in 1794, the first school in Dublin run by nuns.

I remember my youngest brother Tommy making his First Holy Communion. After that he was very nervous about going into the confession box. Well in those days, it was a ritual that all the children went to confession on Saturday morning, so Mammy asked me to take him along with me. I asked him his sins and wrote them down as best I could on a piece of paper and told him just to hand it to the priest, which he did. The priest must have thought my brother Tommy was deaf and dumb because he just gave my brother his blessing. Well, that went on until Mammy found out about it and she put a stop to it. I was making life too easy for him.

The next happy occasion for me was the Eucharistic Congress in 1932. All the little girls wore yellow dresses, white shoes and socks and the boys wore white trousers and shirts and shoes. People displayed holy statues and hung flags out of the window and there was bunting hanging all around. The weather was lovely and all the people walked up to the Phoenix Park for open-air mass by the Papal Nuncio and to hear Count John McCormack sing. He made history that day and it was a great occasion for him and the people of Ireland.

TOWN LIFE A Peep into the Past

Lilian Healy (b 1918)

Dun Laoghaire, County Dublin, 1920s – 40s

Two years after the 1914-18 War was over, my parents who had been living in England (where I was born) came home to settle here in Ireland. My father had been wounded in the Battle of the Somme and at that time he was recovering from the 'Black Flu' from which a great many people died, so he was not very strong and there was very little work to be had after the War. There was not much Social Welfare either. They rented a house on the Main Street, Kingstown then, Dun Laoghaire now. There were about six or seven houses together in a row between shops, with gates and railings and steps up to the front door. All these houses are gone now. My earliest memories are of standing on those steps seeing the Free State Soldiers passing towards the City in lorries and listening to small boys shouting after them, 'Up the Rebels'.

At the back of our house there was a long back garden surrounded by an old wall. There was a break in one part of the wall which led into the garden next door. As soon as I could climb I was in there playing with the children. They had pigs, chickens and horses, rabbits and other little animals. That family had pony and traps and horse coaches and cabs which were used to bring people who were travelling to England to the mailboat and to meet visitors arriving and our own natives coming home here. There were four mailboats at that time travelling back and forth from Dun Laoghaire to Holyhead. Local men were employed there meeting the boats at the pier and at the customs. There were no such things as supermarkets then, Woolworths was the nearest thing to that. Otherwise there were more small shops and a few medium and large. The smaller shops were mostly family businesses with the family living either above the shop or behind it. Everybody seemed to know everybody else in the town. At that time the population was very small compared to now.

I started school in the old Dominican Convent National School, when I was four years old. My mother had gone to that school too. I still remember how the room looked with the nursery pictures tacked to the wall around the room and the big counting beads intrigued me. The cloakroom was so small it was just a little cubby hole. A few years later our new school was built which was a fine building. On fine summer days we would have nature study classes on the lawns. On our way to school through the town we would take a lump of ice from a truck which would be making a delivery of fish to a shop. The fish would be lying in boxes of lumps of ice because there were no fridges then. We did not seem to mind the salty taste. At about eleven o'clock on Sunday mornings during the summer our 'ice cream man' whom we called Charlie used park under the 'fat tree' and stay for a while ringing his bell to let us know he was there. He had a pony and trap and he used keep the ice cream in a big box with loads of ice. It was really only cornflour.

By this time we had moved to a new house. I was five years old. This house was built in the grounds of the very old convent. We had permission to play in the grounds while we were growing up. It was a field with the old convent in ruins but part of it was habitable and a caretaker and his family lived there. The caretaker was the Drum Major of the Town Brass Band and whenever they had a music practice, which was once a week, we were allowed into the small hall to listen to them. We called it 'Murphy's Band' and they assembled every other Sunday morning in all their finery outside the old convent to commence their grand parade through the town with many of the locals following behind.

During the summer months on some fine Sunday mornings a line of horse coaches and sidecars complete with drivers would park along the side of our houses and if any family cared to hire one for the day they could do so and a few families would travel to Powerscourt for a picnic. It was a regular outing for us. My mother used collect ferns on the way. The men enjoyed what was called 'Bona Fide' while travelling (a drink while out in the country).

While attending primary school a large number of girls from the area attended the 'Monkstown Quaker Hall' to learn social skills which were taught us by ladies who gave their services voluntarily. They helped to lead us in the right direction and gave us true values. All denominations were welcomed and those who did go benefitted greatly by learning sewing, making garments, darning, library, gym, singing, games, Magic Lantern ('Foreign Missions'). The 'Classics' were read to us while we worked. For the year of the Eucharistic Congress we had a choir from the girls school in the Phoenix Park for the Mass.

Round about the year 1931 — it could be a bit earlier or even a bit later — it was when the 'Talkie Films' first made their appearance that 'orchestras' were not needed any more. They became redundant and it was so sad and heart-breaking to see those musicians in such a bad state, so down at heel, playing music for pennies on the beach at Dun Laoghaire, beautiful music. It was some time before things improved for them. We used to have the Army Band playing for our entertainment on Wednesdays and Sundays on occasions during the summer months. There was a pleasure boat as well which used to run trips around the Bay. Anyone could hire a rowing boat for sixpence or a shilling to row around the harbour or over to Dalkey Island. Kingstown was a fishing village and many of the local men went out fishing for their livelihood. They would arrive home in the evening with their catch of fish and one could buy a few pence worth of herrings or mackerel fresh from the sea and alive and have them for supper. Now and then when there was a heavy storm at sea in the middle of the night a boat would be in distress and the lifeboat would have to go out and we would hear the siren and people would jump out of bed to go down to try and help if necessary. The lifeboat men were great, always risking their lives for others.

We were sent down to swim in the sea in the months of September and October. We were told that it was good for us because the iodine was in the water then and that the bubbles burst on the seaweed.

In 1891 my father was born in the Rotunda Hospital. It was called the Lying-in Maternity Hospital then. There were two women to a bed. He had a brother and sister and they were left orphans. Their parents died young. They were educated in a school on Carysfort Avenue, Blackrock. It was a Protestant school and indoor. Each child was carefully assessed as to their capability and duly educated along those lines. When they left the school they were 'improvers' in whichever profession or trade to which they were suited and that which they chose to follow as a vocation and a means to earning a living. This was a fee-paying school and the pupils were well cared for and well trained for a start in life. My father became a journeyman tailor; his brother a musician and solicitor's clerk and his sister a leather book binder, no mean achievement in those days.

In the Thirties, Forties and Fifties there was little or no employment either and no universities for the majority. University was for the chosen few. There were a few chronics who never left the Campus. They seemed to stay there permanently. So for the ordinary middle-class person the next best thing was a good trade and to get into a trade you would be a lucky person to have a father with a trade on his hands and that is where you served your time for a number of years, either to your father or to somebody else that he knew or paid a fee to take you. Otherwise you might go and dig the roads or labouring work. The best results were had from 'learning on the job', seeing things done the right and real way, no fooling around. After a few years one could earn some sort of a living.

At the beginning of the 1939 – 45 World War, Dun Laoghaire got a big shock when a bomb fell beside the People's Park on the tramtracks on the main road at Sandycove. It caused quite a big crater in the middle of the road. There was no one hurt but a huge rock went through the roof of a house and landed at the foot of a baby's cot while he or she was asleep. It happened at about seven o'clock in the evening. It was rumoured that the Germans were trying to attack the mailboat.

In the mid-Thirties and Forties to have a bicycle of your own meant freedom to come and go just as much as a car means to the people of today. I cycled to South Circular Road from Dun Laoghaire to work in the City during the summer months. I travelled by train in the winter and we cycled for recreation here and there. During the war years there was no petrol for cars or late night buses so there was no other way to get about. The centre of the City used to be just one big mass of bicycles being taken care of by men and boys who made jobs for themselves doing that while the owners were off at a theatre, a dance or a film. Life was elegance itself in the City, day or night, at that time. Meals were served with grace and decorum, no paper cups. Memories live on events which occurred in the past, sentimental happenings mostly. Reaching seventy-five one has more time to dwell on memories but let's hope we can take what is left of the future in our stride.

THE POWERADDY

Susan O'Driscoll (b 1923)

Off Leitrim St., Cork City, 1920s – 40s

When I was a child growing up some 60 years ago we never heard of pollution, environment or sex, which takes over our lives on TV news of every day. We lived in the middle of all this and didn't even know it or take any notice of same. Everyone heard of Poweraddy. First of all we had the Fever Hospital blowing all the germs over our houses and into our back yards and whenever there was a death there, all we kids went up the hill into the mortuary to see the corpse. Also on our way to school, North Presentation, we passed a pigsty in between the houses in Chapel Lane as it was called at that time, and what a smell. At 3 p.m. on our way home, we came a different way, out the side door of the school to Bulldog Lane. There we had Denny's Cellar, the killing of pigs, blood and burning hair. Yet we all went in there for a rope for skipping. Most of the men were nice and would give us one and we would play with that, till it ravelled away.

Now that smell was bad, but across the road we had the back of Murphy's Brewery called the Grains house; stuff pouring out in heaps on to the main road and facing a row of houses' front doors, John's Street. We also had smoke bellowing out of the big shaft. We got near home then and sat on the wall above Poweraddy river in-haling the smells from Sunbeam factory's coloured water, Cork Distillery, Harringtons paint factory, and anything else that flowed from Blackpool Bridge, and had to come through Poweraddy river.

Education, the more we have of it, the more we have to worry about. How many remember this? My Father, God rest him, had to get at least 10 names in our place, Shandon View, to have gas installed so we got it. Then we got a radio, wireless as it was called but the trouble with that was that we had to take the battery to Burwoods to be charged every few days. A glass bottle with wire handles, you would return one and get another. We also had a gramophone with a big horn and the family two doors away would send us in to tell my mother to turn the horn out the door so they could hear it — all doors were open that time, and one thing I know, we never had a key to our front door. You could go in anytime, so could breadmen, milkmen and friends. I wonder will we ever see those times again. It's so sad we have to lock our doors now, even if we go across the road.

Monday I hated, my poor mother with a bath on two chairs washing on a washboard in the kitchen. What hard work and not a word of complaint and today everyone has stress rearing children, cribbing over washing and all we have to do is put it in a machine and press a button, take them out of that and into the dryer and fold them and put them away. Are we any better for all this stress, tranquillisers and sleeping pills? If we had a cold when we were kids or a cough we all got a spoonful of the same bottle, Mother, Father, boys and girls, but today if our kids sneeze the doctor is called and the child is ordered antibiotics. In our family five girls and two boys, Mother, Father and grandmother all lived in a small house, a few of us in each bed. And to bath, a big bath was taken up upstairs and we all washed in our turns.

We were a very close happy family. When my oldest sister got married we missed her very much. Our family got too big for the small house so in 1948 we moved to a bigger house in Douglas Road. A second sister got married. In 1943 my father died. In 1948 my sister died and in 1949 my brother went to Canada, and the same year another sister got married. In 1950 my grandmother died and my youngest brother went to Canada. So in seven years there was only my mother and myself left and she always said wouldn't the small house be big enough for us now and when I see our own family adding to their homes with only a few kids, wanting more room, I just had to remember all this. So again everyone is bringing the stress on themselves with expenses they could do without, if they only realised the years pass so quickly and the older you get the faster they go.

Now this is not just our family, the same thing went on all

around us. There was no such as keeping up with the Jones's. We all made do with what we had, dresses and shoes were all handed down from older sisters — sizes too big but we just dragged them along, so did all our friends and there was no jealousy and when we got a treat of new shoes it was something special. I remember waking up in the middle of the night looking out at my new shoes hoping for morning to put them on. The kids today can choose which shoes to wear with what, but I still think we were all the better for being unspoilt.

We have lots to look back on, and when I hear some people say the good old days; yes they were good and safe but very poor and we were all happy. We had many laughs and can look back on it today. Can anyone imagine this happening today? My father made up enough stuff to paint the outside wall of our house, and found he had too much, so he painted the woman's house next door. She was out and when she came home her house was finished and all she had to do was say thanks — no money — it wasn't expected either. Now this is a funny part. One day our shopkeeper called my sister and said, 'Now I am very fond of you so I have these high boots they're new and I would like you to have them.' She came in home and opened the parcel and first thing she said, 'I can't wear these I don't like them.' So my good natured mother said, 'You can't disrespect the woman she will have to see them on you.' Well she wore them, and of course they were too big, so she said I should have them, as I was older than her, so mother said, 'you were her favourite you must wear them.' She wore them to school and her legs were so thin she couldn't bend her knees, she kicked every stone and kerb on the way to school and back, and eventually they wore down, so she said Thank God they were worn out. We went to bed happy and laughing about the boots being gone. We also had a good natured father, he saw the boots needed repair and he always had leather in to repair our shoes and yes you guessed it, when we got up in the morning there was the boots as good as new looking at us. When Nancy Sinatra sang that song years ago 'These boots are made for walking' we had a good laugh over it all.

THE THREE SISTERS

Bonnie Freyne (b 1925)

Ballyshannon, County Donegal, 1930s

Maud, Catherine and Louise — the Miss Allinghams as they were known to us children in the 1930s — they were nieces of the poet William Allingham who was born in 1824 in the house next door to where I was born and reared more than 100 years later. The town of course was Ballyshannon, County Donegal. Many 'Golden Oldies' today may have memories of his poems in the Old School Readers — 'Adieu to Ballyshannon', 'Four Ducks in a Pond' which in later years I was to learn from Sr Eustace, our English teacher in St Louis, Carrickmacross.

The three sisters were old, rather eccentric but very kind and lovable. They were very friendly with my parents. Catherine in particular was a keen gardener, an interest shared with my father. I can remember the lovely pansy plants she gave him, a most unusual white and a real deep purple — these she got from the gardens in Lissadell, the home of the Gore Booth family in County Sligo — the head gardener there always advertised his plants for sale in spring.

Maud, the eldest of the three, never left the house and seldom answered the door to callers but when she did, she was most gracious. She was a tall lady dressed in long skirts and high necked blouses. Even though she was old, her hair was a light brown colour, possibly dyed as hair dye, not rinse, was fashionable in those days. She had beautiful blue eyes, a very pale face, rouged pink cheeks. Maud was a gifted artist, specialised in water colours of local places of interest and there were many in the locality — the Falls of Assaroe and the Beach of Rossnowlagh were amongst her favourites.

Louise, the youngest of the three, was like the swallows. She was never seen outdoors from September until May and then only if the weather was suitable. She loved style but her clothes always looked as if they were resurrected from some old trunk. She wore a pale blue flimsy chiffon dress, with three-quarter length sleeves which showed off her very thin arms. Her large straw hat was certainly late Victorian, adorned with roses and daisies and her neat shaped patent shoes had high heels. She was always accompanied by Catherine when she did appear and clung very tightly to her.

Catherine, unlike her sisters, was the most outgoing. She did the shopping and the garden and always had a friendly word for all the neighbours. She dressed in a long tweed coat and wore a green beret, strong shoes and thick stockings. She too had lovely, kind eyes but her weather-beaten face was lined and rough.

The sisters adored and lived for their pets — little Pekinese dogs, about six in all. One seldom saw Catherine without two or three on leads having their daily walk, and very often she carried one in her arms. In winter they wore little coats neatly strapped around their small bodies. They were treated just like children and had what they called a Bone Parade every evening, when the pets lined up and got a special bone biscuit each. When they passed away they were buried with dignity in the little graveyard in the back garden. 'Bubbles' was Catherine's very special pet, he died of old age. She must have cried for almost a year if his name was mentioned. A small photograph taken of him when in his prime was fitted into the frame of her Cameo brooch and worn with pride. Little headstones with each dog's name, erected with the help of old Ned Carrick, who helped Catherine with her garden, marked each grave. I well remember the day I overheard Catherine sobbing to my mother her tale of woe about poor Prince Edward who was suffering from an enlarged liver — young as I was, I was aware of the trouble in the Royal Family over Edward and Wally Simpson's romance in 1936 and thought to myself, well Edward will die now and the problem will be solved, not knowing until mother told us later that Prince Edward was the odd man out in the dog family — he was a little Scots terrier who was ill. Luckily he made a full recovery to the sister's great joy. Miss Henrietta was Louise's special cat and there was much weeping and sadness when her death was announced after weeks of special loving care.

The pleasant memories of the three Miss Allinghams will always stay with me. I treasure the hand-done leather cover Catherine made for my missal when I was going to boarding school. Leather work, including beautiful handbags, was her form of relaxation.

Last year, when visiting Donegal, my two widowed sisters and I (another three sisters) paid a visit to the old churchyard in Mullaghnashee, Ballyshannon, where many of our old neighbours of forty-plus years are laid to rest. It was a cold misty day in September. The church clock struck twelve mid-day — the Angelus bell rang from the Rock Chapel as we called it on the other side of the Erne. We saw William Allingham's tomb, but nowhere could I see the names of Maud, Catherine or Louise. Were they forgotten, the last of the family and no-one left to inscribe their names or perhaps in the misty rain we did not find their grave.

I wondered were the headstones to 'Bubbles', 'Prince Edward' and 'Miss Henrietta' still in the back garden or were they too, like their kind mistresses, completely forgotten?

SHOCKING TIMES

Geoffrey O'Shea (b 1918)

Piltown, County Kilkenny, 1920s – 40s

RADIO BLOW-OUT — ALL-IRELAND FINAL, 1933

In September 1933 very few had a wireless, as they were called in those days. You went to houses who happened to have one; the wet battery ones. We didn't get one until 1950 ourselves. A second-hand one at that.

The largest grocery and hardware shop in the village had one. People walked over from miles around. It was between Kilkenny and Limerick. The wireless was situated in the shop window. A queue a mile long stretched on either side. An exciting match. Three minutes to go with very little in it, a point or two, Kilkenny going for a score, the wireless went dead. There were more than a few Hail Marys said.

Bitter disappointment. We had to go home, go some place, to the local cross-roads that night to hear the final result — Kilkenny won.

THE BLUE-SHIRTS - 1930s

The times were so bad, especially for farmers — the economic war. Dev refusing to pay annuities to Britain. The country was still low after the Civil War, the Troubles, fights, fist fights over politics were common. The bitterness was real. The way it was you were a follower of Dev's, thought him God or you hated him. We were on the hate side. When Eoin O'Duffy started the Blue-shirts, joined up with Cosgrave, Cumann na nGael were going to fight to have the tariffs removed, get rid of Dev. All we youngsters backed him. We wanted to be able to sell our milk and cattle. Survival was what it as all about.

I attended a huge rally in the nearby town, six miles away in May 1934, the year before he took Dev's back hand and left us high and dry. The town was spilling over with people. All cheering and shouting. A number of Dev's followers tried to boo us. We all had our blue shirts on, the girls blue blouses. It was a warm day. Throngs walked for miles, 12/14 miles away. It was a bit of amusement for us too. Easy to amuse us that time.

MARCH FAIR 1936

I was only left school four years. In August would be a young lad of 18. The Economic War was on. Tariffs on all exports going to Britain. Burn everything English but their coal was a familiar saying at the time. During the bad winter of 1947 they would have been glad of English coal. Farmers were badly hit. The butter, cheese, fowl, sheep and cattle, all our exports went to Britain.

We were short of money, I was sent with two shorthorn yearlings for the fair six miles away, set off before dawn. Joined others on the road. Jobbers passed in cars. One lad stopped me and asked me how much. 'Take off the £2 and we might have a deal,' he said. The princely sum of two shillings!

I kept going, stood with them until about 2 o'clock. Not a single bid was I offered. Hadn't even the price of a bit to eat. I walked them home again. Met up with a man two parishes away. He too got no bid. The heavens opened on us as we left town. I had nothing but brogues and a cheap white trousers on me. Not a wonderful top coat either.

Lashed the whole six miles home. I was like a drowned rat when I arrived. The calves of my legs were skinned from the wet trousers rubbing against them. Took off all I could, ate a bit at the fire. Was up the day after, working away without a snuffle.

COMING HOME FROM THE CREAMERY IN THE BLACK FROST

We had a fortnight of hard dry black frost before Christmas 1938. In the morning there would be two inches of ice on buckets of water inside in the kitchen. No heaters or electric blankets, nothing only cold white sheets made from flour bags.

I didn't go to the creamery every day. One particular morning I remember well. Tackled the mare and dray — lifted in my twenty gallon churn. Got there walking slow. Especially down Keever's Hill.

On the way home I had an empty churn, butter and a few bags of cheesings. Was a quarter mile gone, when the mare started to skeet. I untackled. Went in between the shafts, guided her and shoved the cart most of a mile. Didn't know my strength then, a young lad of 20. For years after could lift a house. We did everything by man strength and ignorance in those days. Years after in 1971, a specialist told me I was born with weak muscles in my back. Was in agony with it at the time. I lifted everything that came before me.

BALD HEADS AND BALD TYRES

In the middle of the War years, the 1940s, rubber was next to impossible to get. Petrol was a problem relevant to most of us, keeping the bike going was a major one. My front tyre was bad, to say the least of it. I heard tyres could be got in Kilmoganny. So one Saturday morning, in the summer time, I headed off on my bike, a journey of 12 miles if not more. None to be got I decided to keep going, headed for Ballyhale, ten miles away. The same story. Cycled from there to Mullinavat and into Carrick. A round trip of eight miles.

Tried a few shops, nothing. Tried one last one, wasn't a regular customer. He jeered me saying, 'Only when ye are stuck ye come in here'. I was going to say, your head is baldy enough for 'A basin head' as a wit in my parish called him years before.

Still not willing to give up yet. I wanted it very badly. Banjacksed without a bike. Holding my breath on every journey in case it would blow in bits. There was one possibility left. A man who was able to get stuff on the black market. Though I wasn't a regular customer, the worst I could do was fail. He was obliging anyway. Never insulted anyone.

Six miles more, through Piltown, Fiddown, on the road to Waterford. He had a shop on the side of the main road, sold everything, groceries, oil, some petrol, clothes, footwear. A baldy headed man too. I was in luck, he had a tyre for the enormous price of one pound. I cycled home the eight miles happy. My mother kept a dinner for me. I ate a fine feed. Went to bed tired as a dog until evening. No matter I had a tyre. Could go places with ease.

CAT'S MILK

The year was 1945. Not a bad summer weather wise. My brother was home from the Mill Hill Fathers Seminary for the summer. The War was over since May. The rationing was by no means over. On a farm that time we had little money. Only in September or October you might get some of the milk money, the butter and feed bills might be cleared by then.

Tipperary and Kilkenny were to meet in the All Ireland Hurling Final. We were strong followers. Cycled miles to Thurles one time, on what you might call bad bikes. I had one so high that a neighbour of mine, Sean, used to say, whenever he'd meet me 'How are you all up there, in the sky?'

We worked like hell for the summer. Maurice thinned and stooked. I did likewise, bound corn on task. What would you get for anything then only a few shillings. Our expectations were little. Enough to keep us going, was all we asked.

The first weekend in September finally came. On a wet Friday evening myself and Maurice cycled to Kilmacow, he heard some tickets could be got, a journey of six miles. It poured rain, no tickets. 'Well, tickets or no, we're not staying at home' I said to him.

The next evening, Saturday, we walked to Fiddown, four miles, went on the night mail to Dublin. Arrived at four in the morning. Walked the quays, no-one around only milk carts. Certainly no vandals or thugs like now. The words were Chinese to us then.

We got our breakfast in a place I can't think of its name. If it wasn't sow's milk it was cat's they gave us to put on the tea. Shocking times.

Tipperary beat us. We were scalded after all the hardship. We booked in at Stoke's Guest House for the night. Walked around the streets, chatted to other lads until later, slept on mattresses on the floor. In the morning, a maid stepped over us, going into another room. No trousers on women in those days. We got tea, bread and red jam for our breakfast.

Got home on the train to Mullinavat. Six miles from home. Walked home. Maurice's feet were killing him, he took off his shoes. We arrived home at about two. I changed clothes, ate a bite, went out to my father and stacked oats for the rest of the day until evening and cow time. Maurice went to bed exhausted.

Headed for Jamestown Cross, down the road a half mile in the late evening. One of the principal meeting places those times. Relived all the exploits to the lads. Played skittles. By God they'd no young lads do it today. We didn't know any better.

THRESHING DANCE DURING THE WAR – 1945

In the winter time apart from hops at crossroads, card games, the threshing dances were all the go. Threshing started in late October, went on until early January. A neighbourhood thing. You worked at his threshing, he yours, or if you couldn't go yourself you sent a workman or someone and paid them. Everything was done by co-operation. No machines so everyone gave a hand.

This particular threshing dance after Christmas 1945 sticks out in my mind as being the best I was ever at. The family giving it were known to everyone as being comical characters. Lived in a big ramshackle two-storey house with an underground cellar. Had a school room. Were big people one time. The house is gone now, modern cattle sheds in its place. So are the family.

Dancing went on in two big rooms. The melodeon player played in the hallway between the two. The place was jammed. Some complained they couldn't hear the music. 'No problem' one of the brothers said. He took two doors off their hinges. Tore them down you could say.

Pounding was heard in another room, the parlour. Some thought it might be a ghost. It was known to be haunted. One brave person looked in, there was a work horse inside. Most of the outhouses were down. During a storm slates flew like confetti around the yard.

It was four in the morning before we got home. Got a big supper and all. They had had a good threshing so they made a big splash. Could never hold money.

II

A JOURNEY TO THE COUNTRY

Mary Fitzpatrick (1902 – 94)

County Monaghan / Roscommon, 1911 – 15

I was born in Monaghan town in 1902. My mother was a native of County Roscommon and my father came from County Down.

Every summer when we got our school holidays, myself and my two brothers, who were a few years older than me, were packed off to stay with my mother's people in the country.

I seem to remember that we stopped overnight in a house in Dromod on our way. Then the next day we waited eagerly for the narrow-gauge railway to take us as far as Carrick-on- Shannon. Strange I have no memory of the journey from home to Dromod but I still remember clearly the rickety wooden carriage on the narrow-gauge and how we rattled on at a leisurely pace along the narrow track.

When we reached the station at Carrick-on-Shannon a new adventure was about to begin. My uncle would be there to meet us with a side-car drawn by a sprightly young horse. As we jogged along the road the horse shied and stopped dead at a certain spot and no amount of shouting or coaxing would make her go on. My uncle would have to step down and lead her by the head past the invisible block. We heard people saying that this particular place was haunted! By what I never found out; it was a bit of a mystery then and still is to this day.

SCHOOLDAYS

Margaret O'Sullivan (b 1904)

Ovens, County Cork, 1910s

I was born 8 July 1904 at home, went to school at six, got first Holy Communion at nine and a half years. We were examined on the confirmation day by the Bishop or a priest appointed by him in the long Catechism and Historical, which was a book of short questions and answers, a little bigger than the life of 'Our Lord'. We worried till this exam was over for fear of being put back for two years. We were dressed in a white dress and veil. I think at that time no child got money from relations or friends.

On my first day in school I was given a lovely framed slate and three inch bare kind of pencil, which I leaned too heavily on and broke in small pieces. After a little time I improved. The slate was lined on one side for writing, plain on the other for sums, now called maths. Later I got a jotter and right pencil.

When I got to 3rd standard I got an ink pen. The teacher mixed some powder and water in a big bottle and poured it into little inkwells shaped like egg cups firmed from spilling in circular holes in front of each pupil on our desks, dipping the pen I think I made a terrible mess to paper and hands.

I was very fond of dancing at a young age. We danced in each other's homes, no invitation was needed only lift the latch. Children and adults danced together sets, barn, etc. There were no dance halls or big bands. A member of some family learned by ear to play the melodeon, or the violin, called a fiddle. Some of the floors were only hardened clay made smooth by use. Better floors were fine sand mixed with cement. Our boots and shoes were made of thick rough hard upper leathers and 1/2 inch high soles, a narrow strip of tin was nailed to the heels to keep them level. Our stockings were knitted by ourselves or parents of black 3 or 4 ply wool, long above the knee and held in place with a garter.

The first I got to know of the world outside our own was when the 1914 War One started. It was awful to hear of all the men that were killed. During that period we obtained our divided government from England. Electricity was unknown to us. A paraffin filled lamp of tin was hung on a nail in the wall filled with a burner and covered with a sparkling glass globe.

At Christmas we had no fruit cake only a very high currant loaf which tasted lovely. Through the year we bought no loaves, most people baked cakes in a bastible heated on coals in an open fire, no ovens. Of course there were rich people like extensive farmers who could afford the best. We had only twenty acres of rough land, two or three milk cows. A fat pig slaughtered by a local man cut in useable pieces, salted, packed into a timber barrel for three weeks, then hung from the rafters. Also a half sack of white flour. We were never hungry, three tons of coal. The money for these was spared over the year. So we were warm during the cold weather. We grew plenty of potatoes. We boiled the waste for our few hens. No turkeys only a bought goose for Christmas. We also had plenty of eggs. We went to school bare-footed.

NO SHOES IN SUMMER

Stephen Conroy(1912 – 1991)

County Mayo, 1920s

When I was young most people went to Primary school only. These were small two-roomed buildings with two teachers. Pupils stayed in one room until they reached third class and then moved to the other room where they stayed until seventh class.

All schools were heated by a big open fire. Each family had to provide a cart of turf or wood every year for the fire.

At that time everyone walked to school usually two or three miles. In winter the children wore heavy boots with rows of studs on them which saved the leather from getting worn. I enjoyed sliding on the ice with these boots. In summer we were allowed to leave the boots at home and go to school barefoot.

Corporal punishment was allowed then. Some pupils got very bad beatings from the teacher's stick. Six blows on each hand was the usual punishment for getting the answers wrong or talking. We all believed that a single horsehair across your hand would break the teacher's stick. It never worked for me however.

Most exercises were learnt off by heart, like poems, tables, etc. The problem with this was if someone asked you what SIX sixes were, you would have to work your way up from six ones to six sixes. Another thing wrong with this was we learnt lots of things without understanding what they meant; for example, in Religion there was a book called the Catechism which had lots of questions with long difficult answers, all of these had to be learnt off by heart even if we did not understand them. For half his lifetime someone I knew thought that the third line of the Hail Mary was 'Blessed art thou A MONK SWIMMIN'.

On Mondays, the Parish Priest would visit the school and ask questions from the Catechism; he would also ask us questions about his sermon at Mass the day before to check if we were paying attention. Anyone who gave the wrong answer got a sore ear.

At that time too, the Parish Priest used to walk the roads of the Parish with his blackthorn stick. If he came upon any young people up to mischief they would get a blow of the blackthorn stick. My clearest memory of my school days is of the day I got a blow from the blackthorn stick, when the Parish Priest caught me smoking.

BEFORE THE SCHOOL BUS

Nancy Power (b 1916)

Redestown, County Kilkenny, 1920s

When I think back to my own school days in the Twenties and compare conditions then and now I ask myself how did we survive, not to mention how did we manage to learn? Our school-house was better and bigger than most, having been built by the Earl of Ormond for his tenants in the bad old days; nevertheless it was a cold, damp structure with a fireplace at one end and six large windows which our principal, who was a fresh air fanatic, liked to keep open. That was fine if you had your back to the fire, as she had.

It was a mixed school and we had an average of seventy pupils all in the same room, although the classes ranged from infants to sixth class. I will not dwell on the qualities of our two teachers, except to say that it required a strict disciplinarian to keep affairs in order in the set-up just described. Our principal lived up to all that was required in that sphere. An uncompromising West Cork lady of middle age (in my time), her name is still spoken with awe although she is dead for over half a century. She had no inhibitions about the use of corporal punishment and the sight of the school door in the mornings never failed to sink our spirits and quieten our tongues. Like the school children in Goldsmith's 'Deserted Village' we too could read 'the day's disasters in her morning face'. We never complained to our parents because we knew there was no alternative. School was school and that was all.

There were compensations and this is where, in one very

important aspect, I pity the country children of today. The journeys to and from school were an education as valuable as any we managed to imbibe at school. We had to trudge about three miles over little white limestone roads and through what was known as 'mass paths' through the fields to reach our school.

The seasons were laid out before us from September to June. Who of my generation does not remember the start of the school year in September? Setting out from home on sun-filled mornings with the nip in the air. I don't remember any rainy September days, only the hazy light on the changing leaves. In my mind's eye I can still see the jewelled cobwebs stretched between the blackberry fronds. I can hear the drone of the threshing engine in a neighbour's haggard and I can remember the taste of ripe damsons and blackberries and hazelnuts which we cropped on our long journey homeward on Autumn evenings.

Yes, I remember January days sliding to school on ice-bound roads and blowing on frozen fingers to thaw them after snowball fights. Setting out from home on bitter January mornings to trudge three miles to school was no picnic, to put it mildly.

Suddenly, one morning it was spring. Jack Frost had relaxed his iron grip and the little streams gurgled and danced in the roadside dykes. The fields were alive with young life, the hedges full of birdsong. We were part of it all. It was as if God created this season especially for us. Soon it was Easter and bird-nesting time and the holidays once more.

After Easter it was not long until we could shed our shoes and feel the grass under bare toes and dabble for hours in the brook on the way home.

We had secret places where we copied home-exercises and where the boys had the usual fist-fights which the girls didn't like but endured because our brothers were usually involved. If one of them arrived home with a black eye, we were the ones who were grilled as it was a point of honour with the boys never to tell.

Yes, there were hazards too on our journeys. We dreaded the eve of the fair day when the roads were full of dealers' wild horses. Occasionally we were chased by straying bulls, by mad turkey cocks, by pet rams and even by irate farmers when we strayed from the straight and narrow or trespassed.

Worst of all, we had to pass the witch-woman's cottage, where we were so afraid that we stared straight ahead without even looking because even to look called down her wrath upon us. She was usually out tending her goats by the roadside and was a bundle of rags tied in the middle, with a black hat tied under her chin and baleful narrow eyes peering from a nut-brown face. Even the boldest took no chances with HER.

Our trek to and from school taught us to take the rough with the smooth and we learned early that life was not all sunshine.

Not very long ago we heard great tumult about the school bus. Who should pay and who should go free? People of my generation said things like 'What's all the fuss about?', 'They are all spoilt brats.', 'What did we do?' That's all very well. Times change and as Hartley said in 'The Go-Between' the 'the past is a foreign country, they do things differently there'. With the best will in the world, children cannot get to school under their own steam nowadays because all the little schools which we knew, scattered here and there about the country, are no more.

Experts on the subject of education can put forward arguments for and against the closure of the little schools. When the late Donagh O'Malley had the enlightened vision of a wider education for us all he didn't foresee the difficulties, not least the cost of transport of getting the children to the newer enlarged schools.

Anytime I take a country walk nowadays I relive those school times of ours and think of the companions who shared the road with me. I don't think life would have been so adventurous on a school bus.

CHILDHOOD IN THE TWENTIES

Angela Mitchell (b 1908)

Ballybrien, County Offaly

I am 85. I lived on a small farm with my parents and eight brother and sisters. We had a three bedroomed thatched house with a large open fireplace in which we burned logs and lots of turf which was cut on our local bog by my father and some neighbours. As children we helped to turn, spread and harvest this turf until it was dry in the summer sun. This we did after school. We walked to and from school which was about half a mile from our home. We seldom missed any days from school and I remember being four years without being absent one day. For this I was rewarded with a prize each year which was usually a storybook which I loved, being an avid reader. We were a very healthy family and I don't recall ever seeing a doctor called to attend any of us. We had a very happy childhood playing with neighbours' children and among ourselves. We had lots of pets: rabbits, guinea pigs, birds and young lambs. My brother had a pet goat which we trained to draw a little cart which he made himself with a little seat. I often sat with him in it and we went for little drives. One day we met a cross old man who set his dog on us and poor Bonny got frightened and turned over our cart into a tuft of briars.

Our diet was mostly home made brown bread, freshly churned butter, lots of home grown vegetables and potatoes with home cured bacon. We remained at school until we were 16 or 17 years old. Our greatest joy was taking home the turf in August. We trotted down to the bog in our pony and creels with numerous friends and loaded up the dry turf. We came carefully back with each load to deposit it in the haggard where it was carefully built into ricks by my father to keep us warm during the winter.

In summer we went to crossroad dancing and singing and in winter time there were house parties and we had many happy pastimes.We spun our own knitting wool on a large spinning wheel. Many winter nights I spent spinning wool which one of my sisters corded. This was knitted into very warm jumpers and stockings for all the family and friends.

I remember being frightened when the Black and Tans came and my father made us go to school through the fields as we might meet the Crossley Tenders on the road. This is just a little of past times.

OUR NATURE TRAIL TO SCHOOL

Bessie Byrne Sheridan (b 1919)

Askamore, County Wexford, 1930s

As time moves on and we grow older we recall with vivid and nostalgic memories our journey through our very picturesque and very emerald green countryside on our way to our local primary school. It was located just two miles from our farmstead and it nestled beneath the wooded hillside of Sliabh Bhuide in that most historic and scenic area of Askamore which is on the Wicklow-Wexford border in North Wexford. Unlike Alice Taylor we didn't walk through the fields to school, but travelled the then rugged and stony way which was uphill and down dales. Oh! what treasured and revered memories we retain of those days gone long, long ago into oblivion. No tarmacadamed roads in those days of sparse cash but healthy living. Making ourselves happy with very little was the norm for us all. Those times were known as the 'hungry thirties' which I think is a misnomer because there was plenty of home-produced natural food available everywhere and those that hadn't it shared it with their neighbours.

Armed with our schoolbags and lunch, and filled with excitement of what the day might bring we set off for school. It's now the lovely Spring time of the year, and all the way there it's a real Nature Trail. Before we leave the short boreen leading to our home we loiter to look at a robin's nest in the ditch. Seeing us approach, mother robin is frightened and quickly flies away to a nearby bush where she can watch us. Looking out at us are four little fluffy chicks with gaping mouths. They are a real joy to behold, and we are truly thrilled to see them hatched out as we have been awaiting their arrival for a long time. We then think of the red hen in the farmyard with her lovely clutch of chickens, but she doesn't claim the same appeal to us as the robin and her offspring do. We (as children) imagine the robin and her chicks are our property hence our greater interest rests with them. After leaving our laneway and going downhill we spy a bank of lovely primroses beneath the hedgerow. Quickly we decide to pick a bunch to bring to the school altar. While we are plucking the primroses a wood pigeon flies over our heads carrying some twigs in her beak to build her home. A thrush in an overhanging tree sings her tune, and seems to prolong it for our pleasure. We now proceed over the bridge and along by the riverside. We are now in the valley, and there are bogs on both sides of this level road. Later on the yellow irises or water lilies will deck the bog adjoining the river. As we continue our way a heron or 'cor eisc' (as we called it) with its gaunt and weird ghost-like appearance alights on the road before us, but again takes flight almost immediately. In the meantime a waterhen rushes back into the river after being out picking on the grass margin. Not far away a frog croaks. The beautiful Spring flowers deck the scene demonstrating their many and varied colours that nature has endowed them with — even the river has her lovely white flowers. Now we are halfways to school. Now we pass the old mill wheel (then in use) and look in on the pond, where the ducks are swimming and diving for small fish. It's now uphill so we walk more slowly. While doing so my sister takes the left-hand side of the road, while I take the right side. The road is mostly all our own as there are no cars or pedestrians to be seen except the odd farmer and his cart and perhaps a woman putting out the cows after milking. My sister and I start counting the snails on both sides as they emerge from the side-paths. The day is so kind and mild that they too come out to enjoy the nice weather. From the distance we hear the call of the cuckoo while the corncrake asserts his presence in a nearby meadow. On dewy mornings in the harvest our attention was drawn to the furze bushes on the waysides where the spiders and their cobwebs enthralled us. We watched them as they tried to elude our presence while hurriedly dashing up the bushes. Now we are up near the old derelict school house on the cross where sometimes we caught up with our school pals. Everywhere is very quiet and as we draw near the school we hear a farmer urge his horses forward as he ploughs. No tractors or automatic ploughs in those days. Mechanisation hadn't reached us. Now we have arrived at school having had a lesson in 'Nature Study', and another lesson in Arithmetic rehearsed by counting the snails.

On our homeward journey we see a pheasant and her brood at a distance but when we arrive at the spot she has disappeared to conceal herself and family under some bushes and briars. Further down the road a rat and his mate have a row in a ditch while a rabbit rushes down the way before us. Nearby a whitethorn is in full bloom, but was beginning to shed her lovely white petals which drop like confetti on the ground beneath. We now arrive back at the 'Old Mill Wheel' and we stop to watch it turning with the water cascading down it. The miller is busy grinding the grain for the farmers who have come with wheat to be ground into wheaten meal for baking and oats to be ground into pinhead oatmeal for food for the farm family. He also brings some corn too to be ground for the farm animals. After leaving the Mill we loiter along by the river bank and again watch the water hens as they rush back into the river, and we take off our footwear and dip our hot and tired feet into the lovely cool water. By this time we are near home, and we spy our old sheep dog coming to greet us and welcome us home. Our nature trail is over for one day as we arrive home to partake of our dinner , but tomorrow we will again repeat the same trail.

MEMORIES OF CLONTIFLEECE

Liam Bradley (b 1927)

Clontifleece, County Down, 1930s

We called it the Big Bridge. How small and insignificant it looks to-day. It carried the Ballyvalley Road over the Moygannon River just three miles north of where it emptied into Carlingford Lough. All the world that mattered to us lay within a half mile radius of that bridge. The New Mills, roofless and derelict even in my childhood, was the most important meeting place for the young people of the district. A hundred yards further off stood Clontifleece National School. In the two bare rooms of that old school I acquired skills and knowledge from my third to my twelfth year. A stone's throw away from the school stood The Master's house and there I lived until my late teens, cut off from the new indispensable comforts of electricity, running water and motorised transport. Contifleece is a hilly townland but there, too were our football pitches — little flat patches at the foot of the surrounding hills. Many a name known on the football fields of the province was cheered on first, on these humble pitches.

I was sent early to school. My father was principal of Clontifleece school and at the tender age of three he brought me with him to start my education. I remember well that for the first few days he kept me with him in his own room. That was a new and wonderful experience. In those days the school catered for all pupils up to the age of fourteen. The older pupils seemed to me to be grown men and women and there were great crowds of children such as I had never experienced before. I still distinctly remember the day the good times ended. Lessons were just about to start when my father handed me two sticks of white chalk and told me to bring them into Miss Mehegan's room. Innocent as I was I didn't suspect a thing and marched into the room where all the youngest children were taught. Miss Mehegan greeted me, took my chalk and then began introducing me to all these boys and girls of my own age. She seemed to like me very much for she wouldn't let me go back to my father's room. However, gradually my fate dawned on me and I had to accept that I would have to grow into a big boy before I would rejoin my father's pupils.

Life was uncomfortable for the youngest pupils at Clontifleece in those days. Much of their day was spent kneeling on the rough wooden floor with the pupils resting their slates and books on long moveable wooden forms that stretched most of the width of the room. There we learned our A B Cs and wrote with chalk on our slates. Many a jersey went home showing signs of the day's industry as a duster went missing. Those same forms were frequently borrowed from the school to seat mourners at all the wakes in the district. They were a natural and accepted link between youth and old age. I can't remember being particularly fond of sums, as the study of mathematics was then called, at that stage in my education. That love came later on. But I do remember the wonder of poetry. To this day a verse from one of the first poems I ever learned stands out in my memory. It was about the attractions of the seaside and in particular about the waves. The final verse was as follows:

> Then back they went,
> And on they came,
> And tumbled in the caves,
> I think that I have never seen
> Such happy things as waves.

All I knew of waves at that time was learned from a picture in a book and it wasn't for many, many years that I stood in a cave. Those lines opened up for me a new and magical world and they have remained with me ever since. I am sorry when I meet to-day students who are unable to quote a single line of poetry.

I associate the mathematics of those days with fear. Miss Mehegan had a good book in which we regularly did our sums. This book was a showpiece, to be produced as evidence of success in learning. Correct answers were given a much admired tick with a red pencil and wrong answers a dreaded nought. Miss Mehegan did not take kindly to noughts on these books and each time one appeared was an occasion for trembling. Nervousness on the part of pupils made noughts more likely and I still remember the day I rejoiced that the sums could not be corrected because the teacher was too busy taking the older girls for cooking.

I must have been a sickly child at this stage for I was constantly subject to sties in my eyes. Wee John, a pupil from my father's room, came to me one day and said 'I have a cure for the sty. Bring in ten gooseberry thorns to-morrow and I'll cure your sty.' I told my father that evening and he exclaimed, 'If John thinks he can cure you let him go ahead.' Next day at lunchtime in my father's classroom Wee John asked me to give him the thorns one by one. He pointed them at the affected eye, gave each back to me to be thrown by me over my shoulder and finished by asking me to say a prayer. When I had finished he said, 'Now you are cured.' That was the last sty I suffered from.

It must have been in these years that the machinery was

stripped from The New Mills. I don't remember feeling sorry at the time at the passing of an era; all I remember was the excitement of seeing strangers working so close to our house. Perhaps regret at the disappearance of the familiar from the scene is too sophisticated an emotion for youth. The Monaghan poet, Patrick Kavanagh, has immortalised his regret at a scene similar to that I witnessed in my childhood. He calls his poem 'Requiem for a Mill'. The first stanza goes as follows:

> They took away the water-wheel,
> Scrap-ironed all the corn-mill;
> The water now cascades with no
> Audience pacing to and fro
> Taking in with casual glance
> Experience.

And he goes on to mourn the passing away of an old institution:

> Packaged, pre-cooked flakes have left
> A land of that old mill bereft.

The other day as I motored past what was the Master's House and ivy covered ruin that is all that is left of The New Mills and the modernised Clontifleece School with its electric light and flush toilets and tar-mac yard I could not help reflecting on Kavanagh's 'land bereft'. But I had some little consolation too. Someone had enough sensitivity, despite the modernisation, to retain in one of the original walls of the old school that plaque that I used gaze up at all those long years ago. It read:

CLONTIFLEECE NATIONAL SCHOOL
Erected by Narcissus Batt, Esq. /1839 / Virtute et Valore

A great day in the lives of the schoolchildren at Clontifleece was the day they graduated to 'the master's room'. It was an important stage in the business of growing up. For boys it was just as important as the first donning of long trousers, something that didn't happen in those days until one was thirteen or fourteen years of age. The elevation to 'the master's room' took place when pupils were aged about seven or more probably eight years of age. My father thus had the responsibility of teaching pupils of varying ages between eight and fourteen — a task that would be considered quite impossible today when the clever fourteen year old is almost half way through his Grammar School career. The youngest class in my father's room was Standard Three which would correspond to Primary Five in today's schools. He also taught in that one classroom Standards Four, Five, Six, and Seven — perhaps a total of forty pupils in all.

The total furniture in the classroom was a collection of three, or perhaps four long desks running the entire width of the room, fixed to the floor, and with long benches behind. Around the walls were long stools which could be moved about. Only half the pupils could be seated working at desks at any one time; the remainder of the time had to be spent standing.

To try to cope with this enormous age range my father divided his pupils into two main groups. Standards three and four worked together at similar activities, and standards five, six and seven also worked as a unit. Of course, inside these units the individual standards had to be catered for. Activities involving writing with pens had to be done seated at the benches, but reading activities, and much mathematical work written with pencil had to be done while standing. I still remember writing with pencil on a jotter balanced on my left hand.

Mathematics was a favourite subject with my father, and his pupils had to know their tables off like lightning — six eights had to be forty eight without a moment's hesitation — one hundred and ten pence had to be nine shillings and two pence on the tip of the tongue. Mental arithmetic was a daily feature in our school life. My old school companions would be horrified at the hesitancy of modern schoolchildren in mental computations. The banishment of the chanting of tables from our class-rooms by the inspectorate has left its mark. In those days in the 1930s chanting tables was not a crime, and there was really no need for pocket calculators. One of the advantages of a school like ours was that the younger children were constantly listening to the work being done by the more advanced classes. I was frequently familiar with the work of the senior classes before I reached them. One of the stories from the reading book of the standard six or seven class, I forget which, was a description of the chariot race from the novel 'Ben Hur'. I could recite reams of that story by heart from my lowly position in standard three. The opening remains with me to this day. 'Forth from their kennels like missiles from a volley shot the six fours' — and the extract finished with the overthrow of the bad guy 'and Massala entangled in the reins pitched forward headlong'.

My daughter, just last week, went into the main post office in O'Connell Street, Dublin, to send a telegram to Carrickmacross. The official told her that as Carrickmacross was in Northern Ireland it could not be delivered until after the weekend. Any of the junior pupils in our school could have rhymed off for him the chief towns of County Monaghan as 'Monaghan, Clones, and Carrickmacross, Ballbay and Castleblaney', and of every county in Ireland including Kildare — the chant embroidered as follows:- 'Kildare, Athy, Naas, and Maynooth — my hair, my eyes, my face, and my tooth'. So much for the progress of education. I studied Gography for six years in Grammar School but the Geography that remains most firmly fixed in my mind to this day is what I learned in that bare classroom in Clontifleece National School.

Pride of place in the curriculum of senior pupils of that old school was mathematics — including Algebra, Geometry, and Arithmetic. I was sitting for my Junior Certificate in Grammar School before I had caught up with the most advanced work done in some areas of study at Clontifleece. I well remember the Geometry lesson. The big test was whether one could prove that the square on the hypotenuse of a right angled triangle was equal to the sum of the squares on the other two sides. My father told us that mathematicians referred to this as 'pons assinorum' — the bridge of asses. Apparently less able pupils could not quite pass this obstacle, and could travel no further along the road to geometry. I must have been light footed in those days for I skipped across the bridge quite easily.

In arithmetic books in these days, a problem frequently set concerned the mixing of teas at different prices to produce a mixture to be sold at a certain price. My father showed us a simple way of doing it which infallibly produced the answer in a couple of seconds. The method used he called 'allegation'. When I went to Grammar School, and was confronted by similar problems, I automatically used 'allegation' and produced my correct answers immediately. But Brother M, my mathematics teacher, was not impressed — I was not allowed to use that method — I would have to work through a page of calculations and do it 'the right way'.

I was learning rapidly. But school was not all learning. How we looked forward to lunch break and the inevitable football match in 'The Hollow'. John, now long dead, would scarcely have emerged from the classroom when his call would ring out, 'To the holla boys as hard as yous can hook it, and no foalin' stinker is going to put me out of goals today'. In summer shoes and stockings were discarded, and football and most of the day's activities were enjoyed bare-footed. Each season of the year had, in addition its own peculiar schoolboy activity. Searching for birds nests in Spring in due course gave way to pegging tops, a game I never see played today. Later on came marbles, and a game we called 'Kitty' which was played with a small stick, pointed at both ends, which we struck on the ground so that it flew up into the air. The object was to hit it as far as possible with a long rod whilst it was in the air. In the windy days of Autumn we made kites and flew them from the big hill behind our house.

Long winter evenings kept children confined to home in the country districts in those days. There was no electricity, rooms being lit almost entirely by paraffin lamp. The country roads were in complete darkness. Our house was one of the only two that I knew of to have radio in my childhood. I distinctly remember listening to a play about a County Treasurer who ran away with the life savings of the ordinary people to the Isle of Man where he was safe from prosecution. I can still hear in my ears the cries of the duped people as they gathered outside the robber's door crying out for their money. It wasn't until about ten years ago when engaged in some literary research that I discovered that the play that remained so firmly in my memory was an adaptation of a novel by Tyrone writer William Carleton (1794-1869) entitled 'Fardorougha the Miser'.

Reading was an important winter occupation in our house. Our parents purchased each week a supply of children's reading that many will remember — 'The Skipper', 'The Rover', and 'The Wizard'. These were exchanged, where possible for others. My favourite book in those days was 'The Swiss Family Robinson' which I must have read at least half a dozen times until I knew it almost by heart. Games like draughts, snakes and ladders, and ludo also helped to while away the hours of darkness. I hadn't been to a cinema more than a couple of times until I was in my late teens, and naturally there was no television. I suppose the break with childhood came when I became a Grammar School pupil at the age of twelve. That involved a journey of nine miles by bicycle, reduced during the months of winter when I took the train from Warrenpoint to Newry. During the winter months I set off for school in darkness and returned also in darkness in the evening — a day of nine hours during which, like the rest of my companions, I was sustained by a package of buttered sandwiches. The most traumatic aspect of Grammar School for me was the confrontation with Latin and the Irish language for the first time. This was something completely new and strange. Many of my classmates had studied Irish already, and it was a chastening experience to find myself unable to comprehend what so many others were performing with ease. Time eventually solved my problems, but the story of that is perhaps, matter for another day.

CHILDHOOD MEMORIES

Paddy Hanley (b 1926)

Slievefinn, County Galway, 1930s

The best memory I have of my childhood is when I was six years old. I had been to school since I was four-and-a-half. Being the youngest of nine and five years younger than my sister I can safely say I was well looked after.

On the day in question, I was ready to go to school when my mother told me to stay home and help her for the day. My father and brothers had gone to the fair, so there were a lot of jobs to be done. At about 12 o'clock my mother put a pot of potatoes on the fire and when they were boiled she took them and put ten or twelve on a plate. Being so busy she did not have time to cook meat or vegetables so she got the tongs and put it into the fire until it was red hot. She then got a piece of fat bacon and squeezed the gravy onto the plates. We sat at the table and peeled the potatoes and dipped them into the gravy and the flavour of that is still in my mouth sixty years after.

When we had everything done she said she would go to visit my aunt who was home from America for her first visit. At that time doors were seldom locked. The front door was closed so she want out the back door and told me to put the bolt on the inside of the back door and then go out the little window in the back room. We walked to the house (where my mother was from) which was about five minutes walk and when we went in my aunt was out in her garden. After a few minutes she came in with a bowl in her hands and in it were the loveliest gooseberries I have ever seen. She left the bowl in front of me and told me to eat them — and eat them I did.

After all these years I think that that is one day I will never forget.

THE SCHOOLMASTER

Anon

I was aged between six and seven years and absolutely feared and hated our schoolmaster. Things were so bad that I felt I had to do something about it.

Our Sunday School teacher always taught us that God would give us anything we asked for — so I set to — many were the prayers. I prayed that God would land him in another school! He was rather slow in answering our request. Until one quiet morn and all the pupils were gathered outside the school door and the blinds drawn on the windows.

Some time passed and the School Mistress appeared on the steps and informed us that she had some very sad news for us: that the Schoolmaster had died during the night and that God had taken him to Heaven.

My sense of relief I just can't relate to you. It was fantastic. It was only when the Headmistress called down at me, 'Why don't you show your respect?' I was grinning from ear to ear! And the toughest little boy in the school suddenly piped up, 'Well if he's gone to Heaven there's no loss on him'.

And the question on the lips of all the youngsters was, 'Did he really get to Heaven?'

SUNDAY SCHOOL

Helen McKeown (née Hodge, b 1926)

Dungannon, County Tyrone, 1920s – 30s

I was born on a farm outside Dungannon, County Tyrone on June 1st 1926, one of five children, four girls and one boy. In those days everyone walked everywhere until they became old enough to cycle or go by bus or train. Very few owned a car.

I walked to Church of Ireland Sunday School (about 2 – 3 miles) each Sunday for 11 a.m. On entering the Church one was aware of a smoky smell and a small film of smoke all over the place, because the heating system was solid fuel. The main stove was situated in the centre of the main aisle. This was placed thirty-four steps underground and covered by some metal grating which allowed heat (and smoke) to escape. Two other stoves were placed at either wing, left and right, the Church being built in the shape of a Cross.

Sunday school began by singing a suitable hymn and prayer. This was conducted by the Superintendent or Minister (if present). We all trudged to our separate classes which were made up by age groups. Teachers were usually older girls or young married women, who gave of their time voluntarily. I was given a little homework, verse from a child's hymn, verse from a Bible passage or Psalm, our teacher explained or asked questions concerning our lesson. These lessons increased as I became older, by which time Catechism was introduced in preparation for Confirmation. This act took place every three years when candidates reached the ripe old age of 14 or 15 years. Special classes were held prior to the service in order to explain and prepare us for Confirmation at which we became full members of the Church (partaking of Holy Communion).

HOLIDAYS

Patricia Breen (1933 – 93)

Listowel, County Kerry

My mother was a native of Listowel, County Kerry, and lived on a farm about two miles outside the town. This is where I spent my Summer holidays as a child and what beautiful memories I have of those times. I could not wait for the first day of the school holiday to pack my few little belongings and be ready for my uncle to pick me up. He usually arrived on his way home from the creamery with the donkey and cart. I settled in and off we went. We would go up Ballygrennan Hill, down the 'Black Road', turn right and continue until we came to the small bridge, and there was the thatched cottage with the roses growing up the front wall and over the window. I was always greeted so warmly by my grandmother, aunt and cousins, Sheila, Kathleen and Jimmy.

After dinner we would go straight up to the orchard at the top of the 'Haggard'. We would climb the trees and sit contentedly on a branch and talk about what we would do during the holidays while we chewed apples which were only crabs at that stage. We played around the yard until it was time to get the cows for milking. We usually went up the fields and would drive the cows down the 'Glaishe'. That was a stream coming down from the upper fields and we would walk barefoot down the Glaishe and drive the cows into the barn. I loved the smell of the cows in the barn while they were being milked. 'Betsy' was the quietest cow so I was allowed to milk her on the very odd occasions. Milking over, they would be driven up the Glaishe again.

The work went on cleaning and scalding the tanks so they

would be clean for the milk going into them. Tea time would be home made bread, home made apple tart and possibly currant bread. My aunt used make the bread and bake it in a pot which was raised over some red hot coals and more hot coals heaped on the cover of the pot. They had to be replaced about every fifteen minutes and kept red hot until the baking was over. The coals would be taken from the fire which somehow never seemed to go out even on the hottest days. I loved the evenings with all the noises coming from the farmyard. There were six doors leading off the kitchen, three to the bedrooms, one out the back yard, one to the front which was a half door and the other to a store room.

My cousins and myself slept in what was called the lower room and it had a massive bed with a beautiful feather mattress which you would just sink into. We loved going to bed in it and would talk for hours about school and things. I loved it when dusk was falling and my uncle would have to light the paraffin lamp and the glow would light up our bedroom.

My grandmother's house was what you would call a rambling house. The neighbours from some distance would come along to the house and chat well into the morning. We would try and fig-ure out whose step was coming towards the house each time. The latch was lifted and the greeting always was, 'God Bless all here'. There is something very comforting in the sounds of voices com-ing from the kitchen when you are tucked up safely in bed. After some time my uncle would tell whoever was present to go on their knees and the Rosary was started. He would call on different ones to say a Decade and we would be warned if we were not an-swering the prayers. My grandmother had so many trimmings and all the neighbours were prayed for.

It was always men who did the rambling and they would have a flash lamp to show them the road home. They would have tea and currant cake usually. Sometimes they would start telling ghost sto-ries and we would be under the blankets at this stage. There was a special kind of pleasure in those days in getting up in the mornings when you were living on a farm. Everything was moving around and the half door was open with the sunshine streaming in.

How I loved going out to the hen house and getting a fresh egg for my breakfast, woe betide anyone who left a hen out before they had their eggs laid. They were on perches with straw under them and the eggs would still be warm. The big event of the morning would be the arrival of the postman. He would prop his bicycle up against the side of the house and my grandmother would be so pleased to see him. It meant of course that there was a letter either from England, America or Australia from one of her children. Dennis would lean over the half door and produce the letter and would then be offered a cup of tea which he rarely refused.

The work of the farm went on and the hay was getting ready to be cut. The men from the neighbouring farms always came to help with the cutting and saving as they did with the turf cutting also. My uncle in turn would give them help also. We loved it when the hay was being drawn home and we would take the tea and bread up to the meadow to the men. The ride on the hay cart was a special treat.

The latter part of the Summer saw the big event of the killing of the pig. We were not allowed see it or go anywhere near the barn where it was being done. We could hear the pig squealing but saw nothing. The neighbours were there to help in the skinning and cutting of the meat. The blood was cooked and made into black pudding and we looked forward to having porksteak and pudding for our dinner the next day. The barrels were all ready for the meat and some of it was salted in the barrel and more was left hanging from the ceiling. This was all kept in the store-room.

My holiday was almost over but what lovely memories I collected along the way. As I got older I used walk to my grandmother's and spend the day there. After all it was only two miles out the road but to me it was another world filled with simple things and nature at its most wonderful.

THIRTY-THREE YEARS TEACHING
IN LISLEA

Catherine McAleavey (b 1923)

Armagh 1950s

I had mentioned to the late Canon Peter McDonnell that I was next on the list for a parish school. One day I arrived home from Clady School — a long arduous journey by bus and bicycle — to find Father McDonnell waiting at the house to tell me he was appointing me as second assistant to Lislea School. Such were the informal methods of appointments in the 50s.

The enrolment had increased and a third teacher was needed

but there was no accommodation, so I shared the classroom with my great friend Josephine Quigley. Jo taught infants and first class on one side of the black sateen curtains, and I taught second, third and fourth on the other — an unsatisfactory arrangement. Soon a building was erected at the bottom of the playground; Josephine and I moved down there. It was still open plan as it was intended to use the school as a Parochial Hall but this time the red screens from the Cathedral Sacristy separated the two groups.

In the early days I rode the bicycle to school, timing myself by the familiar landmarks — a long push past the Primate's Gates, an even run past the dips to the Fairy Steps at the end of the Demesne Wall, a steady spin down the Keady Road, past the wonderful giant oak tree, past the Clock Face where I always thought of Grantchester, ah Grantchester — a push up to the level crossing at Beechhill and a rush to school to sign one's time in the master's roll book.

You knew it was spring when a child was waiting with one or two snowdrops wrapped in a small damp piece of newspaper that crumbled away from being held so tightly and lovingly in the little fist. Then came the pussywillows and celandines and later bunches of primroses and bluebells for the May altar, from the back down the Navvy.

At playtime the girls skipped and sang 'Down on the Carpet' and 'Jenny Sits a Weeping'. The boys played marbles and ran in and out of the wee girls' dust houses. The year wore on — the beech trees came into leaf and the children who lived near the River — they never called it the Callan — brought in jam-jars of spricks. In the third week of June as regular as the clock the wild roses bloomed and you knew that Summer was here and the next week brought the holidays.

When we came back after six weeks the huge red poppies were in bloom in the rockery; they were cutting the corn on Mulligan's Hill, swallows were gathering on the wires and the beech-mast covered the ground at the top of Ballyards Hill. I could go home from school the back road. It was a good haul to the top of Ballyards and there at the very crest the twin spires of the Cathedral came majestically into view. The easy spin down to the lowest part of the valley took one past McShane's and McAuley's and half way up Linen Hill — the bleeching greens of long ago. I went over the hump-back bridge of the Butterwater, past The Three Piers, the Lonesome Houses, Red Barns, the Sheep Walk and onto the main road again. Sometimes I went home by Milford, the dismantled bridge on the Ballyard's Road, a reminder of the Armagh-Keady railway. Then on past the village football and cricket fields where once Catholic and Protestant played together.

When the school-leaving age was raised we had a very full school and at that time I remember a big effort to raise funds to improve the playground. Every child paraded in fairy dress. I wonder does Cathal Gamble remember being a Water Rat (Customsman) with white uniform cap and real car. Brigid Traynor was the Goosegirl and when the wayward goose wanted to stray Brigid gathered it up in her arms and followed The Beautiful Miss Bradys in their private ass and cart.

When the girls left for the Convent Intermediate School the boys had to stay on, as St Brigid's was not built. Those were difficult years — hard on them and hard on me. Reading, writing and arithmetic were a good discipline in the morning and in the afternoon hoping they would have exhausted their high spirits in a game of football, I read to them, 'The Green Cockade', 'Tarka the Otter' and 'Tom Sawyer'. They painted, clay-modelled, played the recorder and wrote poetry. We even grew cabbages and lettuce one year. I met one of the boys — or man — a few years ago and he said to me, 'We gave you a hard time.' They did – but when I see these handsome bearded young men shepherding their off- spring to First Holy Communion and Confirmation all is forgiven although not forgotten! One boy was marvellous at clay-modelling. He became a baker and I often thought how dull it must have been to be turning out uniform loaves instead of magical monsters and dinosaurs.

When Fr Clarke was our manager he appointed a caretaker so we no longer had to sweep the floor or light the fires. It was a red-letter day when he gave Lislea £100 to spend on equipment. (A year ago, Mrs Maureen O'Toole, who succeeded me as principal was authorised to spend £300 on Science alone.) Electric clocks were installed and I got one American Eight Day clock which I have in my kitchen and Michael John Corr got the other.

We had some visitors. If a car slowed up and it was not 12 noon on a Friday, when the priest called, you were suspicious. It could be one of the inspectors for all subjects — all very friendly and helpful people. But it might be a specialist — an eager beaver for Physical Education or the Needlework inspector who, once in a school, far from Armagh, found rusty needles in the children's unfinished garments.

St Brigid's Feast was celebrated by the making of crosses. When we had a Brigid, she knocked at the door and we — on our knees inside called out, 'Tar Isteach Bhrighid'. The making began with varying degrees of efficiency. I hope Lislea keeps up that practice.

FINISHING SCHOOL

Eileen Dempster (b 1896)

Andersonstown, Belfast / Neuchâtel, Switzerland, 1914

I never went to a proper school. A governess came every day and taught my young brother (until he went to boarding school) and myself. The governess came by train to the nearest station and we used to go and meet her, hoping that she would not come but she always did! Looking back she must have had a hard life! Quite a long walk, before she caught her train and another walk before she reached our house. In those days Andersontown was a most respectable area, later an IRA stronghold. There was a tennis court in front of the house and a huge beech tree. The tram terminus was about 200 yards on and we got to know many tram drivers and conductors. If they had not too many passengers they used to have time for a smoke and a chat before they went off.

My early days were very ordinary until I was sent to a finishing school in Neuchâtel, Switzerland. There seemed to be always a war on. I was sent out by my brother just before war broke out with Germany. I went out with a girl from Holywood, County Down, one Frances Leslie, known as Frankie. We were met in Paris by one of the owners of the school and there I stayed for about a year.

I didn't enjoy it much except when we went for holidays once to Venice. One day when we were there we were taken to a glass factory. The glass was supposed to be unbreakable. To prove this I threw mine on the floor where it broke into dozens of pieces and I was in disgrace.

In the summer holidays we were taken to Zermatt where we did a little mild climbing. My unfortunate parents had to pay extra for these excursions. I was laid low with scarletina shortly after the Zermatt trip and was whisked into hospital so that the entire school would not get it. I found this a pleasant change.

Shortly after I got back we were joined at the school by one Aziza Sakit Bey, Turkish, I think. She arrived smartly dressed including a pair of high heeled boots. These were at once taken from her and the heels chopped off. When Aziza got them back she was so angry she threw them onto the railway line which ran behind the school leaving her with nothing to wear on her feet.

I was known at the school as Emily as there was another Eileen at the school. We were supposed to speak French all the time but of course we didn't.

First Communion and Confirmation

COMMUNION AND CONFIRMATION
Michael McDonnell (b 1908)
St Patrick's Church, Ringsend, Dublin 1914 and 1919

It was in 1914 I made my first Holy Communion. I was only seven at the time. I remember my mother not letting me eat the night before. I had to fast from 12 the previous night till the next morning. It was a very strict fast as you couldn't drink or eat anything until you received Communion the following day.

Every piece of clothing was brand new. Everyone was dressed up but of course not to the same extent as you now. My mother was very proud of me dressed up as I was like a sailor in my shorts and top. Making your Communion was a very nervous thing to do as in my day while you were in the church you were asked questions on the ten commandments and the six precepts of the church. You had to be well versed in them or you would shame your family and friends and be in trouble with the church.

After Communion I went home and a large white sheet was put on me to prevent me 'mucking ' up my new clothes. I also had to wear a communion medal. I was brought on a tour to family and neighbours showing me off. You never knew whether you were lovely or not but they always said you were. I was then brought to town to get a photograph.

I thought things would change after I made my Communion but it didn't. Everyone (young) that was going to school had to go to Catechism classes after church (it was very like Sunday School). You were taught about the Pope and the clergy. To attend these classes were very strong points of view on parents; the bells of the church used to ring out after 12 Mass to make sure to remind us all to attend.

CONFIRMATION

It was in 1919 I made my Confirmation. I was twelve at the time. The preparation was a lot that went into making your Confirmation. Months before I was made learn all my Catechism which was a lot of hard work for a child to do.

At my Confirmation all the priests of the parish was there including the Bishop of Dublin. At the ceremony the Bishop used to go through the whole congregation and ask all those to be confirmed questions on Catechism and God help you if you didn't know the answers. Actually, I'd dread to think if you didn't know as the school masters were there along with your parents.

The Bishop sat on the altar with all the other priests of the parish and as far as I can remember I kissed his ring and he tipped me on the cheek to let me know I was a soldier of Christ, confirmed by the Bishop.

Dressing up was all part of the act. Of course the usual sentence came out of my mouth as I visited my neighbours, 'my mother sent me around ...' — when you were dying of embarrassment as well when the old relations came in contact (relations you never set eyes on for years, you'd be looking up!!). Visiting people was mostly good fun. The whole family used to go with me but now it seems like 'little enough for myself without bringing all of ye around'.

I also had to go to Confession growing up in my youth. Our Church was a hell of a lot different to the Churches in Dublin nowadays as in my day you had the Women's Sodality, the Men's Sodality and then the Children's. You wore a green medal for the 'special' 9 o'clock Mass. This was a different kind of Mass as the men's Mass was first.

The different sexes sat on different sides of the church — they weren't allowed to sit together. When the Women's Sodality was on the queues would be huge. The queues would start at 6 when Mass was at 8 — they'd have to shut the doors before 8 because the church would be overcrowded. The Rosary was said while a ceremony took place also; I often laughed while the women would be chatting before the Rosary — getting and revealing all the gossip they had.

With the Benedictions or Sodalities the whole thing of Religious ceremonies were very well attended in those days — I don't know about now.

MY FIRST HOLY COMMUNION

Mary Brien (1917 – 1994)

Menlough, County Galway, 1920s

I made my first Holy Communion when I was seven years old in 1924. It was always held on a Sunday and I had my first Confession on the previous Saturday. I was not allowed to have any breakfast before the mass as I had to fast overnight.

It was 8.30 a.m. Mass in St. Mary's Church in Menlough. I wore a white knee length dress with a lace collar and lace cuffs on the sleeves. I had white shoes, white socks and white rosary beads. I was very proud getting dressed that morning and we travelled by our own pony and trap to mass as there were no cars in those times. The Church was decorated with flowers for the occasion and we were all very happy.

I met all my school friends when mass was over and then we all left for home. There were no special feasts laid on in those times just our breakfast when we got home. In the afternoon I visited all my neighbours. There was very little money then but we all had a wonderful day on our First Holy Communion in a very simple way.

SPANISH SILK

Tilly Blanchfield (1917 – 1994)

Athy, County Kildare, 1920s

I made my Holy Communion when I was eight years of age. At that time everybody had to fast the night before they received Holy Communion. I made my Holy Communion at nine o'clock because of that rule just in case any of us fainted.

I had lots of older sisters. We had to share the same Holy Communion dress. The dress was originally my grandmother's dress and it was cut down to size for us. The dress was made from Spanish silk. I felt very proud wearing the dress.

On the day of the Holy Communion I arrived at the church at 8.45 with my mother and father. I remember the church was full of beautiful flowers and glowing candles. I felt very special. The mass went on for about an hour and a half. And by the time mass was finished I was starving.

The nuns in the convent had arranged a special breakfast for everybody after the mass. We all ran into the convent very excited because we had never been allowed into the convent before.

Everything in the convent was gleaming and polished. It looked lovely. We all sat down in a big dining room where the table was set with a snow white table cloth. For breakfast I had rashers, sausages and a fried egg and toast and a glass of milk. Beside each place was a holy picture and a pair of rosary beads which we were told were blessed by the Pope. I thought it was great.

After the mass we walked home and some of the neighbours

gave me a penny each. In those days a penny was worth a lot.

My mother made a special dinner for us all. All my aunties and uncles came to our house to visit me on my Communion day. They all gave me a small present. I was thrilled with everything.

After dinner we had a party and everybody was singing and dancing. I had a great day. I'll never forget it.

A SLAP ON THE CHEEK

Frank O'Callaghan(b 1919)

Dolphin's Barn, Dublin, 1925 and 1928

I don't remember very much at all about my first Holy Communion, but I can be excused for that as I was only six years old. In those days children made their communion at a much younger age. The year was 1925 and it all took place in Dolphin's Barn Church at the 9 o'clock mass. Of course I wasn't all dressed up like children are these days. I wore a basic grey flannel suit with short trousers and long socks. The ceremony is a blank, all I remember is that Canon Deasy was present (in later life he died and left a will of £50,000 and was the talk of the town!). Father Hawk said the Mass (I used to cut his grass for a shilling a month). After the mass I was taken around to friends and neighbours. In all I got two shillings. I still have the black and white photograph taken on the special day.

Being confirmed was another kettle of fish. I was about 10 years old and attended Rialto boys school. Confirmation was the horror of horrors as we had to learn off by heart our catechism and religious knowledge as we didn't know what questions Archbishop Byrne would ask us. Every boy was asked a question and if we got it wrong the school master would make sure we knew it when we got back to the school with the help of his cane.

The question I was asked was 'Where do souls go when they die if they die with venial sins on them?' My answer was 'People who die with venial sins on their souls go to purgatory where they suffer for a time before they go to heaven'. We were then all marched up to the Bishop and he gave each of us a slap on the cheek to remind us that we were soldiers of Christ. I considered myself to have looked very smart on the day. I wore a skull cap, a dark suit, with short trousers, long socks and new shoes. I had two medals pinned to my lapel — the confirmation medal and an emancipation medal as that year, 1928, was the commemoration of the Catholic Emancipation.

These days children go for trips and have a meal in a hotel on their confirmation. There was nothing like that in those days — I was just brought around to friends and neighbours in the hope of getting a bob or two. Altogether I got nine shillings, my mother took most of it off me as every bit of money was needed. I still have the photograph of me and my class mates and can remember most of their names.

CHINA DOLL

Maureen McLoughlin

Clannbrassil Street, Dublin, 1930s

I made my Holy Communion from Warrenmount Convent Primary National School near Clanbrassil Street. As the only grandchild in the family my grandparents had bought my dress and corded silk coat in Walpoles and the bonnet with silk frills. My mum Nellie came with me and it must have been one of the saddest days in her life as my dad had died when I was only five years of age. However she went to a lot of effort to make the day as special as she could, making a cake and getting minerals and ice cream for a party. All my cousins and friends were invited to the party in the Daniel Street artisan's cottage. I got money from my aunts and uncles and also from my grandparents.

The 1932 Eucharistic Congress was in the Phoenix Park and all the children who made their Holy Communion were brought back in groups to the Phoenix Park. Trams were in Dublin the method of transport but there were some excursion buses, charabancs to bring people to special events. The Holy Communion children were allocated special places at the Mass in the Phoenix Park. There was also a special Altar erected in O'Connell Street for Mass. I enjoyed all the fuss and attention but I never realised until much later in life what an effort it had been for my mum to have made my Holy Communion Day so special for me. There weren't many studio photographs taken then and the only photo available is one taken with an old Brownie Box camera.

My aunt Bella gave me a present of a beautiful china doll for my Holy Communion and it was my pride and joy and dearly loved by me. The dress and coat I wore for my Holy Communion was a short dress as this was most popular at the time. I tried to bring my lovely china doll with me to the Holy Communion and there were a few tears and tantrums because I wasn't allowed to do so but my mum was very strict and a great disciplinarian but I had my doll at the party when I came home so all was well with my very special Holy Communion Day.

THIRD CLASS TICKET

Jim Sweeney (b 1920)

Kilcormac, County Offaly, 1930s

I am one of a family of twelve. When I got confirmation at ten years my mother requested the PP to put me forward despite the fact that I should not go for another three years. Confirmation was every third year in our parish, Kilcormac, County Offaly. If I had to wait for another term two more family members would be going with me and it would be impossible to rig us all out at the one time.

So I was put forward and had my exam at the back of the Church (actually in the Church yard) the day of confirmation, together with those who failed on the day of examination some time earlier. The main part of the story is this. There was great distinction on the day of confirmation. All the children went up the middle aisle of the church to the rails where the Bishop was. By class distinction, there was first, second and third, depending on how you fared on exam day. Red tickets for 1st, blue tickets for 2nd, yellow tickets for 3rd, pinned to a cord around the neck. Children examined at the back of the church that morning automatically got number three, so it goes without saying that I wore a yellow ticket.

III

GOD BLESS THIS WORK!

Rural Ireland as it was

HARNESSED ERAS

Florence Moynihan

Drumcree, Drumsna, County Leitrim, 1930s

HARNESSED ERAS

Under the kitchen stairs
A dark press
The pine door creaks
Polished leather and Brasso
    permeates

Beams of shadowy light
Glinting on hame and stirrup
Horse and earth smells
Mingle with your tobacco

Motorisation
The final thud of the bolt
Entombing your beloved
    harness
Years of dust, cobwebs, must

A mildewed collection
For an antique dealer's van
Last memories for you
Harmony, leisure and toil.

The horse was very precious and my father used him with great love to the full — ploughing, harrowing, mowing, bringing home the turf and hay. Sometimes galloping for the doctor on horseback when one of the family or a neighbour needed urgent medical attention.

For each event or job there was a set of harness, rough 'tackling' and working harness for farm work, dress harness for when the horse was tackled for the sidecar and a beautiful leather saddle for riding purposes. All had to be greased and polished. On wet days my father spent hours polishing and shining the horse's 'wardrobe'. The rough 'tacklings' were greased — goose-grease from the Christmas goose was kept for the purpose. Brasso for the brass ornaments and hames and polish from a gallon-sized tin for the riding saddle and dress harness. All was then stored in a purpose-built press under the kitchen stairs.

Sadly, by the mid-50s the horse and his era became redundant. My father never drove a tractor or car. His gentle fulfilled world was gone for ever. I would love to see this poem published to his memory, his era and also to our faithful animals, especially Dora Grey!

FIFTY YEARS AGO

Ernest M.A. Scott (b 1929)

Ballynure, Ballyclare, County Antrim

The ring of steel-shod hooves is heard along the lonely road
In winter's dusk, man and horse, each makes for his abode
But master yet has work to do, his charges he must feed,
The plough tomorrow must be pulled, it is the urgent need.
In breeches warm and leggings tight a warm bran mash he makes,
With contented puffs at plug-filled pipe sweet smelling straw he shakes,
Not yet for him the cosy fire, horse and cow come always first
Or maybe yet a sickly sow, or a calf which must be nursed.

Seedtime's age old miracle is here, Scotch oats the sower wisely buys,
The corn fiddle's happy song the lark drowns out in clear blue April skies,
The ploughing's done and winter's frosts left seed beds in good cheer,
The potato pits have gone, the hedges trimmed and sloughs are
running clear.
In May the creaking cart winds right o'er the headrig bare
And patient horse shall stop and start in drills like arrows there.
Placed in the dung, the sprouted spud life's cycle bravely starts,
A ten-fold yield with loving care, the prayer in country hearts.

With swishing tails the clegs to beat the horses bravely plod,
The reaper's song drowns out the corncrake's screech o'er stubble sod.
A blazing June, a Constable scene, the hay-ricks sprout apace,
No panic here, with fork and rake, man's toil is blessed with grace,
The grass seed hay is saved, potatoes hoed and turnips growing fast,
The ewes are shorn, the wool is sold, and flies o'er trout are cast.
Copper sulphate and the soda-ash over potato haulm is sprayed,
In Ireland memories slowly die as when the hungry years dismayed.
The August days go slowly past, the meadow hay is saved,
The valley's filled with golden grain with each breeze the ears are waved,
In each sheltered farmyard, thatched and roped, the pikes of hay abound,

An expectant hush is felt, once again the harvest is almost round.
The binder's out! The sheaves fall fast, the stooks in rows are set.
And as at dusk, when looking round, the farmer nods, and yet
He feels a Higher Presence there, his faith to Him is dear;
Seed time and harvest shall not cease, this is the promise clear.

In each haggard, row upon row, the corn stacks against the sky
Stand out like Zulu kraals as the hunters pass them by.
October frosts are light as yet but the grain is safe and snug
And a bigger task appears when the spuds have to be dug;
A fortnight off from school and a shilling for each day,
Each mother anxious waits at the weekend for the pay,
New trousers to be bought and the old ones handed down,
To be rich nigh fifty years ago was no more than half a crown.

For man and master in those days, each contented with their lot,
Toiled long and hard, money in hand before a single item bought.
At Harvest Home, in lusty voice, their Maker's praise sing out
Their heartfelt thanks for another year with no room for any doubt.
Ill fares the land when men like these will eventually pass away.
And I in the Hallowed Acre kneel and feel guided there to pray
That I may yet become like these, before I cross the Bar
And maybe reach the Golden Shore, if Jehovah thinks it's not too far.

LIFE IN GLANGEVLIN

Kathleen Sheehan (1894 – 1985)

(Written for her family and grandchildren), County Cavan, 1900 – 20

What I am going to write about now is the hardship and primitive way of life that was the lot of those who lived in the first twenty years of this century, in that part of Ireland where the poor inhabitants were banished by Cromwell — 'To Hell or to Connaught'. This part was a wild mountainy district in West Cavan.

My first memory is of going to school. I was about three years old, and was carried most of the way by my father, or a neighbour who was a big strong boy. It was a sunny day, and when we got to the top of the hill overlooking the school, I saw the teacher standing at the door, dressed in black, with a white shirt, and tie. He was watching for us — my brother who was two years older than I, and Barney. That was the beginning of my schooling. The teacher was a relation — the Manager (our Parish Priest) induced him to study hard and go to college and qualify as a teacher. He was the first qualified teacher to come to that part of the country. The schoolhouse was new — two classrooms with big windows, and a walled-in playground divided in two, with a privy. This school caused a lot of bad feeling between the Manager and parents of children who were going to the old school and the old teacher who was a woman of about sixty years. The parents refused to send their children to this new teacher and consequently the average was not enough for the teacher to get a Diploma. I was one of the small ones to make up the average. This teacher got on very well. He had to walk a long way to this school, and later on I learned that he had a bad wetting going to school, and developed pneumonia and died.

How the pupils survived the long walks to school is still hard to understand. The children who went from our townland had to go over hills and rivers in between, and when those rivers were in flood, my father had to meet us and carry us across. I must mention the drawback for the children attending this school. The Manager would appoint a teacher who would stay for a few months, and then for one reason or another would leave, and the school was closed for weeks. My schooling therefore was an erratic affair for some years. There were five schools in the Parish then, and now I am told there are only two. The children attending these two schools have buses to take them to and fro, but we had to walk for miles, with no roads — only bad boreens. In those days men and women had to walk everywhere, except those who owned a horse. I can still remember a man on horseback with his wife sitting behind him and holding on, often with a big basket of groceries, after they had been to the village and sold their eggs. Later on, those who lived near the road got a side-car or a trap. At that time the houses were small, with tiny windows. The farms were small too, and the families big. There was no income from the British Government for anyone. The first relief was the Old Age Pension — ten shillings (50p) — each week for those over seventy years. It was a Godsend to the people, as before that a lot of old people died in the Workhouse. The old people got this ten shillings on a Friday, and one old man called Friday 'Silver Morning'.

The houses were small, and I remember when our house was renovated — two rooms added. My maternal grandfather was very clever and could do most things. He did the building with the help of my father and Thady, a man who worked with us for years. The stones were carried from the mountain, about a mile away. Sometimes the men carried those stones on their backs, but mostly on what they called slide-cars. Those cars were like a large door and were pulled by the donkey or pony, down the fields from the rocks. In this way they also built a large barn, a stable and a pigsty.

There was altogether a cluster of houses that could be seen for a distance of twenty miles or more, a landmark to my family in later years when we enjoyed our summer holidays there for many years.

My childhood was happy. I was the third child and first daughter. Nine children survived. My early recollection of my father was of a tall, strong man with a beard. My mother was fair and lovely. She wore her hair coiled at the back and arranged on her forehead with neat little curls, and when she wore her bonnet and veil she looked lovely. A neighbour said to me at some point — 'Your mother was the loveliest bride ever to be married in that Chapel'. It was a made match. My paternal grandmother had a hard life. Her husband was injured in a faction fight and died while the children were young. Grandmother worked hard, and even when my father brought his wife home, she did not relax. She made life hard for my mother in many ways — no love or sympathy. My mother enjoyed working in the fields, in the bog, helping with the hay, and later on, digging the potatoes. In spite of all the work, she found time to help others. She could laugh and be gay at a wedding or céili, and she could be a doctor or nurse in many emergencies. She was always ready to walk miles to deliver a baby, perhaps at night even, when a man could call for her, complete with his lantern, and they would set off over the hills and fields. I am well aware of the mothers and babies whose lives she saved. It usually took hours for the doctor to arrive. At one time he too was on horseback — a slow way of travelling in an emergency. Grandfather had that gift too. He was known far and wide as 'The Doctor'. He had a cure for most diseases and knew what herbs to use. If a neighbour had a sick animal, he was there to help. He was a tall stately man who loved to sing. The songs I remember are favourites with my grandchildren today.

Later on, the Government appointed a trained Midwife to the District and a doctor to the Dispensary. The doctor was there on a Monday, and vaccinated all the children at an early age. He attended my brother when he had pneumonia, and used linseed poultices back and front. He said to my grandmother, 'Don't worry, Granny, he will be able to jump the ditches in a few weeks', and so he was. He came to my grandmother later on, who had a nose bleed. 'Nature's way', he said. 'It will put ten more years on to her life' — and so it did, and a lot more! She lived to be ninety years. Her's was the only wake I can remember.

All wakes lasted two nights. There was porter to drink, and

tobacco cut and ready for use, and clay pipes. The men smoked all night, and some of the older women took a 'draw'. The neighbours and friends would come during the day. It was the custom to pay one shilling 'comnoro', an Irish word for gift. If not a shilling, then some tea or something of that value. The Priests were very much against this and eventually it was abolished. The 'Offering' which was given to the Priest, remained for years. The near relatives gave the most — five shillings, ten shillings, or a Pound. The day grandmother was buried it was wild and wet. The men carried the coffin over the fields, all the way to the graveyard, in relays of four. All coffins were carried this way, as it was some time before the hearse was in use.

My maternal grandmother died when I was about nine years of age. She was very petite in her cloak and bonnet and was very lovable. She was always busy. The local teacher stayed in her house, which was a large house with golden thatch. The outhouses were fabulous too — a large byre, piggery, hayshed, and a big farm. They kept sows and litters of pigs. My uncle would often stay up all night, having a fire in the piggery, to watch the sow and keep her from lying on one of the litter.

Our farm, or farms, were small — enough for four cows, their calves, and some dry stock. Those bullocks and heifers my father would drive to better grass in Roscommon — some twenty or thirty miles away — to fatten and sell later on, and buy more young stock. This happened for many years, but when some died of 'blackleg' he gave up. Mother kept one pig for home bacon, and hens, ducks and geese. Bacon was mostly for every day use, while fowl was for special occasions. The down, plucked from the geese, was carefully kept for pillows and mattresses.

It seems impossible now to visualise how even the children worked so hard and continuously. Before school, we carried the water from the spring well. Turf had to be brought in from the bog, cows brought from one place to another, and so on, and then run all the way to school. I learned to do most things at an early age. I milked the cows and made butter, made bread in the pot oven with hot coals on the lid. I made boxty and potato cakes for the tea, while my mother was helping with the work in the fields. I hear a lot about boxty these days, and it is a favourite with my grandchildren today, made in the same way, as follows: well washed unpeeled potatoes, raw and grated, with flour added to the consistency of pancakes, and also a little salt; baked by dropping onto a hot pan, and turned; kept hot and eaten with butter and sometimes with bacon. To everyone's amusement I could attend to the butter when the men had finished churning. The churning was done by the men before they went to work in the fields. The butter was salted. So much was kept for home use and the rest put into a box for the market. My mother was noted for her wonderful butter and it was always in demand, and in the market she was very proud when the buyers came to her specially. The making of butter required great cleanliness, all utensils being scoured, washed, and lastly scalded in boiling water. The crocks were placed on benches in that part of the barn kept so clean, and the crocks covered with wooden lids which were made by the cooper. He made the boxes too, and also the churns and the churn-dash. This dash was moved with the hands, up and down, until the butter was ready. The fresh buttermilk was lovely to drink. It was used for baking, and it helped to mix the feeding for the fowl, pigs and calves. My father often did the churning on his own if Thady was not there, and when my brothers got big enough they too would help by taking the dash for a few minutes. If a stranger came in while the churning was in progress, he or she would take the dash, so that the owner would not lose the butter. It was a custom from generations back, perhaps when witchcraft was prevalent. There was a time when the 'Good People' were busy in that part of the country. I know there are books written about their activities in Ireland, but thanks to the Mass, those souls have not troubled the people for years. At least that was how it was explained away!

To put into writing how hard the people worked, is beyond me. At that time everything was accomplished by the sweat of the brow. The ground was first of all prepared for the spring planting of the crops, such as potatoes, oats, vegetables, etc. Manure was spread on the fields, especially where the potatoes were to be planted. This manure was carried by the donkey in 'pardoges' - creels, with a shutter at the bottom. When the donkey got to the spot where the manure was needed, the wooden peg which held the shutter in place was removed and the manure dropped to the ground. The ground was well selected - perhaps a new piece which had not been used for some years. After the manure was put in the drills, the soil was turned over with a 'loy' pushed into the ground by foot, and the seed potatoes were laid on it - about one foot apart. The oats were sown where the potatoes were the previous year, and were shaken over the ground by hand, after the ground was harrowed and the soil made fine enough. The harrow was home-made, like a wide rake, and drawn around by the pony.

Cabbage plants were planted out about this time, and later on the seeds for turnips, mangolds and carrots were sown. If the weather was fine towards the end of May the turf was cut. This was done by hand and a slean was used to cut the sods. The sods were wheeled out in barrows and spread on the hard ground among the heather. When they were hard enough they were footed, that is, put standing on end, say five or six sods supporting each other.

In this way they dried out, and when they were ready for burning, they were stacked on the bog and thatched, or if time permitted, brought home and stacked and thatched with rushes. At this time there was weeding to be done, earthing up the potatoes, and so on. The making of the hay started when the meadows were ripe, and those meadows were cut with a scythe.

Using a scythe was an art, and it was back-breaking work, but I never heard the men complain. It was the only way then and they took it in their stride. At the haymaking, all the family helped, shaking out the swards, and later on gathering it into laps to dry. It was then gathered into hay cocks (or ricks) and left until it was ready to be taken to the haggard and piled into a large rick and thatched. It was some years before the farmer got a mowing machine or had a hayshed built. During all this work the neighbours helped each other. You could borrow your neighbour's donkey to draw home the turf or put out the manure, and the men would help each other with the scything, and there were always quite a few helpers (a meitheal) at the bringing in of the hay. There was usually a can of porter to quench the thirst, and heaps of potatoes, bacon and cabbage for dinner and home-made bread or boxty for tea.

The oats were ripe around this time and ready for cutting. The crop of oats was very important. Like the potatoes, it was the main food of the people. When the oatmeal was ready, the family had stirabout for breakfast, and for supper too. The process of converting the oats into meal was a hardship indeed. When the corn was ripe the men cut it with hooks and tied it into sheaves, long enough to handle. It was then stooked, six to eight sheaves standing on end, supporting each other. The stooks were left in the field for a time before they were brought into the haggard and stored in stacks and covered. The threshing took place later.

Looking back now, the threshing was an unbelievable feat of endurance. First of all the barn was cleared and the flagged floor scrubbed clean and then my father and his helping man, Thady, and a few of the neighbours who knew the art of wielding a flail, commenced the threshing. The flail was made of two strong sticks tied together at one end with strips of strong leather. The sheaves were already stacked in one end of the barn. To begin, the sheaves were put in the centre of the floor in a bundle of five or six. Each man wielded the flail in turn until the oats were separated from the straw. The oats were then put into sacks and the straw put carefully away for thatching. It was the work of a few nights depending on the amount of corn. The men were glad to take a rest and enjoy the tea and oven-baked bread, or perhaps a mug of porter, away from the dust of the barn.

Next came the winnowing - getting rid of the chaff. It would have be to a special sort of a day for this work with the wind blowing away from the house, and not too strong. A large sheet was opened and spread on the bank at the back of the house. The sacks were brought from the barn and my father or Thady would fill the container, which they called a 'whyte'. This container was like a riddle or a sieve, but made of skin. They held this aloft and the oats fell to the ground while the chaff was wafted away over the valley. To have the oats made into meal was hard work indeed. The mill was in the centre of the valley, approximately five miles away. The pony and the donkey did their share of the work. They carried turf in creels to heat the loft, and they also carried the sacks of oats thrown over their backs and held there while they travelled over the rough ground. When the loft, which was made of tin, was hot, the oats were spread on this hot floor and the men had to keep turning them over until it was ready to be ground into meal. The meal was coarse, with husks, and when they got it home some of it was sieved with a fine sieve, for porridge or for making oat cakes. The oat cakes would stand on a griddle before a bright fire and turned until baked. It was very sustaining and good with plenty of butter. I think all the animals had a share of this oat meal in winter. So much for the threshing!

The potatoes had to be dug before the frost came. We children had to do our share — picking the best ones and stacking them. The stacks were thatched with rushes and covered in clay to keep the frost out, and so the winter comes and there is plenty of work for all to do. We children also had our homework to do after our usual chores.

My grandmother loved to spin, while my mother made the rolls from the best wool — lambs' mostly. For all this work the light was from an oil lamp, hanging in a special place so that we all had some light. My father made the scallops for keeping the thatch in place. Later on he would thatch the house or barn or whatever. The scallops were made from sallys grown near the river, cut to about one and a half feet and pointed at each end.

I can remember the card games and particularly one that was held in the barn – perhaps twenty-five — and the winners got a goose each. This was the chief entertainment for the men and they enjoyed going to the different houses. My father did not play himself but my brothers did. We all loved cards and could play at an early age.

The making of flannel I must write about! The yarn was spun by my mother. The wool was mixed, so much black and say twice as much white, and the thread spun as fine as possible and rolled into hanks. Those hanks had to be converted into flannel. There was only one weaver and he lived ten miles away. The loom was old and the cloth was woven by hand, very loosely. I can remember the weaver throwing the shuttle from side to side, and twenty yards of flannel was put together. It looked like a mottled tweed. The pony or donkey was used for carrying it home. Then came the task of thickening it. It seems to me now to be a strange procedure. All those yards of flannel were arranged on a big board on the barn floor. The men rolled up their trousers and they so arranged themselves that their bare feet would meet the flannel. My mother or helper would pour warm water over it and the men would move the flannel vigorously with their feet, left, right, and so on until it was the desired thickness. Next day it was washed free from soap and put to dry on the hedges. Some of the flannel was coloured - a reddish brown. The moss for colouring was picked from stones in the rocks. I think that was the only colour. The flannel was made into shirts, waistcoats and perhaps underpants and petticoats for the old people. I think the first pants the boys wore were made from this grey flannel. It was great wearing and lasted for years. I have what I am sure is the only hand made bedspread in this country. The reddish flannel was tacked to a frame and lined, and the women stitched it back and forth and crossways, until it was finished. Later on I saw bedspreads made, but they were sewn on a tailor's sewing machine. My mother managed to make a few petticoats for some of the old people who were so very poor.

This whole thing was the only sort of life — comings and goings — and still the people had plenty of enjoyments, like weddings and ceili. After the old people died, or the young left, they were there in their sorrow to help. Now, years afterwards, the houses are empty — no-one to take care of anything — the old have died and the young have emigrated. Eventually the houses were only ruins — the children finished their schooling and left.

'HUNGER IS GOOD KITCHEN'

Brigid O'Donnell (b 1923)

County Donegal, 1920s

My father was a fisherman and farmer combined but the sea was his love. My mother used to remark that he'd go fishing in the harvest 'if the corn was a shaking'. When I was very small I used to go down to the small port where my father and his neighbour had their wee punt. The repairs to the boat were done with brown paper and tar which made the neighbours worry and worry when they put to sea. However my father was happy. He brought me with him once when I was about four, much to my mother's displeasure, who always feared the worst. We first went down to Bunagee where my father and Bob caught sand-eels in the sand with a hook for the purpose. The eels were used for bait. We came back up the bay and into port where my brother was waiting with tea, bread and butter. It was heavenly I thought.

Then we set off out again, my father and Bob rowing. Sometimes they would stop and bale the water out of the bottom of the boat with a three quart pan which was known as a milking pan. Then they rowed off again out to different anchorages named The Bow, Esklin, The Chimneys and The Trees. These were located by certain marks on the land. My father was really in his element, sitting in boat with his line in the water. He caught a different lot of fishes, sheelog, mackerel, gubog(known locally as rock salmon), grey fish, puckers (small fish), creilógs and blind hays — the latter were very unwelcome and were thrown back into the sea. I saw what my father described as herring hogs sticking their noses out of the water.

We dined on fresh fish. My father always gave the neighbours fish. What we couldn't use immediately my mother salted. She was an expert at the job. She had a big wooden tub and coarse salt which was purchased in the nearby town. She put the fish which had been thoroughly cleaned into the tub in layers and the salt was liberally scattered between the layers and over the top. After some time she took out the fish and put them on a long form. Weights were put on top to flatten them out. Little slivers of sticks was placed in each fish to keep them flat. Then they were placed on the shed roof when the weather was good to dry them. When they were thoroughly dry she placed them in a ten-stone clean meal bag and they were hung in the kitchen. They served us during the winter as 'kitchen'. Kitchen was a term used locally to describe food for dinners. The proverb used was 'Hunger is good kitchen'.

I remember the little three legged pot used to boil the potatoes for our dinner. It was also used for making 'Brochon' for our supper. The potatoes were scrubbed clean and the fish was put in the middle of the potatoes and boiled. It gave the potatoes a unique flavour.

We all went barefoot from April. We had about a mile and a half to go to school. When the roads were wet how much we enjoyed seeing the clabair (muck) coming up between our toes. There was a pond at Sarah Ann's brae; it has since vanished, and we used to spend ages watching the frogs' spawns. We loved getting rides on the horse carts and a highlight was getting rides on the horse roller when the corn was being rolled. Coming from school in the harvest time was great, we had blackberries, heather berries on the Gort-hill, haws, 'fatties' from the fuchsia bushes, sugaís from the marshy areas, and we took swede turnips from our neighbours' fields. Pesticides were unknown. We were never hungry. My mother had a spinning wheel which my father bought in Carndonagh when they were married in 1906. She got white wool fleeces; black and white. She washed the wool, we teased it, she greased it with butter and made it into rolls which were neatly placed in her little roll box. We were never allowed near her wheel which was her pride and joy. She spun and knitted socks for all of us. She made the thread into what she called 'slippings' (hanks) and in a bag someone of us took it on the mail car to Malin Head where the weaver one Mr Molloy made it into blankets. I still nostalgically keep a piece of one of those as a memento. She also spun as much in black and white yarn rolled in balls which the weaver made into tweed for a suit, overcoat and cap for a local gentleman who wore it with pride some sixty five years ago when Báinín was not fashionable.

RURAL LIFE SEVENTY YEARS AGO

Ann Burns (b 1923)

Mullaghmore, County Sligo, 1920s – 40s

As children we were very happy and carefree. We lived in the country on a farm with one sister and two brothers. It was a beautiful seaside resort, a very safe strand and a beautiful big castle called Classeybawn. I never liked school as we had a big tall teacher who shouted at us a lot. From April on until October all the children went to school in their bare feet which we loved, people in those days were rather poor. When the cold weather came we had to wear shoes. The class-room was very cold and pupils had to give one shilling weekly but those who could not afford the shilling had to bring a sod of turf under their arm each morning to provide fuel for the school. It was a two classroom school, one room for juniors and the other for the senior pupils. Fifty-two pupils in all! Some of the families who lived there were fishermen. They earned their living fishing in small sailing boats. We loved to watch the fishermen mend their nets, it was just like weaving. Those who had a farm saved the hay, when it was cut in June. As children, we had to first shake the hay, which was cut down with a scythe by my father. My mother always helped too, of course, and she was very hard-working, as was my father. The big weeds were picked out of the newly mown hay, it was then rolled by what was called a rake, a wooden implement with a long handle, a head which had about twenty wooden teeth in it. Those rolls of grass were called 'wind-rolls'. After a couple of days the hay was made into little bundles called lappins, after about two days more the lappins were gathered into larger lots and made into several heaps dotted all over the field and called hay cocks. After a few weeks of fine weather, the hay was well saved and again gathered into a field, nearest the dwelling house, and dragged by a horse with a rope around the bottom of the little hay cock and made into a much bigger hay stack. We, as children loved that part of saving the hay, as some of the neighbours, the males of course, would help with this enormous job. Meals would be provided, a special dinner at 1 pm of beautiful homecured bacon and home-grown cabbage or turnips and homegrown potatoes. In those days every household had their own fields of potatoes, cabbage, turnips, parsnips, onions for their families and mangolds which were cooked for the cattle. The real big day came when all the hay was saved and usually in August or September all the big hay-stacks were taken into the yard at the dwelling house and made into what was called a rick of hay. About eight men would come from around the neighbourhood, plenty of food and drink was provided. The drink was usually stout, or porter, as many called it. Everyone worked very hard at the hay while my mother and grandmother prepared the meals and we would help with the washing up and tidying afterwards. All that work lasted until 7 p.m. or oftentimes longer. Everyone who came to help would stay after all was finished and lovely songs were sung by some of the men who had excellent voices. Stories were told, most of which were ghost-stories. I would sit next to my grandmother, listening attentively and at the same time I was terrified. People were very superstitious in those days too and believed in fairies. If a baby died suddenly some people believed that the fairies took it. They also believed in the 'Banshee' even though I'd never heard one! If someone came to visit and entered through the back door, they would have to go out the same door or it was believed, if they went out the front door, they took all the good luck with them.

Most people, if they had cows, collected the milk in large crockery containers called pans. After a couple of days when this milk was thick it was put into a big container called a churn, or creamery can, with a special lid with a hole in the centre, into which a utensil called the dash was used. The dash with a long handle was just pulled up and down through the milk for one and a half hours until the butter appeared at the top of the milk. Now, if a neighbour called or even passed by the house during this procedure, he or she must help with the churning of the milk and if not it was supposed to be very bad luck and no butter would appear on the milk.

There were old cures too. If a child had mumps he was taken out the back door of the house, around the house, and in through the front door with a donkey's harness over his head. A cure for jaundice was ferret's milk. The ferret got milk to drink and whatever he left afterwards was given to the child. Nettle juice was given as a cure for measles.

I remember when the World War broke out a neighbour came to tell us. My poor mother started crying and everyone was terrified. Prayers were recited non-stop and always the Family Rosary. Here again if a neighbour called or if one was passing by all knelt down and joined in the rosary, together with lots of trimmings. People in those days had great strong faith.

As we lived beside the sea, in that beautiful sea-side resort of Mullaghmore, County Sligo, there was a hut built up on a hill overlooking Donegal Bay and Innismurray which

was then inhabited. Eight men who were in the Local Defence
Force manned this hut, two at each time, a period of nine hours
all day and all night, keeping watch for foreign intruders. Everyone in the neighbourhood was warned to keep heavy dark blinds
on their windows during lighting-up time in case a plane would
lose its way from England and drop a bomb on our houses. It was
the Germans everyone was terrified of. Hitler was on everyone's
lips.

Few people had radios then and the lucky ones who could afford
one, had to have the battery charged every now and then, whenever it
became silent. We had newspapers (Irish Independent and Irish
Press). Whenever we heard the noise of a 'plane we were terrified. I
remember two 'planes crashing. One huge one, on the strand, it was
American and a crowd of us rushed down to see it but no one was injured. The other 'plane made a crash landing not far from Classeybawn Castle, in a place called 'The Burrow'. Then of course came the
food rationing. It was desperate. Ration books for everything. We
were lucky to have our own butter, eggs and fresh vegetables. But the
flour was awful. We called it black flour! Of course it was a novelty for
us to get baker's bread from the shop. Most people always had a big 7
stone bag of flour in the kitchen. My mother or grandmother baked two
big cakes in an oven on the open hearth every day and the home-made
bread was only delicious, but not so with the black flour. It wasn't really
black but a dirty shade of brown with a horrible taste.

The groceries and other goods came on the black market: 2s 6d
(two shillings and six pence or half a crown) for one ounce of tea
which was an awful lot of money then. One pound of tea cost 3s
(three shillings) at that time, before the war. Sugar, one stone bag,
was 2s 9d (two shillings and nine pence). Each person in every
family got a ration-book. Times were extremely hard. There was
no electricity nor running water, all the water for domestic use
had to be carried in two-gallon tin cans which we would buy
from the tin-smith. In those days there were many tin-smiths and
their wives and children would carry cans big and small and sell
them to anyone who would buy them. Those people or travellers
were called tinkers in the olden days and every house in the
neighbourhood had four or five cans which were used for milking the cows and drawing water from the spring wells. We usually had to go through several fields to get to the water. The cans
when filled with water would be very heavy and one would have
to take a rest for a few minutes from leaving the well, before
reaching home. The spring water tasted lovely and fresh, it was
used for drinking, cooking and washing. Our bath was a big tub,
filled three-quarters with lovely hot water which my mother

would heat on a big fire in the kitchen, in a big kettle. Our light was an oil lamp hanging on the wall, it was filled with paraffin oil, with a piece of hard material which was called a wick coming through the centre and covered with a globe which had to be cleaned carefully every day so that the light would be bright.

KETTY

George Sheridan (b 1912)

Killesher, Florencecourt, County Fermanagh, 1910s

As long as I remember, Ketty was there. She had come to help my mother when my eldest sister was born and it seems she took great delight in watching this baby progress to walking and talking stage. I was second in the family and, it seems, never made a great impression with Ketty. I suppose I was maybe three years old when Ketty gave my mother some advice. 'In troth ma'm, if you don't give that lad the rod, you will have another Paddy Bruiser.' It seems that Paddy Bruiser was a wild youth in Ketty's close neighbourhood. Ketty was long gone from our home and I was in my teens before I knew she had another name. She was Ketty Melanophy from the townland of Skeagh. She had never married. When she came to our house she was in her seventies because she was in receipt of an old age pension which, round about that time, 1913 – 14, went up to ten shillings old money. She had been housekeeper to a man who went terminally ill and, as all belonging to her had died, poor Ketty was homeless. So, my uncle Sandy, who was a brother-in-law of her late employer, took her in and she helped look after his two wee ones until my sister was born. Then she came to our house and, as the babies arrived in both houses, so Ketty moved back and forth.

Ketty was a firm believer in the fairies, or the wee people. If she was in charge of our house any time my mother would be away, and if Ketty had to leave the house to go out for turf, she would put the tongs on the side of the cradle in case the wee people would take or exchange the child. And when she washed us and prepared us for bed — for there was no bathroom, or hot and cold taps, in Gortaree at that time, just a small bathpan that Ketty would empty outside the back door - and if it was after sunset, she would say before she threw the water 'hugita ugitas, iskey sollagh'.

A few years ago I talked about Ketty with my sister Annie. She told me she remembered going down the path to Dolans' with Ketty. The Dolans were in a house belonging to the Reids. They were poor people and the biggest treat they could give the child was a fistful of sugar set on a chair. This was before 'hygiene', the goddess of health, had come to Ireland, and the child could pick up grains of sugar while the grown-ups exchanged grains of gossip, and all was well and life was simple. Ketty was in Legolagh, my uncle's place, when she got ill. She was able, with help, to walk the padroad to our house and it is one of my oldest memories to see poor old Ketty going off in the sick car to what the old people called 'the favery hospital', which was part of the old workhouse. She left her life savings with my uncle, £7 10s 0d, and asked him to see she would be buried in the family plot in Old Killesher.

I am not so sure how long she lingered. I know my uncle used to visit her in hospital and, when she died, he carried out her wish. Francis Dolan of Blacklion was the undertaker. He supplied the coffin and the hearse. A few neighbours dug the grave. There was the tobacco and clay pipes passed round, and Ketty was laid to rest in the family plot in Old Killesher. Sometimes I try to picture what Ketty really looked like, because I looked at her through the young eyes of a child. What a tough life she had and how many people of her generation, who worked their fingers to the bone, were laid to rest in cheap coffins ... and now make the rich dust and unwritten history of Old Killesher?

CURRAGH HAY

The Curragh was the flat land on the lower shore of Lough Macnean and it belonged to Lord Enniskillen, and was probably 100 acres. He set it out each year in meadow, in one acre or two acre plots (Irish measure), and it was reckoned a good day's work for a man to mow an Irish acre with the scythe.

Most of the farms in the Marlbank area would take two acres — about eighteen or twenty rucks of hay — because the sheep in our area ate the meadows 'til May Day and there was no fertiliser then, so the Curragh hay was a great extra. It was very coarse with a lot of sprat in it, but, if it was won without rain, cows in the byre would eat it, and it was great for making ropes to tie down thatched stacks.

It had to be drawn up to the hills of the Marlbank on asses. Most of it came up the old Killesher lane with the bundles of hay hung on the straddle pins. This was before the Marlbank road was made.

The hay was tied in bundles with thumropes made from the long hay. The bundles had to be perfectly even so as to balance when linked on each side of the ass. One man was so good at this job that a local songster, canvassing for the making of the road wrote in verse:

Young white Murty can tie so purty,

Half an acre of Curragh grass

And with precision make division

And tie four bundles for every ass.

Two bundles would then be put into a strong rope. These were made from a jute bag that could be cut into a long strip, then twisted and doubled to make a very strong rope.

NO TIME FOR LESSONS

Hannah Mulhall (b 1927)

West Cork, 1930s

I can recall many, many memories from an early age. I was born on February 16th 1927. I am now heading for sixty-seven. I can remember the birth of my younger brother on December 18th 1931. I was then three years and ten months. He was born at home. The bed was brought down stairs to the parlour. The nurse came and a good neighbour who knew what to do. At the same time my poor father had rheumatic pains and was spending a lot of time in bed. My poor mother had to do the milking and tend the cattle as well as take care of me and my six-year-old brother. She had no 'mod cons'. She had an open fire in the kitchen. On it, she cooked and baked bread in the bastible by putting the red sods of turf on the lid. The same bastible boiled the spuds. She had a smaller one for boiling the bacon and cabbage or whatever type of cooking took place.

The usual thing to do at the time was to fatten a pig, kill it and salt it in a wooden barrel. Then when fair day came once a month, and an animal would be walked ten miles to Bantry fair and sold for very little, my father would buy a piece of fresh meat. That was a treat and with the lovely fresh carrots and parsnips and onion which he grew in the field and the potatoes, there was no one hungry. Another treat in the meat line was to catch a chicken or hen in the yard and kill it. Boil it in the bastible with pepper and salt and an onion and we had lovely chicken broth when that was cooked.

We also had lots of fish. My father was a great provider. He got up early and went fishing off the rocks in summer. We had beautiful fresh fish and we also had salted fish. They were put in a tub with coarse salt for a few days, then taken out and dried in the sun on top of the slates of the cow house. When dry, they were hung from the rafters of a back room. Then to cook them, it was necessary to steep overnight in cold water. Boil them, take out the bones. Make a white sauce from milk and flour, pepper and salt, and a nice lump of butter melting in the middle of it, to that mixture add the fish and nice floury potatoes. (Num-num, delicious).

We also had our own eggs, wheat, oats and barley. The wheat was ground into flour. The oats were crushed, also the barley made into meal, it was used to feed the calves and cows. The horse got whole oats. He also got furze. It was ground in the furze machine by hand and dropped down a little trap door into the manger. My father also grew mangolds and swede turnips. Some turnips were used for the dinner but were mainly cut up with the mangolds and fed to the cows on top of the hay under their heads in the cow house. They would also get a handful of crushed oats on top of the mangolds. We had a separator to take the cream off the milk. The cream would then go into a barrel to make butter. We all took turns at the handle until at last the butter appeared. The separated milk was fed to the calves. The buttermilk was used to make the brown bread, so you see we only had to buy tea and sugar and breadsoda and paraffin oil for the lamp.

We had no electricity. We had our own turf cut in the bog, saved and drawn home with donkeys and baskets and benched up in the hay shed under the hay. My dad cut the hay with a scythe, saved it and drew it in with the horse and cart. He ploughed the fields with the horse. So as I say, we had our own turf for the fire, our own flour to make the bread, our own meat, fish, milk, butter, eggs and vegetables. We also had sheep. When the wool was taken off their backs, it was sold and the money used to buy shoes, clothes and blankets. There was no dole, or children's allowance or handouts of any kind. We had six cows, some sheep on the mountain, a donkey and a horse.

My father spent nine years in the Rocky Mountains. He brought home a Rocky Mountain saddle in his trunk. That was in 1923. My sister has it at present. There were six boys in my father's family - no girls. Two of my father's brothers died in Casper, Wyoming, USA, from the 'bad' flu. Two other brothers died there at a later date. They all herded sheep. We heard great stories about the lambing season and the foxes and the coyotes and moving camp and getting frost bitten and falling off horses, etc. His other brother went to England, he was home only twice during his time there. He married and had one son and is buried in England. My dad was the only one to come home from USA at the request of his mother who was a schoolteacher. She gave him the place. The other four never returned. They were buried in the USA. My father's father died young. My dad was only three years old. His mother got married at the age of thirty-nine and had six sons in seven years; so she was fourty-seven by the time the sixth child was born.

We had to work, there was no time for play. The water had to be drawn in buckets from the well before we went to school in the morning. The cows had to be driven out to the hill, also the calves. Turf had to be brought in to keep the fire going, to keep the kettle and the pot boiling. After school I had to feed hens, bring in the eggs and clean them. They were sold at the shop to buy the groceries. I had to wash the separator and put it back together and have it ready for the milking. The job I hated the most was washing the dishes off the table and sweeping the floor and taking out the ashes. During the summer when the turf was getting cut I used bring tea up the hill to my father and maybe a helper. Then I'd go and try and find the cows and bring them home.

We had hardly time to do our lessons. We had poor light from the candles and oil lamps, but we knew we had to know them off by heart or be killed in school next day. The hardest thing I ever had to do was teach my younger brother his Catechism and Life of Our Lord for his Confirmation. I thought it would never end. I am sorry to say he died in April 1991. My father and mother are also dead. May they all R.I.P. My mother was a great woman. She made all our clothes and quilts and pillows and did all the washing by hand. She worked in California for four years and met my father on the boat coming home. Her mother was sick and requested her to come home. There were nine in her family, four of her brothers went to California. They never came home and are buried there. My mother had a return ticket. She never went back. She married my father six months later. She was a native of Kerry. My dad bought a horse and trap in Killarney and drove to Bantry. As I have already said he was a great man. I remember bringing tea to him in the field and to the rocks when fishing. He would let me hold the fishing rod and if I got a pick he would have it in and oh the excitement to get a fish. He used crabs for bait. Now I love to go fishing and have caught a lot of fish over the years.

I went to National school — mixed boys and girls, only one teacher to teach all classes. I stayed on until I was sixteen and in 8th class. From there I went to Domestic Science college for two years as a boarder. I was like a fish out of water, a backward country girl. I got a job from there in a convent orphanage in charge of the children in April 1945. The pay was £36 a year and my keep. When my stamp was taken out of it, I got £2 16s 7d a month. I got married in

1954. At that time girls had to give up work at marriage, so now when I applied for my old age pension I was told I had only ninety-four stamps after 1953 and need 156 to qualify so I get no old age pension, although I had stamps since 1945. They don't count.

I have just touched here and there and given you a glimpse of bygone days as it comes to mind, I always wanted to write a book. I have so many different memories to relate.

BIKE ON THE FOOTPATH

Con Moloney Snr (b 1917)

Mountrath, County Laois, 1930s

Should the phrase 'the good old days' be rephrased to the 'bad old days?' I often ask myself this question. Then, reflecting on my past, I know some things will never change, like memories, thoughts and feelings.

Twenty years ago you could leave your bike on the footpath and nobody would touch it, but not today. Everybody had time to talk and you didn't have to jump out of the way of lunatic drivers behind the wheel of fast cars. The element of time has been blown completely out of proportion. 'Jack', I say, 'have you got the time?' 'Haven't a minute!', is the reply. No-one has time to spare, time to spend to talk. Or there's the time-wasters. The ones who think taking it easy and slowing down means sitting down and having a few cigarettes while drinking a cup of coffee, watching the day go by.

Years ago, work was work. You began and ended at a certain time. There was no overtime. They didn't need it. Up and down every day behind a plough and horse we'd go, doing half an acre a day, six days a week. No complaints. Of course there was the talking and humour. While beside one another in the field the farmers spoke to each other. It had to be done and they were doing it in the best way they knew. A man said to his son 'Tommy, I think you should be a barber instead of a farmer', because in those days, it was 3d to get a haircut and 3d for a gallon of milk. Today it'd be almost a pound. Wages were a pound a week and if you had a good job, three! At three shillings a day you'd be a long time becoming a millionaire.

If sport tickled your fancy, a train excursion ticket to Croke Park cost two shillings. Admission to Croke Park was a shilling. Who said you needed a lot of money to have fun? 'Pitch and toss' was a popular game usually played at the street corners. We'd gather in a circle, then throw the money in the air and catch it. Dancing at a crossroads was also a spectacular event. That cost a shilin' a set! In 1939 was the farmers dance and all the farmers' daughters would line up against the wall. Then, the men would come and take their pick. The 'wallflowers' left would sit and wait and wait for a partner. Once, I chose one and she wanted to know why I had done so! At that time it was fifteen pounds to hire a band for the night and they were one of the best!

Those were the times, I must say, but I can't really be biased. There were bad times too. When winter came, there was no electricity. Television, radio, videos they are all added luxuries, and even I love the radio. Things are made easier now but I can't help debating whether or not some need have been. New inventions are discovered every day. At the moment, there is a jet which travels faster than sound itself! One can only go so fast. What will they do to make it faster? Cars will soon turn into rockets and soon the cars will out-number the people. Machines are overtaking the human race almost as quickly as we, the humans, overtook the animals. It's easy to say that life is becoming advanced and great. But the 'golden' days were a lot safer. I could go on and on but I'll leave it up to the reader to make the choice.

'HORSE PLOUGHS I DROVE'

Jennie Buckley (b 1929)

Mohill, County Leitrim, Geashill, County Offaly, 1930s

Early to bed and early to rise makes a man healthy and wise — a composition that won me a prize in school. My mother and father — Daddy and Mammy we called them in those days of the 30s — had three of us, my brother and sister and I (the oldest), up for school early. But we had our jobs to do first. After we had our breakfast of home made pin-head porridge and plenty of milk, not pasteurized, we got our three-legged stool (Daddy made them to suit our sizes) and got our bucket and had a cow each to milk and baby calves to feed. Then change our clothes again and walk three miles to school.

We were often kept in if we did anything wrong or talked in school. Our teacher was hard, the odd good slap, but she always, if kept in, gave us a penny in case we were hungry going home — we got a three tier bun for that, sometimes two. Walk three miles home. Sit down to good stew, our local butcher when Daddy got his stew

beef often gave a big bone for soup with plenty of meat on it. Local butcher in Mohill, County Leitrim, long since gone. Or we got
good home cured bacon and cabbage, a good chicken soup and
farm yard chicken and eggs. Those days were lovely. Then we
went out in the fields to help Daddy. No homework till night —
Daddy and Mammy helped us. But the farm work had to be done
first.

Cutting the corn, wheat, barley and oats with a scythe, reaper
and binder and often a reaping hook. It had to be stacked and
brought in and the threshing mill would come later and a band of
men came and threshed all. And then the big tea; home-made
butter, eggs and big currant bread my mother made, and of
course the dinner would be cabbage and bacon again.

There was always lot of work on the farm. Horse ploughs I
drove. Picking of potatoes, picking weeds, thinning of turnips
and vegetables, picking of stones, even the fruit in field and or-
chards was used. We had to make hay. Daddy made small forks
for us to turn the hay and then cock the hay, later brought it to the
hay shed. Our farm kept us going, we bought nothing except tea,
sugar, rice and sultanas. The rice pudding was our Sunday treat.
We sold eggs and Mammy churned the milk and cream and made
home-made butter, buttermilk was lovely to drink. She said she
churned with one hand and rocked the cradle with the other.

Now our pocket money was we had a hen each and collected
her eggs and sold them and when that hen stopped laying we
would ask Mammy for another. We were real happy children,
never got bored. Two pigs were fattened and killed every year.
We all fed them. I did not like the man who did the killing. He got
a piece of the bacon going home. We had no TV or even a radio,
just an old gramophone.

And long winter nights, we had to carry the stable lamp for
Daddy to feed the cattle. Sheds for cattle not like now, in those
days the sheds were all over the place. Cattle, horses, foals were
all in different sheds. Daddy trained horses, young fillies, wooden
bits and long reins on the roads and he told me he often rode horses
and was often near caught on the roads with the Black and Tans,
would put the horse to a gate when he would hear the Tans coming
and jump the gate into someone's yard till they passed by.

At night Daddy and Mammy would tell us old stories, fishing
at night, etc. They helped with the homework and after Daddy
would say, 'any shoes to be mended' the old last would come out.
I (as a child not more than 8 or 9 years) would make the wax end
and he and I would sew all the shoes. He would put in studs in
the soles of the shoes and another night the steeped sally rods

would come out and we would make lovely baskets and creels from the rods, our kitchen was a mess. But those days the floor was cement. Mammy would be making a patch work quilt, knitting or baking or ironing with the box iron, no electric. Just oil lamps. No water laid on, water from spring well.

Nice featherbed. Foxford blanket and patch work quilt and good home fire and the odd neighbour in for a good chat. No car then. A treat on a Sunday was a pony and trap drive. I could go on.

After I left school I worked hard in a drapery shop, came home on the bike at night. I worked serving my time for two years for nothing. Did the books and even had to turn the collars of shirts for one of the bosses. Two sisters and a brother ran the shop.

My first job was ten shillings a week in Tullamore. I met my husband. We reared nine children. I worked hard on the farm, we both did. I kept dogs and poultry and gave each child secondary education.

Now my husband is dead ten years God Rest Him. I have knee arthritis and hope to get replacement knee joints in March.

But life was never boring for me. I get it hard to sleep. I live alone now so I am writing this at two o'clock in the morning. I often said I would like to write about long ago. I really never got down or had the time to tell my own nine children this, of the good old times. Children get a lot these times. They are hard times to bring up children.

EGG SMUGGLING

Eileen Meehan (b 1924)

Smithboro, County Monaghan / Roslea, County Fermanagh, 1930s

We would carry the eggs to Paddy Flynn's shop over the border into County Fermanagh. He had a shop on the Free State side and one in the north. So if we met the customs we'd say we were going to the hut with them— that was the one on the Free State side. We would have to take over the fields for a mile and a half to get to the Northern Ireland shop. We'd get more for the eggs there — this was about 1934.

But this one day I'll never forget it, two neighbours Bridie and Rita and I were going and I had 2 baskets of eggs and they had two — one in each hand. We had to cross over the road at Amerson's hill. Bridie said, 'you go out Eileen and see if there's any customs about.' He'd be on his bicycle in them days. So I went out and I looked round the corner, up and down and I could see nobody.

And we went out and here he was on the road on his bicycle. He was going to take the eggs off us too. We said we were going to the hut with them and he could do nothing about it. But we had to bring them there then and he stayed and watched us till we went. He had a shake in his head and we called him the 'shakey' custom man.

We'd buy things in the north that were cheaper sugar, flour, bread. We used to get white bread in the north when there was only black bread here. I remember my father going away off to Roslea and getting white bread for the matron in the hospital in Monaghan. It was to make Christmas puddings I think. It was Christmas time anyway. I think he got her half a dozen loaves. He went into Roslea and then he rode his bike into Monaghan about nine miles. She was so delighted and I don't think she gave him even a penny for doing it. She was a nun.

The butter was cheaper in the north too and we used to carry butter back over we'd put it in the lining of our coats. But it was only an odd time we'd get it because we churned. This neighbour used to wear a belt and she'd have two bags made out of flour packs hanging down for the butter and it would be under her coat. But this one warm day, she was passing the custom man and he asked her had she anything to declare. She told him she hadn't a hate — that she was visiting friends. He kept her there for ages and the butter started melting. It wouldn't run down your legs but it would get soft and oily and then you'd have to go home and put it in spring water — that's all we had in them days.

FARMING HALF A CENTURY AGO

Mary Lyons

Clonakilty, County Cork, 1940s

I am ninety years old and a retired National Teacher. The enclosed are my own recollections of farm work and its many phases. I married a farmer who had returned from San Francisco, where his nephews and nieces still reside.

Farmers, even owners of small farms, employed a hired workman to help out. He sometimes lived in a cottage nearby or in a thatched house or some resided in the farmhouse in a little room off the kitchen called a linney where he had a wooden bed and chair and a wall rack on which to hang his garments. The pay was meagre but there were no dole queues waiting in lines nor social welfare benefits. The fare was shared with the family consisting mainly of potatoes boiled in their jackets in a large three-legged pot hung on a crook with holed iron hangers by means of which the pot could be raised or lowered and the potato water drained off. The potatoes were served with bacon, cabbage or turnips on a huge dish in the centre of the table usually hand sawn and nailed by the local carpenter, and the cloth was of flour bags the colour and ads washed and re-washed by the farmer's wife with the aid of washing soda. No amenities existed then such as vegetable stores or supermarkets. Rationing was unknown. The small local shops supplied bags of yellow meal bran, white and brown flour by a bagful or stones or half stones weighed on a large scales scuff (able to rotate in order to be seen from all sides) shaped. Every farmer killed a pig monthly himself or there were special pig killers in the area. The pig was hung outside on a tree limb until all the blood was drained off. The intestines were then removed, the blood being retained and used by the housewife to make the homemade black pudding mixed with flour, oatmeal, onions, etc., a savoury fried with fat also from the pig, rendered and stored in jampots. Potatoes sometimes were used for the three meals and so when the blight appeared through the years causing the potato failure then followed the famine when half of Ireland's population dwindled and the famine ships departed with their starving victims. Some men savoured stirabout for supper made of yellow meal boiled and served with milk. The heart and liver made tasty snacks and the pig's bladder blown served as football for children.

Every farmer sowed acres of oats, wheat and barley as well as an acre or two of turnips, carrots, parsnips, table cabbage and cow cabbage. Ploughing was begun in late Winter or early Spring. Two horses and a furrow plough were the normal as well as herds of cows milked by hand. In every farmyard were the stalls for cows, a calfhouse and stable. The horses were stabled about November 1st. They were then fed during winter with cut furze and also mangolds. If there was no furze on the land it was purchased from a 'furze-owning' neighbour by the load. Then the hand-operated furze-machine was used to cut the furze to provide fodder for the horses supplemented by sliced mangolds. Then the furze machine was also used to cut up cow cabbage which, when mixed with yellow meal, was fed to the bonhams or bonnives if you wish to call them, the progeny of the sows. There was also a bonham-house in the yard in the centre of which was a huge iron trough, spaced where heads could enter to drink the sour milk left over from the cow herd when they were mature enough after the suckling period was over. There may be two sows or more and the male, the boar, was the property of a neighbouring boar-owner.

Potato planting began with setting the early crop in ridges about six feet in width. The sciollans were cut usually by the housewife and planting was done by dropping each sciollan into an opening made by a spade from a bagful on the shoulder and closing the opening by pressing the spade firmly on the soil. The main crop was set in drills by operating a horse-drawn drill plough in furrows and then closing the drills. There may be an acre or two, of the main crop called the champions, a forgotten name nowadays. Then there were acres of cabbage, table variety and cow cabbage, mangolds stored in heaps in the haggart covered with earth. Then began the sowing of the corn, wheat, oats and barley. The soil was prepared beforehand by scattering loads of sand drawn from the seashore if convenient, or long journeys to a lime kiln with two horse loads to scatter. No silage or bag manure was known then. The corn flourished unless a rainy season set in when disaster occurred and it lodged as they said. If everything went well the reaping started in Autumn early . No reaper and binder then. Simply a moving machine operated by two and drawn by the faithful old farm horse. One man sat on a high seat the other on a lower with a four-pronged-rake with which he cut the corn in swathes or swarts as they called them. Firstly a swathe was mown all around the corn field to make way for the machine. This was accomplished by a scythe. Then the helpers came along and gathered the cut corn into armfuls to form a sheaf, tying each with a binder of twisted corn stalks. These were later lifted to form a triangular shaped group where they were left to dry out completely. Afterwards these stooks were put together to form a stack in the corn fields. Then followed the drawing in to the haggart where big stacks were raised by two-pronged pikes to await the big day, threshing day, an event indeed.

The threshing engine owner was consulted two weeks before so that a fixed day was arranged. If a farmer possessed a large holding the threshing went on for a full day. If it was a small farm it required only a half day. The owner of the machine was boss and called out the orders in stentorian voice. He manipulated the wheel while his helper stoked the coal. Of course the meitheal gathered, each group its special task. Some stood on the thresher receiving the sheaves from the men on the stacks and pushing them through an opening on the thresher. The straw emerged from one point and the grain from another. A group piked the straw to form a rick while another group, the bag-men, filled the emerging grain into sacks secured by twine. Another group carried these on shoulders to the barn usually over the cow-stall, the wheat in one section, the oats in another. Many hands make light work. One must admit it was far from light.

Meanwhile the housewife with her helpers was busy in her kitchen preparing the dinner served in both kitchen and parlour. She has a huge pot of potatoes hanging from the crook over the open fire. They must be watched carefully lest they become a spoiled mash from over boiling. They are strained by grasping the three pot-legs with an over sized cloth. Also, there is a huge potful of table cabbage and perhaps another of the home grown turnips. Already she has baked cakes of brown and white soda bread served with huge mugs of tea. The workers troop in, including the great engine owner in the parlour, others around the kitchen table sit satisfying their hungry stomachs with this wholesome fare followed by tea and the homebaked bread. Who would dream of desserts in those days? Then when all was over, the tierce of porter or the keg was tapped with a device that served as handy opener and all drank their fill. Some got quite jolly and songs were sung with throaty gusto sometimes until the small hours. Nowadays to the amazement of young folk they have old time threshing demonstrations around the country.

Another great day on the farm was the day of the hayrick. No silage then. The hay was mown and then cocked and when quite dry was drawn into the haggart. A small meitheal helped to pike the hay into a rick by two pronged pikes. Pullers caught up the loose strands all round until the rick was smooth and neatly shaped. The hayrick was covered over neatly with a thatch of rushes from the bog. It provided fodder for the cattle during the winter, cut in swathes with a hay knife. Then a couple of jars of porter supplied the drinks. These jars were of yellowish earthenware with tops of brown and still are seen in the restaurants as specimens of ancient culture filled with dried flowers or pampas grass.

The hay makers holding the two pronged hay pikes tested their skill and agility by leaping over the garden wall while holding on to the pikes. Again huge meals are provided in the kitchen by the housewife, washed down by the home baked bread and sometimes jam, blackberry. Butter was also a home product. Before the advent of the churning barrel, the milk was placed in keelers made of wood until the cream setled on top. This then was skimmed and beaten into a semi-solid mass. Two butter spades were used to form a large roll which was served with the home baked bread. Some was also sold in the butter market as there were butter and egg buyers in the towns.

FOR THE SAKE OF ONE CROW

Michael 'Gossie' Browne (b 1908)

Roosky, County Roscommon, 1920s – 40s

Patrick Conboy used to go round with a horse and van sellin stuff — groceries and the like, during the War. He used to come in and he'd put his back to the fire and say, 'Sugar is gone to hell and tay is gone to blazes'. Things was always goin up as it was during the War.

Patrick was an honest man. He once told a story that he was pestered with crows going about their business in the Spring time of the year in the chimleys of the house. 'Begod, I sorted them out', he said, 'I got down the gun, loaded it and blasted them, straight up the chimley'. 'Did you get many of them?', asked a curious listener. 'Begod an I counted ninety-nine of them dead the next mornin', replied Patrick. 'Ah, wouldn't you make it the round hundred', scoffed the questioner. 'An tell a lie for the sake of wan stinkin crow', was Patrick's reply.

I was a dealin man most of my life. I dealt in pigs and cattle mainly, and sheep an odd time. I also bought turkeys for the Christmas market, killed and plucked them and sowld them on to exporters to England. I travelled all over the Counties of the West of Ireland and Counties Leitrim, Longford and Cavan, and I even went as far as the Counties of Limerick and Kerry to buy suck calves.

We had some great times and some hard times and I have lots of stories and yarns to remember them by. I made many friends at the fairs and on the road. They were horrid dacent men and would always do you a good turn and indeed you wouldn't be stuck in most parts for a place to put up for a night. When I was only fifteen years of age I was buying eggs with a neighbour called Tommie Cox. At first he had a horse and van. Then he got a lorry that had solid wheels behind and pumped ones in front. We used to bring eggs to Dublin and sell them around the shops. It used to take more than eight hours to get to Dublin as we travelled at only about ten miles an hour.

I first went on the road for myself about 1930 when I was twenty-one or twenty-two. I bought pigs at the fairs and would sell them to anybody who'd give me a profit on them. Later I bought for the Webbs in Ballyhaunis who were buyers for the Bacon Factories in Castlebar and Claremorris. I used sometimes drive a lorry to the North Wall in Dublin with lambs for export. Dublin was a different place in them times. There were no one way streets and no traffic lights. We used to go in along the Quays and across O'Connell Street to the North Wall. We would get a pound note for petrol and other expenses. Petrol was only 10d a gallon, cigarettes 10d for twenty and you'd get a great feed of steak in Noone's Cafe on the Quays for 2s 6d. I often had a ten shillin note left for myself out of the pound.

I had some very special friends among the dealin men going to the fairs. We would help each other out when necessary. I was once at a fair in Ballyfarnon. A man told me he had a 'chancy' bullock. I looked at the bullock and could see nothing wrong with him. I asked him what he was lookin for and he said, 'eight pound'. I bid him five with a luckpenny of five bob an he agreed. I put me mark on him and he was brought down to a yard. Later a dealin man who was buyin for a factory asked me how much he stood me and I said, 'fourteen pound'. 'I'll give you a quid on him and take him off you', he said. 'No', said I, 'I'll have to get five'. Another man was watchin this and he took out a tenner and a fiver and handed them to me and he took out his raddle and raddled him. I went down the fair and paid the owner. The poor man didn't have change for the luckpenny. 'Ah, you're alright amack', said I, 'he's lucky enough'.

It was great when your luck was in or when you took your chances. Unfortunately, there were other times as well. Falling prices were bad enough but losing stock was worse. I remember one time a pig was smothered on me but through the quick thinking of another dealer, Jim Harte from Kilmactranny, County Sligo, there was no loss, as Jim caught the pig in time and stuck him on the spot. Another time in Cavan, men with me on the lorry told me to go down to Malones for a feed while they put the pigs into the factory. When I met up with them later they told me the pigs were weighed in — dead one and all!

Turkeys like pigs were graded in the later years and you had to be a good judge of how the live animal would grade when it was killed. During the war years there was no grading, and people were glad to get any kind of turkeys or other fowl — according to my cousin Tom Connor they were selling *blackbirds* in London! One exporter that I knew well had his own methods of 'grading' or 'regrading'. He had two tools for the job, a round wooden mallet for the rough work and a porter bottle for the fine grading. With practice he had become very good at it. He would straighten out crooked breasts and flatten thin ones with the mallet and then put the final shape on them with the porter bottle.

DACENT WOMEN

I met many dacent women as well as dacent men in my travels. I think the women I met in Galway were the dacentest of all, although their turkeys were sometimes full of lice! I mind one time my bacon was saved by a widow-woman in a town in the County Longford. I used have a scales there to buy pigs by weight. The finance for the job came from a cheque from Jim Hanley, the founder of Hanley's Bacon Factory in Roosky, which I would cash to get the money to pay the men for their pigs. This day anyway I had seventy-eight pigs weighed and bought and the men waiting to be paid. When I got a message from Roosky to say Jim Hanley didn't want the pigs I was in real trouble and thought my reputation as a dacent man was under threat. I thought later on that Jim Hanley to whom we were related by marriage was intending to take me down a peg.

I decided to retreat to the Post Office for the 'feed', saying I wouldn't be paying out until afterwards. The postmistress, who also did feeds on fair days, etc., was a widow-woman with three childer and a big farm of land — over seventy acres. When she heard my story she took out 500 pounds in cash and a signed chequebook and handed them to me saying, 'You're a dacent man, Gossie Browne, take them and go down and pay for the pigs.' I was very grateful to her and sur what else could I do in the circumstances only take the money and pay the men.

It's a hard bind when a dacent woman has a notion of you and does you a good turn to get you out of a hole, unless of course you get a notion of her as well! I thought a lot about the widow-woman's proposition and of course I brought her back her money as soon as I sowld the pigs. I often wondered if it was a mistake to throw up the seventy acres. I got married some years later and meself and the Missis had eight childer, four boys and four girls. Still you wonder what would have happened if you took a different course . . . But sur they're all dead now Lord ha' mercy on them dacent men and dacent women.

THE DEFENCE OF BUNCOCA

The War affected everything in the middle part of the lives of the people of my generation. Everything was scarce or rationed. Most vehicles (including my own) were off the road because of the scarcity of petrol — you could only get eight gallons a month and sur that wouldn't do me for a week.

For those who could get the petrol, there were good opportunities, and some businesses really got going during the War.

There were constant rumours that the Germans were going to land or had landed. Some of the local men were in the LDF (the Local Defence Force) and some of them were very patriotic and took their duties very seriously.

There was a straight piece of road across the bog above Cloonfour School. One of the local LDF commanders recognised it as an ideal location for the Germans to attempt an invasion of the country from the air and ordered that it be put on a defensive footing. It was decided to mount an anti-aeroplane barricade on Buncoca Bridge (which is not much more than a bog kesh). Asses' carts were put across the bridge and poles sunk in the bog and the whole job secured with wire and whitethorn bushes. It must have been an great sight from the air.

Anyway the Germans never came, and after the War we got back on the road, maybe never telling a lie *just* for the sake of one crow, but always being dacent men and dacent women.

(Editor's Note: Taken down in conversation.)

THE FAIR DAY

Hannah O'Donnell

Kildorrery, County Cork 1940s

It's a wickedly windy Thursday, January 6th, heralding the beginning of the first Fair Day of the New Year. At six a.m. the household are awakened, with the sound of the cattle being rounded up for the long tramp to the village fair. The cattle selected for sale would be housed the night before in the paddock beside the house.

The kettle would be boiled over a turf fire, that domestic chore could take some time, as the turf could be wet and the firelighter

had not yet been invented. After breakfast the gates of the paddock would swing open, the owner and his helper, armed with
lanterns and blackthorn sticks, would shout 'let them out' and the
long march would begin.

In the early Forties the motor car was a rare sight, yet one or
two of the better off farmers owned a Morris Minor, and they
would arrive in style hours later, looking for a cheap bargain, or
to give their wives a day on the town.

In the cold light of dawn with the mist still on the hills, the master
and his stock would trudge on, a stop now and then to light his pipe
and the smell of tobacco would fill the morning air. At this time
dawn is beginning to break, the wind has also changed, it's now
blowing from the south, that could very well mean a snowfall. 'Sure
the Fair Day never lost it', the master would say.

As they marched along by the sleepy houses, the silence was
broken by a sound in the distance of a horse and cart, two hardened hill farmers, overcoats pulled up about their ears, caps down
about their eyes, a big bag tied around their shoulders, to keep
the bitter east winds out, a sharp contrast to how the poor animals
were feeling, steam rising from their beefy flanks, as they stop
now and then to do what nature intended. At long last they reach
the village, the place is a hive of activity, the drovers and tanglers
are moving about, testing udders and flanks.

Dandy, the little Kerry cow, bought at the Fair in Dingle fourteen years previous is being sold. She had served her master well
throughout the years, a bucket of milk at peak time, she looked
sad. I suppose she was missing her grain of oats given her every
morning by the mistress of the house. A young black bull takes an
interest in Dandy but she resists his advances, with a nod of her
head and a shake of her tail. He gets the message and moves on.
Dandy's days of romance are over.

Meanwhile the Fair is in full swing. It's almost twelve noon, the
Angelus bell rings out, stomachs begin to rumble, it's time for
grub. One man stays behind to mind the stock, while the other
hits off to the Hole in the Wall, a restaurant run by a lady called
Big Biddy, a woman of substance. She greets her regulars at the
door calling each man by his christian name. It resembled the
meeting of the cartel without the oil barons or the ten gallon hats.

The kettle is on the boil, the eggs are being prepared, plates of
homemade brown bread are placed on the table, the menu, while
plain is good and nutritious.

A bachelor farmer, who fancies himself as a kind of a Romeo,
fancies one of the waitresses. Although no Page Three Girl, she
does have alluring assets. As she brushes close to the bachelor his

eyes light up and he tries to put an arm around the young girl's waist. 'Give us a kiss', he moans. She stumbles and lands on the bachelor's lap, a big cheer rises from the table, as the men shout, 'Go for her, she'd warm any man on a cold January night'. A shout from Big Biddy brings the young girl back to her senses. 'You're paid to do your job', she cries, 'and not to tempt the men'. The bachelor digs deep into his pocket, counting the pennies and halfpennies, a miser of the highest degree, he pays for his meal and leaves.

Outside the dealing and wheeling is in full swing, the farmer's wives are walking about the stalls looking for a bargain. Poor ould Mary Ellen sits on a butter box sipping a drop of the 'creature'. Her face is a well written book, due to her life and times, her clothes laid out hoping for a good 'kill', after all it's the Fair Day.

A shout comes up from the crowd, 'Get back!'. Men, women and children scatter. A 'stage coach' comes thundering through the main street, heralding the arrival of the travellers. It resembled the Charge of the Light Brigade. Their arrival instilled fear in the eyes of the owners and dealers alike. A row is the norm when the travellers breeze in.

The Fair Day is good for business, the town is alive. At long last there is a battle for poor ould Dandy, she is about to change hands. 7s 6d is the first bid, spitting and hitting of hands is part of the ritual, 10 shillings and she goes, the buyer and seller set off to the Castle Gale to seal the agreement with a drink, trade is in a blaze. Danny, the blind fiddler, sits in a corner, his cap on the ground, hoping to make a few bob. That beautiful old ballad 'Moonlight in Mayo' echoes throughout the haze, visibility is reduced due to the tobacco smoke. A loud bang and the door swings open, the dreaded moment has arrived. Paudie the traveller and he spitting fire, moves up to the counter. 'A pint of your best porter sir', he cries, his blackthorn stick swinging to and fro, like a cat ready to pounce on a mouse. Danny stops playing, an uneasy calm fills the air, Paudie is drunk and abusive, shouting and cursing, a fight is about to break out, only the strong arm of the law moves in and restores normality.

Night time is fast approaching, the cattle have left their trade mark, buckets of water, sweeping brushes and the old reliable Jeyes Fluid helped to clean the flags and walls of the business houses. Meanwhile some farmers who had families to support, were on the offensive so to speak, scouting for bargains. Tea, sugar, bread, etc. were all rationed, it was during the Emergency. The Black Market was the order of the day.

The poor horses were getting tired, having been tied up at the OK Corral since early morning, the night is getting cold, the women are getting tired, it's time to pull the menfolk out of the pubs, that's an art in itself. Having tried gentle persuasion, some ladies used harder tactics like a kick in the behind with their hob-nailed boots, the latter usually did the trick, and her beloved usually answered the call, it's time to hit the road for home.

It was a good day, a few bob had been made, clothes had been bought for the children. A January moon shone down, lighting their way home. The journey seemed endless, feet were aching, blisters were beginning to appear, facing home to the woman of the house was no easy job, yet the men of that era were used to rough treatment. They usually forgot that their menfolk had to walk to and fro, yet the Fair Day was worth all the trouble and hassle, after all it was a day out.

A thought ran through the master of the house, 'What if a cow should decide to calf tonight?' A few hours in 'the labour ward' was a frightening thought, a pan of warm water to ease the aching feet, a warm meal and a cosy bed coupled by a little romance, the Fair Day is gone forever in this country, but the story of adventure that was the Fair Day will live on. This is part of our heritage.

'A PENNY A SOD'

Mairéad Ní Dóige

Edenderry, County Offaly, 1940s

When I was nine years old I was fostered to a lady in the Midlands. Having left the South of Ireland when my father got transferred from 'Bord na Mona' to this midland town, I wondered what my new home would be like. I needn't have worried for the minute I saw my foster mother, Bridget, I knew this lady had won my heart and my respect.

She was born in Dublin and she possessed a sense of humour that Dublin people are gifted with. Looking through the eyes of a nine-year-old, our house was like a picture postcard. There were roses around the door and on a Summer evening the scent of the roses would fill the air. We had no running water but we were lucky as we had a well in our back garden. A lot of people didn't have running water in 1945. We didn't have a wireless or any mod cons but we were content and happy with our lot.

There weren't many cars about then, my father cycled to work which was nine miles away. Hail, rain or shine he never missed a day from work. On pay day my father would drop into his local pub, change his pay cheque and have himself a large bottle of stout; that was the extent of his drinking. Our Parish Priest at this time was totally against drinking and preached this quite a lot. He also loved horses and would ride his favourite horse down our main street. One evening my father was cycling home from work as usual when he met Father John on his horse. Something happened to the horse and suddenly Father John and his horse knocked my father off his bike. Father arrived home a bit shaken and a while later the Priest's handyman arrived at our door to summon my father to the parish priest's house. About an hour later the only hackney car in our town pulled up outside our house and linked a very drunken father into the house. We always laughed every time we heard the sermon about the evils of drink.

Bord na Mona was at its peak during this time; in our area there were three camps to house over a thousand men who came from the west of Ireland to work on the bogs. There was no machinery on the bogs so those men drained and levelled the bogs. They also cut the turf by hand with a slane. They mixed with the town people and eventually married local girls. We had a lot of fun when Bridget's relations came down from Dublin to visit. They laughed and drank the night away and they would rise the roof with 'Molly Malone'. Bridget's sister refused to drink tea if the water was boiled on the peat fire. 'Ah, Bridget', she would say, 'don't ask me to drink that tea and the smell of the turf blinding me between the two eyes'. Now this sister was a dab hand at making clothes and I well remember the lovely 'Shirley Temple' dress she made for me. I wore it until the seams burst.

We had hens and chickens, two cats and a dog who all got on well together. We were never short of eggs or a fowl for a Sunday lunch. Father was a keen gardener and our back garden kept us supplied with food all through the year. He sowed the potatoes on the seventeenth of March every year. This was insurance that St Patrick would take care of them.

There was a lot of boats in the harbour then and we children would spend hours sitting on the canal bank watching them. Another favourite pastime was riding a bogey. The bogey was used to take the hay from the meadow into the barn. Milk was delivered by horse and cart and bread was delivered also by horse and cart. Turf men would come in from Allenwood with a cart full of turf and sell it for a penny a sod. They would make two or more journeys into town in the one day. I remember in the forties there was a lot of emigration and you couldn't travel to England without a passport. In our local cinema DDT was sprinkled on the floor to kill fleas who invaded buildings such as these.

In our kitchen which was very homely we had a mantlepiece and on this sat an oil lamp, a clock and Bridget's snuff box. By the light of this lamp I would try and read the evening paper for my father. I didn't understand every word but it gave me a love of reading that remains with me to this day. I loved school and I loved it when Father John would visit the class; he would tell us to take our books out of our school bags and he would take us up to his orchard where he allowed us to fill our bags with apples.

I remember it all, the love, the fun, the laughter of growing up in a rural town. If I close my eyes I can still see Bridget my wonderful foster mother, baking griddle bread on our turf fire, or leaning on the halfdoor chatting to friends as they passed by. I can still taste that buttermilk that was kept in a crock in the corner of our kitchen. It quenched our thirst on many a hot summers day. As Alice Taylor wrote in one of her books, we were free to be children.

KNITTING

Terry Conville

County Westmeath

I offer you this snippet of my childhood as Teresa Dalton, reared in an isolated house in the Westmeath countryside, when one invented games and made 'toys'.

Mother was essentially an accomplished knitter, and as a small child one of thirteen in the family I soon took to knitting at about four or five. I started on my own with the quills of crow feathers as needles, then I progressed to using cycle wheel spokes cut to size. I knitted my first dress for my dolly, which was two potatoes, one for the head etc. I am now regarded as an expert, having knitted for my own family and friends over the years, but looking back it never occurred to me that I could have knitted shoes or sandals to a skin (hide) or leather, because all my childhood was spent in bare feet. Yes, I am still at it now for my grandchildren as well.

BAGNELSTOWN FIRE BRIGADE

J. Rea (b 1925)

Bagnelstown, County Carlow, 1940s

I joined the Bagnelstown Fire Brigade in 1943 at the age of eighteen. Mr Eric Browne of Browne's Mill was the patron of the Brigade and encouraged many of his workers from the mill to join but there were problems with the Pump and someone who was handy with machinery was needed. That's when I was drafted in because I was working in my father's garage in the town. I wasn't in it very long before I was pushed into leading the Brigade when the Officer-in-Charge left.

It was an entirely voluntary organisation in those days and headquarters was a small hut on Church Street, just opposite St Mary's Church of Ireland. There we kept all our equipment, such as it was. The mainstay of the Brigade was the Pump, but it was a very modest gadget compared to the equipment they have today. For training we had to drag it by hand down to the nearby River Barrow where we practised using it.

If a fire happened to be any distance from the town, one of two or three cars and commercial vehicles, which were willing to help, had to be found in a hurry. We would hitch the Pump to the back, throw the equipment in as best we could and climb aboard. It was all a bit haphazard and rather a confusion. On one occasion we were nearly a mile down the road before we discovered we hadn't got the Pump. No-one had hitched it up!

It's rather difficult to separate memories of individual fires. Things were usually so hectic and busy that you hadn't time to notice particular things about particular fires. There was one bad fire in The Labour Hall and one in Connolly's Bakery, and I dare say that there were many others which I could mention, if I could remember them. The one I remember most was a forest fire in the Drummond Wood in the Summer of 1952. It burned partially underground and lasted for some days. We were short of water at one stage and we went home to have a meal until the tide backed up on the Barrow to give us enough to make an impression.

Alarms were raised by a Klaxon siren at the hut. Telephones were not as common then as now. Very often it was easier and quicker, when a fire broke out anywhere, for someone to go direct to the Fire Station and set the alarm off there themselves. The men, about eight or ten of them, would then have to drop whatever they were doing, wherever they were doing it, and get themselves to the headquarters as quickly as possible.

None of us was paid. It must have been four or five years before the local authority decided to give us all a regular Christmas present, about £37 if I remember rightly. Of course, that was a tidy sum in those days. It was some years after that again before we got a regular payment. Altogether I served in the Brigade for fourty-one years and enjoyed every minute of it.

THE SCOURING OF THE OWENSCAW

Ned Kennedy (b 1921)

County Limerick, 1948

On the twelfth of September, Nineteen Forty Eight
We met at the bridge of Bunoke
To scour the Curragh river and terminate
The bluff of T.D.s who just spoke.
'Twas a wonderful sight to see our hopes rise
As the priest raised aloft his camán
'We'll do it together all the ways hether
To the brown bogs of Clouncourivane'.

It was Father Culhane from well-famed Ahane,
He who trained our young hurlers to score,
With skill and with tact he was now in the act
The floods to keep back from our door.
With very few words he embarked on the scheme,
The neighbours they liked his comhrádh
The twelfth was a Sunday and on the next Monday
We marched to the River Owenscaw.

We liked Sonny Guiry so tough and so wiry,
As ganger he suited all hands.
The spade men and pike men and all men united
For one common cause the half dozen townlands.
Simon Browne and Mahoneys they brought out their ponies
And big trees from their roots we did draw
Barry Mack's creamery tractor was a very big factor
In the scouring of the River Owenscaw.

We laboured three weeks till Curragh Bridge came in sight
And the Curragh boys they started loud cheers.
'When we reach Kennedy's inch I'll throw a big night'
Said Ben Madden who's been flooded for years.
Jim Fitzmaurice worked alone on his own native shore;
So Ballydoorty worked its way to Gurtskeagh
And a million tons more was flung up from the floor
Of the River that's called Owenscaw.

On the eighteenth of October the job was well over
And the waters flowed back to the Deele,
Thanks to Father Culhane who was first in the van
For his courage and patience and zeal.
That night we felt new at a party we threw
We sang and we danced for old Éireann Go Bráth.
For years we did wait but we'll never forget
The scouring of the River Owenscaw.

I wrote this poem in 1948 to mark the cleaning of the river Owenscaw in County Limerick. I was then a young Garda and I finished up Chief Superintendent and retired in 1982 with fourty years service.

A WET DAY

Edward McNerney (b 1924)

Corclara, Edgesworthtown, County Longford, 1930

The smoke from the turf fire was diverted around the skillet of porridge hanging on the crook and the rain that fell down the chimney and sizzled on the lid, we called sootdrops.

The rain it fell from a dark grey sky with no sign of a clearing and my father paced up and down the floor like as if someone had died. The kitchen was full of moving feet as we all sorted out our favourite spoon for a milk and porridge breakfast. It was late in March and we had started to cut turf the day before and my father was a determined man and it wasn't easy to stop him.

My mother packed the lunch bag and she checked every item, calling aloud as she counted on her fingers, bread, butter, sugar, salt, milk, eggs, spoons, a knife and tea. This was the usual pack for a feed cooked on the bog.

A neighbour called and we knew before he spoke that he was going to say, 'I wonder will it clear?' My father and himself walked out to the yard and got well away from the house so that the horizon could be inspected. With one match the two pipes were lighted and after a few puffs the smoke could be seen heading toward the ground, a bad sign, and we kept within earshot for the verdict.

'If there was the size of a half crown of blue sky at the butt of the wind I'd have hopes', the neighbour said. 'There's always the danger that the wind would wheel, and there was a ring around the moon last night and the curlews were crying for the past couple of days', my father said. As a concluding gesture both heads looked upwards and agreed that it would be no day for the bog.

Then the neighbour mentioned that he had pigs to ring and my father went to give him a hand. When he came back my mother said that the hoops on the churn needed to be tightened and the handle of the dash was loose.

Once he got the hammer in his hand there was no end to the jobs he got. Studs in the heels of boots, bucket handles that got bent, and as the day went on and no sign of the rain to stop, everyone settled to accept it as not a complete loss. There were sheds cleaned out and the yard swept and a lot of little things that would never be done only for the rain.

IT'S A LONG WAY

Eric Read-Jones (b 1909)

Behamore Castle, County Tipperary / England, 1920s

Little did I realise when as a child I heard that well-known song, so reminiscent of the First World War, that it heralded for me, my future wife coming from Tipperary. It must also appear strange that I, an Englishman, can relate to the way of living in Ireland during those early years.

I was born in 1909 and my wife a year later. We first met in 1926 when she came to England to take up employment as a children's nanny. She died last year after fifty-five years of happy married life and I decided to revisit Ireland to see all her relations and friends and recall the happy memories of past years in and around her home in Tipperary; also to plant a tree in the garden of her old home in her memory.

My wife's maiden name was Hassett and her family had a small farm in Behamore Castle near Cloughjourdan. Her father had died in 1919 when she was eight years of age, leaving her mother to cope with managing the farm and bringing up the family. Initially, her neighbours gave valuable help but eventually her three sons looked after the farm and crops whilst the daughters were sent elsewhere to work. Kitty, my future wife, spent most of her time looking after and nursing children in the neighbourhood; an experience which was to serve her in good stead when she eventually came to England. It proved to be a real wrench from her mother and family but she was fortunate in getting a post with a Scottish family in London and always maintained that the wife became a second mother to her.

The farming community in Ireland always fared better than the townsfolk during the difficult years of the First World War and its aftermath, because of their self-sufficiency. They were able to live off the land, needing only a few extra but essential items such as oil, tea, clothing materials and the like from nearby towns. Clothes were generally home-made and cast-offs handed down to younger members of the family. It was indeed a case of 'make and mend' in the interests of economy.

The Hassett family was a happy one but hardworking. The main mode of transport was a small pony and trap apart from a shared bicycle. The home was about three miles (Irish!) from Cloughjordan. The farm was well managed with the help and advice of relatives, but there was always a wonderful spirit of camaraderie abroad, especially amongst the menfolk of neighbouring farms, who helped each other in time of need, pooling their resources, their tools and other equipment. This was particularly noticeable during haymaking and at harvest time when even a threshing machine with its steam powered tractor was available to all concerned. I have many happy memories of giving a helping hand out in the fields, being the butt of many an Irish joke or blarney, in view of my inexperience and possibly clumsy efforts to do some of the jobs. On these harvest occasions one was rewarded with a good old Irish farm-house dinner of bacon and cabbage at the host farm.

Many a tall story would be told at these gatherings, including one where a somewhat dim-witted farmer, failing to get his horse to move a heavily laden wagon from a field, decided to light a small fire with straw beneath the horse to make it move; the horse moved on a yard or two and in consequence the fire was positioned beneath the cart which caught fire and was a total loss!

The small village school, long vacated and presently used as a

barn, served its purpose in basic education for several generations. Kitty, in due course was able to make up for its deficiencies
when she arrived in England. She often related a small anecdote;
she was seated one day in class with her younger brother beside
her. He had fallen asleep and the teacher noticing his inattention
hit his hand with the ruler. Kitty's reaction was immediate. She
grabbed the ruler from the teacher and hit her hand in turn! There
were no repercussions Kitty had made her point. The incident did
however reveal her innate love for children which continued for
the rest of her life.

During my recent tour of Ireland I visited the Heritage centre in Nenagh
and also Bunratty Castle in County Clare, where I saw collections of
paraphernalia consisting of farming implements, household utensils and
cream-making equipment which I was able to identify with, having seen
them in use at the Hassetts and other farmhouses. The Hassetts' farm was
typical of all that I had seen, with its main living room and a spotlessly clean
creamery attached. The open fire in a wide fireplace with cooking utensils
arranged around it and an ever-present iron kettle of hot water suspended
above the fire providing a constant supply for all the kitchen chores and every
other need — water being obtainable from a hand pump in the yard. This was
the room for working, cooking, dining and socialising. I recall many a party taking place accompanied by the usual fiddle and the Irish dancing. The old Irish
songs too, were often heard.

Sadly, traditional Ireland, as I knew it, has largely disappeared. Many old
homes, as at Behamore, still stand, looking forgotten and forlorn whilst alongside or nearby, a newly-built bungalow type dwelling stands, very often
unfortunately completely out of character in the countryside; several, far too
pretentious in such a setting. The camaraderie too, has also gone. There is a
scarcity of young people due to emigration and the effect of this on village life is
quite noticeable. Small farms have disappeared along with the husbandry.

Nevertheless, I still have a great love for Ireland in spite of all the changes over
the years and in any case changes are happening the world over. I know
there will always be a friendly welcome when I come again and I am happy
in the knowledge that my devoted wife came from Tipperary and not such a
long way after all.

IV

RETURN FROM THE DARDANELLES

Ned Gilligan (b 1907)

Mullingar, County Westmeath, First World War

I have clear memories of eighty years ago, before the First World War which began in 1914 after the assassination of the Arch-Duke Ferdinand in Sarajevo. At that time Mullingar, like all other county towns, was garrisoned by regiments of English soldiers stationed in a large barracks on the outskirts of the town. These regiments went on regular route marches on the roads around the town led by brass or pipers' bands playing martial music with the object at that time of stirring up the young men to join the English Army and fight the enemy, 'Huns' as the Germans were known at that time.

In the early stages of the War recruiting agents for the English army were busy in every garrison town encouraging young men to join up. They paid special attention to licensed premises which were visited by young men after their week's work on a Saturday night. When the agents succeeded in getting a promise of joining up, usually from someone somewhat merry from intoxicating drink, the volunteer was given a shilling. This made it a binding contract, and even years after if the soldier was lucky to return home from war service he would always be referred to as, 'Oh! He took the Saxon shilling'.

The English Government also used the postal service to further their recruiting campaign. Recruiting letters were sent to all males, regardless of age, urging them to join the army and fight for the freedom of small nations. Across the top of the long brown envelopes were the words 'ON HIS MAJESTY'S SERVICE'. The postman who delivered those letters at six o'clock in the morning wore a black uniform piped with red, and rode a bicycle with its frame and mudguards lined with red stripes, and having a large permanent carrier in front. There was also a later postal delivery at 10.30 a.m.

I remember receiving those letters when I was seven years old, as also did my two brothers who were younger, and I also remember them being taken by my parents and burned. All the grown ups, young and old, received them also.

As the war went on I have vivid memories of two young men who called to my parents' home in khaki uniform and brass buttons to say 'Goodbye'. One of them never came back; he was buried in the muddy trenches around Verdun.

The one who came back from the carnage of the Dardanelles was so changed that the neighbours feared his strange ways. One Saturday night he burst into my parent's home in a drunken rage as we were polishing our boots for Sunday morning. He caught our pet dog sleeping by the fire and sat on the lower steps of the stairs holding it on his knee, and then choked it to death. I remember that night well. It is nearly eighty years ago.

SHOOTING IN THE DISTANCE

Janet Broderick Regan (b 1912)

East Wall, Dublin, 1916

In 1916 I was four years of age. Easter Weekend was special because we were taken by my mother to visit my aunt, a nun, in the Sisters of Charity at Milltown in the south of the city. Dressed in all our finery, my brother Tommy and myself were the joy of my mother's life. She was a young Scottish woman, born in the Persian Gulf, before coming to Ireland at age fourteen and eventually marrying a Dublin Metropolitan Policeman, settling in East Wall on the Northside.

Going to Milltown was a great adventure because the nuns fussed over us and gave us tea and biscuits. We were really having a great time when the convent's senior gardener came to us saying he was sorry it was time to go because some kind of war had broken out in Dublin, at the GPO. The older man seemed very worried and said we better leave right away so he could lead us home to East Wall by safe ways he knew. My mother seemed very frightened. We clung to her hands as we made our way towards the city.

Closer to town the streets seemed very deserted and eerie with no people about. Then we heard the shooting in the distance and had to wait in doorways every time soldiers rushed by, waving and shouting at us to get off the streets and indoors. It took us hours to go down the lanes and back-streets, all the time making for the safety of our home in East Wall. Somewhere on the way I lost my little straw hat and Tommy fell once and cut his knee. The older man was very brave and when we got to East Wall he said goodbye and God bless.

My mother at the time was only twenty-six and I remember how she carried me up West Road in her arms and her face all flushed with excitement and worry. She kept telling us to be brave and that we would be home soon. All the time we could see soldiers and policemen running along the railway lines and hear gunshots away at the Liffey.

We found out later that the old gardener from the convent got to Milltown two days after he left us and said we were the bravest children he had ever met. My mother wrote him a lovely letter and we all signed it, with xxxxs for kisses. We went into Dublin a week later with my father and saw the whole place in bits, with the buildings all black and rubble all over the streets. People kept saying the Rising this, the Rising that and the Rising the other. Confusion was everywhere. The strangest thing I remember was the moment we got home that evening from Milltown after all our trouble and adventure. We burst in the door, my father was sitting in his reading chair, reading the paper, half dozing. We began shouting, telling him what we saw. He looked at us like we were mad. He was completely unaware of what was happening in the GPO, the shooting, everything. It was like everything about that Easter Weekend that changed Dublin for ever.

Now nearly eighty years later I can still remember my little straw hat, my button-up coat, Tommy's rust-coloured top coat and knee breeches, my mother's lovely rose, excited face and the old gardener's quiet voice. I remember too my father's shock and disbelief, the gun-shots and the fear in people's eyes. We all slept in my mother and father's bed that night and that was the best part because we felt safe and secure. All those people are gone now but the memory lives on.

DISPATCH RIDER HERO

Thomas Lynch (b 1913)

Dunshaughlin / Dublin, 1916

James Fox was a member of the Irish Citizen Army, who died in the 1916 Insurrection.

I would like to inform your readers of some of some of the historical facts that surround this young man. He was born in the Spencer Arms Hotel, Drumree, as it was then known. His father was known as P.J., one of Meath's greatest sportsmen on the football field or in the boxing arena and other grades as well. His mother was an English woman and P.J. and herself met on the hunting field. Seamus was their first born, he also had a brother and sister called Todd and Connie. P.J. sold the hotel in 1916 and went to live in Dublin. The reader can conjure the awful heartbreak it was for this man to part with his hotel where the Lord Lieutenant of Ireland wined and dined and where Charles Stuart Parnell held his meetings.

When in the city father and son kept themselves fit by giving lessons in shadow boxing, the father on his knees and the son on his feet, the father being six feet two inches tall. The father teamed up with James Connolly and helped to form the Dublin Citizen Army and young Seamus, who was only sixteen years old, became a dispatch rider.

On the first day of the rising he was carrying a dispatch from one garrison to another when a sniper's bullet found his brave heart and laid him low at St. Stephen's Green gate. It was some days after his father got word down to my father, who was signalman at Drumree Station, to have a grave opened for Seamus in Knockmark Cemetery which he duly did with the help of two other men, William Doran and Paddy Carolan, known better as 'Paddy the Crow'.

The rising was over when that heartbroken father brought his heroic young boy down for burial and he had his first sitting down meal in my father's house, my father and P.J. being blood relations and great pals from boyhood.

I feel proud and honoured to write these few lines thanking the young people (refers to students at Grange Community College who were involved in the initial collection of these memories) who will play a part in keeping this young boy's memory alive. I marched with many young men from many parts around Dunshaughlin to the cemetery to erect the fitting memorial you see today.

I will conclude by writing one of P.J.'s musings:

> The old mill field and the chestnut trees,
> Where in youth I used to lie,
> That home was yours, my boy,
> And I long to lie beside him yet,
> Contented there to lie,
> Over Meath's green fields,
> Where the bees go buzzing by.

MY PET HEN 'SPECKLE'

Sheila O'Brien (nee Lawton b 1913)

Timoleague, Bandon, County Cork

I remember one morning I was in the farmyard with my mother and a soldier appeared and said that the soldiers were coming and to collect her eggs because they would eat them all. We had collected them when six men arrived in uniform and went searching around. I had a pet hen I called her Speckle. She had different coloured feathers and they found her in her nest and when they didn't find any eggs they took her out in the yard and cut off her head. It was terrible to see her body going one way and her head in the other direction. My little hen was gone and I didn't have my little brown egg any more.

Some time later it was winter time. It was dark outside and the lamp was lit. We were washing the ware after the tea when we heard men's voices outside. My mother and father were sitting by the fire and the schoolgoing were doing their lessons. There was a loud bang at the door and it opened in. He wanted to know where the big Boys were. My big brothers were gone to a neighbour's house playing cards. The soldiers were very cross and they were opening presses and banging things around. There were two bags of flour on a seat, one was brown, one was white. The soldier pulled out his bayonet and split both bags open leaving the flour to go all over the place. That was our bread for the week. Thirteen children and my parents.

PÁDRAIG MAC PIARAIS – The Storyteller

Diarmuid Ó Dúill (b 1911, A pupil from Scoil Éanna)

Killester, Dublin

This poem was written some years ago by Diarmuid Ó Dúill now 84 years old. Diarmuid has quite a history attached to his life. He attended Scoil Éanna in Rathfarnham, the school founded by Pádraig Mac Piarais, where he was taught by Margaret Pearse. He later took up employment as a driver to Douglas De h-Íde, the first President of Ireland. He has many fond memories of his years working in Áras an Uachtaráin and his friendship with Douglas De h-Íde with whom he travelled the country, often visiting Douglas de h-Íde's summer home 'Rattra House' in Co Roscommon. Diarmuid has in his possession many of Douglas de h-Íde's writings. 'The Storyteller' is so called because of Pearse's great love of storytelling.

> The little children gathered 'round his feet,
> And listened to his tales of long ago.
> Of Tuireann, Lir and Usna, Deirdre's fate,
> And bold Cuchullan of the 'hero glow'.
>
> The little children 'list with widening eyes,
> To Epic tales of heroes long since gone.
> And perhaps some wondered, under Irish skies
> How such great deeds were done.
>
> When summer came again those children heard,
> Of trouble in a city far away.
> He came no more; this man no wee one feared.
> Their storyteller sleeps beneath the clay.
>
> And so this quiet man who told old tales,
> To little children on a Connaught shore,
> In life's blood wrote an Epic for all Gaels
> To Irish hearts he speaks for ever more.

THE TAN WAR

Charles O'Connor

My father was coming from eight o'clock Mass one Sunday morning with his mother on the jenet and trap. As they talked peacefully they could hear the convoy coming, so Daddy fled through the fields.

There was a bridge down and the English were trying to catch men to mend it. They caught a few of his neighbours but left my granny. After all she was a woman. One man had a brand new hat that had cost fifty whole shillings, and they took it.

The next day, while eating dinner, they were still looking for Uncle Tom (not real name). The door which led into the kitchen only opened forward and there was a stack of coats behind it. Three Black and Tans made their way into the house. Uncle Tom slid in behind the door and waited. The door opened.

'Where is 'e ?', the English soldier asked.

'Ach, sure he's gone up the fields to the neighbours this two hours!', the family told him.

Finally they left.

Uncle Tom was eventually caught and spent six to eight months in the Curragh prison, simply for fighting for his rights.

WANTED — FOR SAVING A MAN'S LIFE

It was the year 1920. The Black and Tans were on the rampage in Ireland. Uncle Tom (not his real name) was making his way home from town one evening, when he noticed an English policeman and a drunken Irishman arguing. He stopped to lend his assistance. Suddenly, the Englishman produced a gun. Uncle Tom grabbed the gun, threw the policeman a punch and turned him upside down. Then he went off home with the gun.

About a week later, when the soldiers found his name they landed in the yard of his house at about three o'clock in the morning. His brother and he were upstairs. When the startled workman who slept in the kitchen heard the racket he raced upstairs, asking where the gun was. Uncle Tom told him to go to the pantry and with shaking hands the man gave over the weapon.

'Will we shoot him?', the English voice asked.

'Nah.. but we should shoot the other man upstairs!' They laughed wickedly and drove away, leaving the household in disarray.

OUT OF THE MOUTHS OF BABES

Anne Le Matty (b 1930)

Glasnevin, Dublin, 1922

My father, James Davidson born 1903, was involved in the Troubles in 1920. During those days he was courting my mother. The story goes (according to my mother) that her family were never involved, her mother being very strict on her sons, indeed she was terrified of them coming to harm.

My mother was the eldest girl in a family of seven, two boys and five girls. The youngest was a little girl called Kathleen, a lovely child with a head of brown curls and beautiful brown eyes. She was a very happy little girl. She idolised my father and every evening she would wait at the cottage door, she seemed to always know when he was going to call. My grandmother would insist that my mother would take her for a walk, she would say, 'Mary, yourself and James take Kathleen down to the park and let her feed the ducks.' Kathleen would skip along happily between the loving couple. I am sure there were times when they could have done without her.

During this time there would be references made about the 'Black and Tans' and I expect about a lot of confidential things. Nobody ever thought about the little girl who seemed to be quite happy playing with her dolls.

Then one night my grandmother and the family were sitting around the fire. The younger children were in bed. All was quiet, my mother was not seeing my father that night. She was busy washing her hair. Suddenly the door of their cottage was burst open by the Black and Tans. The peace of their humble home erupted into a horror scene. Grandmother was a tall stately looking lady. She demanded to know what they were doing there. They said they were looking for my father, mentioning him by name. 'He is not here', cried grandmother. They ignored her and proceeded to search the house. Now my mother, unknown to anyone, had been given bullets to mind by my father. She had hidden them on a Sacred Heart Altar over her bed. All the girls slept in the same room. As the soldiers burst into the bedroom, my mother felt as though she were going to die of fright. The children were all huddled together crying except Kathleen. She was sitting on my mother's bed, cuddling her rag doll.

The soldiers pulled the beds apart. My mother pleaded with them not to harm the children. One of them stood up on the bed to reach the Altar. He pulled everything from the Altar. My mother could hear her heart beat with terror. She could not believe it when he found nothing.

They eventually left, and she collapsed on the spot. When she came to, she told her mother what she had done. 'What happened to them?', my gran cried. 'Are you sure you left them there? And how dare you do such a thing. You could have had your brothers shot.' Just then a little voice piped up. Yes, it was Kathleen, their baby sister and she said in her childish way, 'Me got bullets under my oxster' (a word used for under the arm). Everyone was dumbfounded. They kissed and hugged her.

Kathleen however was not destined for a long life, she died in child-birth at the young age of twenty. As my father looked down at her, in her coffin, that lovely face he loved so much, still lovely, even in death, his tears flowed unashamedly. He was remembering the little girl who had saved his life on that night all those years ago.

THE NIGHT OF THE TANS

Norah Tobin (b 1913)

Booterstown Avenue, Dublin

The night was dark and cold but I felt warm and safe as I sat on my little bed munching my Marie biscuit and drinking my milk. The reason for my secure feeling was that within two feet of me was my gran quietly reciting her Rosary in her large comfortable bed. No goblins or ghosts could get me here, I thought, with my lovely gran so close to me. It was a big Victorian-style bedroom and the embers of the fire still cast a warm orange glow on the walls surrounding us. Suddenly, this peaceful scenario was interrupted by a thundering noise on the road outside. As the noise got louder I recognised it as those awful lorries again.

I ran to the window, and just as I did, one of the lorries stopped and out jumped about ten soldiers all carrying rifles. They began to scatter and started running up and down the road banging on doors and shouting in very loud aggressive tones. 'They're drunk, as usual', said my gran from her bed, 'come away from the window, dear, they can't touch us'.

Just then there was a loud banging on the door downstairs. Ignoring my gran, I flew out to the landing — my Auntie Clarke emerged from her room holding her candle and trembling. Downstairs in the hall stood Mary, our maid, looking helplessly up at both of us. 'Open the door you fool', hissed my aunt under her breath. 'Do you want us all to be killed in our beds?'

Poor Mary did as she was told and in rushed the soldiers running up the stairs and hammering on all the doors, 'Give us your guns you bastards or we'll blow your bloody heads off'. I ran up to my gran to protect her. 'Don't touch my gran, she's an old lady.' I was shaking like a jelly. I looked at my gran. She was sitting bolt upright in the bed with a very vexed look on her face. 'Get out of my house this instant, you are all drunk' she said. 'Shut your mouth, Granny', the leader of the men shouted. He was swaying from side to side. My gran stared at him intensely.

'I am an employee of the British Crown', she said, and I noticed one of the soldiers slowly lowering his rifle. 'I am Post Mistress of Blackrock Post Office and I intend to report you to your Superior Officer for your disgraceful conduct.'

Just then the door burst open and two older men came in. 'Get out, get out you stupid bastards, you're in the wrong house', one of the men shouted. He turned to my gran and said politely, 'I am deeply sorry about this Mam — I shall see that you receive a full apology from my Commanding Officer first thing in the morning'. He bowed and was about to make a quick retreat. 'Just a moment young man' said my gran, 'I would like to give you a parting present'. The man turned around looking uncomfortable. 'There is a book over there', she said, pointing to the round table by the window. 'It's called "The Life of Queen Victoria" — I won't be wanting it any more'. He took it and made a quick exit muttering apologies as he left.

My gran looked at me and said, 'Now I'm going to learn Irish'. She put her arms around me. Auntie Clarke was still standing shivering in the corner. 'Sit down Katie.' My auntie sat in the chair sighing with relief.

'Now child, fetch the Holy water from behind the shutter and sprinkle it all around and let us all thank the Good Lord that we're not lying dead in our beds this night.' I did as she said.

'Now I think we should all have some nice hot punch after all that excitement.' She smiled at me. 'Go downstairs dear and help Mary with the punch — tell her to make them extra strong and to have one herself'. She lay back on her pillow — 'Take more than a drunken Black 'n' Tan to frighten Jane Fennell'.

FALSE ALARM

Phil Walsh (b 1926)

Abbeyleix, County Laois, 1920s

It was during the troubled times in Ireland in the 1920s when the Black and Tans were causing widespread fear and devastation all over the country. My father had a grocery shop in a small town. One of his employees was rumoured to be a member of the IRA so there were constant sniper shots fired into the house and shop. We children were shown the bullet holes in the wooden shutters of the windows in the living area, years later.

One night there was an almighty crash downstairs. My father and mother jumped out of bed and crawled out onto a flat roof at the back of the house, in their night attire, and in through a skylight window to the house next door. They sat in fear and trepidation all night. Next morning they climbed back and crept around to see what damage had been done — fearful of what they would find. When they got to the kitchen they found the large earthenware crock, in which the milk was kept, in pieces on the floor and milk all over the room. The cat had tried to get at the milk and knocked it down.

WAR MEMORIES AND MURDER

Mary O'Sullivan (b 1916)

Waterford City / Dublin, 1921 and after

THE CIVIL WAR

Memories, sandbags at all windows, constant shooting. Soldiers kicking in front door, taking my father and wouldn't let him put on a jacket even though it was very cold. I recall looking at his braces holding up his trousers and my mother crying. He returned some time later to our great joy. It was mistaken identity.

THE SECOND WORLD WAR

I married at twenty and was a widow at twenty-four with three children, youngest eleven months — it was as a result of a German bomber machine gunning a sinking Irish ship. 'The City of

Limerick' was the name of the ship. Two killed, my husband and the other man had the same name as the man I later remarried.

After a few years my parents looked after my children as I trained as a midwife in the Rotunda. It was hard but I liked it. Started work at 7.30 a.m. until finish at 9 p.m. — 3/4 hour off for tea. Worked seven days a week — 1/2 day on Sunday — three months night duty a year — three months at a time — followed by one month holiday.

I was on duty as a student nurse when a patient was admitted from somewhere, I think the Midlands, supposed to have died as the result of an eclamptic fit. Her husband crying, we all felt so sorry for him. Dr Raymond Cross did a caesarean hoping to save the baby but he also was dead. I took specimen of urine, tested it for albumen, it was clear, showed it to the sister-in-charge.

Body sent down to Path. Lab in Rotunda — husband was convicted — was last man to be hanged in Ireland, he was a Dutchman — named Leaman.

HOW WAS I TO KNOW

Elizabeth Caraher (b 1929)

Cork and Dublin, 1939

I wished they'd stop talking about Hitler. I didn't know who he was. I'd never met him, but he didn't sound like a very nice man. Anyway, why should I care? I was off to Dublin next day to spend a holiday with my Gran and my Aunt Kathleen.

I came on the train on my own. Mom and Dad brought me to the station at Glanmire and asked a porter to look after me. Now, HE was a nice man, he put my big case up on the rack and I also had a little tin case which Mom had packed for me. It had comics ('Film Fun' and 'Comic Cuts'), fruit and my favourite chocolate bars, 'Half Time Jimmies'. I think they came in a red box with a picture of a goalkeeper on it. There were nine squares in each bar and they were delicious.

I cried just a little bit when Mom and Dad and my baby brother said 'Good-bye', but the porter came to see if I was all right, and he stayed with me while we went through the long dark tunnel after we left the station. He told the other passengers that I was travelling alone and they all spoiled me with lemonade and sweets. It was great.

I loved that journey but as we got closer to Dublin I became very excited. I'd often been there before but never on my own. (After all, I was only nine). My Gran and Auntie were there to meet me and I thought I'd be squashed by all the hugs.

We went to their house in a horse and cab. I remember the cabbie was a funny little man, full of jokes, but he had only one eye and Auntie told me that he'd lost it in France. I thought this was really silly but he cracked his whip and off we went.

I was thrilled as we went through the city towards Drumcondra, looking out at all the lights and the river. Oh, it was a lovely holiday, visits to aunts and uncle and cousins, everybody fussing over me. We went shopping in the city where a lady in Moore Street gave me an apple and an orange because she thought I was a very nice little girl but I thought it was because Gran bought lots of things from her.

Gran bought me a lovely sailor dress in one of the big shops, it was a white pleated skirt with a blue top and a big collar with three stripes on it. I thought I looked like Shirley Temple, curly hair and all! My Gran called me her little pigeon, and I knew she really loved me, she spoiled me so much.

We visited lots of places and we had a big picnic one day on Dollymount Strand with all the family. It was August and it was hot and sunny all the time. We had great fun and I was very tired when we got home. I just fell into Gran's big bed and I remember the sheets had a lovely scent of lavender and I could hear the trams going clickety-clack as they hurried into town. I could also hear my gran's friends talking away downstairs. She always had lots of friends in and they played records on her gramophone, it had a big horn and somebody had to keep winding it up. I remember hearing a song called 'Three o'clock in the morning' and lots of lovely waltzes and Grace Moore singing 'One night of love', I thought that if I could sing like Grace I'd forget about looking like Shirley Temple, but I could still hear a lot of talk about Hitler as well. Anyway, I fell asleep then.

I was to stay in Dublin for a month, when Dad was due to come up for the 'All-Ireland' and to bring me back home. I didn't know whether I wanted to go or stay but, on Friday morning we heard a great commotion in the street and I looked out to see a newsboy wearing a big placard, like an apron and there was just one word on it 'WAR' in big black letters. It was September 1st and I was terrified. I was so upset that I decided that I would start crying and I would keep it up until Dad arrived on Sunday and I did. Nothing would stop me, all day Friday, all day Saturday, and part of Sunday. I thought my family in Cork would be killed and that I would never see them again.

Early on Sunday morning Gran and I went to Mass in Gardiner Street church (there being a temporary lull in the crying before I went to Holy Communion). There was the most awful thunderstorm and fierce rain. We ran from door to door trying to get some shelter. Gran was a big lady and she was wearing a lovely black sealskin coat, she put me in underneath it for shelter, but we were still drenched.

Dad arrived and I was never so pleased to see him. He went to the 'All-Ireland' with my uncle Jim. Cork and Kilkenny were playing and Kilkenny won 2-7 to Cork 3-3. (I thought that God didn't like Cork people that day).

We went back to Cork that evening and I was very sad to leave Dublin but, at the same time, I couldn't wait to get home. The train was pitch black as all the lights were turned off and all the stations were in darkness too. At some of the stations soldiers got on and they were wearing helmets with funny bits of hedges and shrubs stuck on them. Someone said that this was in case the Germans came and Dad said it was camouflage. I didn't know what that meant but it frightened the wits out of me. At last we were home and Oh, the hugs and kisses I got from Mum and all the stories I had to tell. It was lovely to feel safe and warm with my family again, and I hoped that that was the last I would hear of Hitler.

How was I to know? After all, I was only nine.

HOW TIMES HAVE CHANGED

A Country Lady

County Mayo, 1940s

I grew up in the 1940s and have many memories. It was a time when there was no dole or no children's allowance, but as we lived on a small farm we never were hungry. We lived on good food which had no added chemicals. We kept our own flock of hens, ducks and geese, even guinea fowl. The eggs had to be washed and packed in baskets and ready for the egg merchant who called to the gate. In return for the money obtained for the eggs my mother bought all the groceries for the week and often had change. We milked our own cows and made our own butter.

We didn't ever buy creamery butter, altho' the surplus milk went to the local creamery. We killed our own pig and it was always a great time of feasting when we made puddings and had liver and pork-steak for weeks afterwards. The bacon was cured and packed into boxes for the winter, some extras were given to the neighbours, as there would be a lot of pork-steak and ribs and puddings. We had to work hard when growing up. We had to fill water for thirsty cattle, there was no water on tap. We had a big well which kept the village supplied with lovely clean water when most of the other sources dried up in dry weather, water flowed from under a huge rock. Many a happy hour was spent by myself and my girl friends, as we used to plan to meet there at a certain time. Our pastimes were few then — the local dance which only happened once a month. Finding the two and six to go to the dance was difficult as money was scarce. We laughed and discussed the goings on at the dance and it was always great fun. We visited each other's houses and danced to the music of a gramophone and planned our next dance. We used to have to cycle in those days in hail, rain or snow. We didn't mind so long as we got there. There was a war and everything became scarce. Although Ireland was not involved we suffered because commodities were very scarce. We had no electricity then and had to rely on oil lamps. The oil became scarce and after we had to do with candle light if we happened to have one. We reared turkeys and the Xmas food was bought from the money received for the turkeys. We ourselves had to do with geese (which were lovely) for our Xmas dinner. Pleasant memories I recall are of rising early and climbing to the top of the hills on a lovely summer morning to bring in the cows to be milked. I would sit at the top of the hill and view the valley below and a large part of the countryside and see the lakes, also trains puffing in the distance. Everywhere was so peaceful and still and one was reminded of the Creator who painted this lovely scene. I used to love to be the first in the house to find the new foal born during the previous night, seeing him gallop down the hill and he only a few hours old beside his proud mother.

I left home and worked in the city for some years. I married, returned and now I live with my memories and husband as our family are all emigrated. These are only some of the times in the far off past. One thing I thank God for is my health and that of my husband.

I left out the haymaking and the corn saving and indeed the bog and turf. I could on and on but then I'd need to write a book like Alice Taylor. I will finish now as my hand is getting tired. I would rather not give my name.

THE EMERGENCY

Elizabeth Connolly (b 1932)

Rathmines, Dublin, 1939 – 45

I remember I was seven years old at the outbreak at World War 2. There was great excitement where I lived in Rathmines, on the south side of Dublin. At that time Rathmines was like a village, everyone knew everyone, and the only people with cars were doctors or other professional people and even they mostly used the 14 or 15 tram which ran on tracks with leads onto overhead wires. They made a lot of noise and the 'joke' among us children was 'is that a German bomber or a 14 tram?'

Within weeks of 3rd September 1939 every adult and child was fitted with a gas mask and there was a sort of carrycot with a cover and air pump for babies. There was also a blackout imposed and everyone had to buy black blinds or curtains for their windows.

Then at school we were all issued with forms nominating a relative in the 'country' (rural area) who would be prepared to have us as evacuees. When I brought the form to my father (an eight generation Dublin man) and mother (three generations) my Dad said, 'Sorry, Bette but you will just have to stay here and face Hitler'.

Other than having to eat brown bread and having no fruit other than native apples and pears, plums, blackberries, etc. and sweets being off the shelves, we got plenty of good food, and felt sorry for people in England who had strict rationing. The only fuel available was turf and logs but I can never remember being too cold. New clothes were seldom bought and people 'made do and mended'.

I remember grown-ups being very upset by occasional bombing attacks (once in the adjoining parish of Terenure) through which we children slept. We always prayed in school for the merchant seamen who risked their lives to bring vital supplies to Ireland. We enjoyed seeing the army out marching behind great brass bands and also enjoyed hearing the Air Raid Warning practice and seeing the search-lights in the night sky.

The war was referred to as 'the Emergency' and we had an LDF (local defence force with brown uniforms), LSF (local security force, blue uniforms) ARP (air raid patrols) and many of our mothers joined the Red Cross.

We just took it all as normal and played our games and went to school as usual. The war ended in 1945. I was then thirteen, so you could say I grew up during the 'Emergency'.

TALL TALES FROM THE PAST

Nan Gannon (b 1919)

Fermoy, County Cork, 1940s

I am seventy-five and over my lifetime many recollections come to mind. In small towns the local shoemaker often worked late into the night and local men would gather there. Such was the case in Fermoy and into his establishment filtered a motley crowd each evening during the War — battles were fought and the gossip of the town was discussed. One of the regulars was an ex-USA Army man who fancied himself as a military expert. He arrived each evening after the 9 p.m. news and would regale the boys with the position of the troops, etc, his favourite topic being the Burma Road Campaign. The boys were 'bored to tears' with him and so one evening he arrived as usual with his opening gambit, 'Good evening, boys — any news?'. He was just about to open the map which always travelled with him, when he was answered by one little man who boasted of his illiteracy — 'Yes, Mr Mac, we have very good news tonight [you may find the following a bit risque] the War is nearly over — as the Japs have taken Cascara [laxative] and the Burma Road is destroyed'. Needless to say he was not seen there very often after that!

People were pretty gullible also long ago and parted with money to strangers who entered the town with mad schemes. At one time they were conned into thinking that a film of the 'Colleen Bawn' was to be made on the hill overlooking the town. A most unusual and unsuitable place. The shooting was to be made at dawn and the budding film stars and extras climbed up at midnight getting themselves sorted out and excited. The producer and cameraman had ostensibly departed to Cork to pick up equipment and other necessities to produce a blockbuster. It was the wettest night that was ever recorded and the 'actors' were not left 'high and dry' but high and very wet and crawled home feeling foolish but wiser — and many bills were left unsettled and even the hotels and banks cried.

FERMOY LDF, 1940-45

Raymond Kelleher (b 1930)

County Cork

In 1939 when war was declared
and the people were frightened to death.
An Taoiseach De Valera stood up in the Dail
and said we were not beaten yet.
He formed a band of well-armed men
the 'Local Defence Force' by name.

They are spread out all over the nation
We have a group here in Fermoy
When on Parade they jut unafraid
and the people behold them with joy
They have a uniform the like has never been seen in any land
The tunic is like something out of a dream.
The breeches the colour of sand.
The sleeves came up to the elbow,
The tunics don't fit them at all.
And the breeches two sizes too small
But what they have got is really a lot
For the boots don't fit them at all.

I remember well one Sunday afternoon
the Locals were training that day.
Some of them went to the 'Pictures' to pass a few hours away
The 'Picture' was just getting thrilling,
When a voice from the 'Mike' very shrilly said -
Hey boys get your guns and stand ready
the Germans are on Corin Hill.

Some took the News like the heroes they were
And rushed out the door like the wind
But the cronies you know, they didn't go,
And their country they said they'd defend.

They assembled outside the 'Garda Barracks'
and Marched up the Hill to the fight.
When they got there Corin was bare
and the Germans were nowhere in sight
They remained all that night up on Corin.

though the frost penetrated their bones.
They suffered no loss for they slept 'neath the Cross
And on top of the Big heap of Stones.

They went to Youghal for their annual training
The Soldiers down there jumped with glee
For half of them fell down a farmyard well
And the rest nearly drowned in the sea.

Now five years of war has passed us by
But we have a country that's free.
And 'Twelve Bob' every week on the dole.
And through the Sad History of this Lonely Isle,
Their record will stand out in fame.

The above 'parody' was written about an incident which happened in 1942 (as a small boy I can faintly remember it) during WWII, known here as the 'Emergency'. It was reported on that Sunday that a German paratrooper had landed on Corin Hill, Fermoy, by some local wag. The LDF were on training exercise that day and were requested by the Garda to investigate the matter.

The LDF (Local Defence Force — Ireland's Dad's Army) later known as the FCA was formed in 1940 to assist the Army locally should the country be invaded. Their uniform was brown in colour (like a habit) of a cotton or overall material. It consisted of a Forage-Cap, Tunic, Slacks and Brown Boots and Gaiters. (The Boots were very welcome in those 'Frugal' days — like the Russian peasants of 1916 they joined for the Boots — I kid you not).

LSF (Local Security Force) Uniform similar to LDF but was Navy Blue in colour. The Boots and Gaiters were Black. They were there to assist the Garda. They were the forerunner of the Civil Defence.

The ARP was also formed in 1940 in case of Air-raids. Their uniform was similar to the LSF. They were the forerunner of to-day's Fire Service. That was the year Fermoy got its first Petrol-Driven mobile fire-pump. As kids we used to watch them go through their fire-drill outside the Courthouse on the Green, in the Summer evenings. Before 1940 as far as I can remember all we had was a few fire-hoses and a ladder mounted on a Hand-Cart.

P.S. You can see the Cross (erected 1932) just outside Fermoy on Corin Hill on the Fermoy to Cork City road. Some LDF members were at the Sunday matinée in the Royal Cinema, Fermoy, that day.

IRISH WOMEN IN THE RAF

Mabs Sinclair (b 1919) with Molly Maguire (b 1918)

Cloughjordan, County Tipperary and other places, 1919 – 61

We were both born in Cloughjordan, County Tipperary, and spent a good deal of our youth there. Though we have since sojourned in various parts of the British Isles, soldiering some-times together and sometimes apart, we have remained lifelong friends and indeed still address each other as 'Baker' and 'Ma-guire', our maiden surnames. I now live in Donabate , County Dublin, while Molly lives in Rostrevor, County Down.

I was born in 1919. My father was the Postmaster in Clough-jordan. He was a Methodist — there was a sizeable Methodist congregation in that area. I remember the Post Office was a fine big room that had brown wooden panelling bearing large posters advertising the Cunard Shipping Line. I remember my father tap-ping out the telegrams in Morse code on a gadget for that purpose and indeed as a child I had a go a few times myself. My father also had a number of business 'sidelines'. These included running a bus from Clough to Portumna - the bus driver was Ben Percy who first taught Sir Henry Seagrave the famous racing driver to drive. The bus was a beautiful open-decked gleaming contrap-tion, of which I still have a photograph. My father also had a corn store, a fine building next to the Post Office, still there. My fa-ther's brother owned a shop next door, now the bank. My father would spread out the corn on the windowsill to see if it was good for seed and if suitable he would buy it and store it for resale in the Spring. Indeed we must have been an enterprising lot as I re-member as well having rhubarb from our garden for sale outside the Post Office on fair days.

On the fair days the animals used be penned against our front door, something which used drive my mother berserk! My mother was Church of Ireland but later became interested in the Christian Scientists. My maternal grandfather's name was Corri-gan, a Gaelic name, so I presume they must have 'taken the soup'. Indeed religious and race pedigree are more mixed in Ireland than is often thought. Molly's family were well established in the Church of Ireland tradition though her surname, Maguire, is Gaelic, and her father came to Tipperary from County Roscommon, to which the family migrated from County Fermanagh, their ances-tral territory.

I was driving cars from the age of thirteen. My father had had one of the first Model-T Fords in the area. A cousin of Molly's mother had one also; indeed the two men were very friendly and in earlier times used ride out together on penny farthings. I attended Rutland School in Rutland (now Parnell) Square, Dublin, for two years. My mother's death in 1932 when I was thirteen was a watershed in my life. My Father (who felt I needed a woman's touch) later sent me to stay with my mother's sister in Southampton — her husband was an engineer on the passenger liner the *Mauritania*. My friendship with Molly was to continue there as she had been sent to do a course in Domestic Science in London.

WAR COMES

In 1936 I returned to Ireland and attended Alexandra College in Dublin, where I did Secretarial. I used to drive back to school in Dublin from Cloughjordan — I had driven to Dublin since I was fifteen. After qualifying in Alex. I got a job in Brittains at Portobello Bridge, the company that assembled Morris cars. I was still a regular visitor to Clough and enjoyed the social life there, the hockey dances and tennis dances and the hunt balls. Then the War broke out, and like many others of our generation, it changed the course of our lives.

I decided to join up in 1940, primarily out of a sense of adventure. Many of the young people around me were joining up. I didn't want to be left behind at twenty-one, on my own in Clough for the rest of my life! Catching the last train before they closed the border, I went to stay with my friend Molly who was now in the North of Ireland and there awaited my call up. We joined the Airforce because Molly's brother was already in it. I wanted to go in as a driver, or as a plotter (plotting the whereabouts of aircraft on missions, training flights, etc.). I wasn't accepted as a plotter — Molly was — because it was felt that as an alien and returning on leave to neutral Southern Ireland, I might give sensitive information to the German Embassy. I wasn't given driving either — some said the reason was that people from Ireland couldn't drive! However, the real reason was probably because my secretarial qualifications in shorthand and typing were of more use to them.

My call up came within six weeks and I returned to England, now a member of the Women's Auxiliary Airforce (WAAF), after the War called the Women's Royal Airforce (WRAF), with the job of clerk. During the War, we were stationed in various parts, the Cotswolds, Yorkshire, Lancashire and Wales. Ironically in view of my being seen as a possible security risk, my most interesting postings were in Scotland, first as a secretary to the K and Q officer for the whole of Scotland — the K and Q were dummy airfields and dummy marshalling yards which were lit up to act as decoys to draw German air attacks. I was stationed at Petreavie Castle in Rosyth. Later I was stationed at Turnhouse the RAF base for that area. The CO was the Duke of Hamilton and his secretary was Pearl Highett with whom I was friendly. That was the time when Hess landed on the Hamilton Estate and we as a result of our work were aware of some of the 'top secrets', although I don't think we fully appreciated their significance at the time.

Though in the Airforce the only flying I did was on test flights with a boyfriend! — with CO's permission of course. All through my war service, we got leave three times a year and usually I returned home to Ireland. I used get a travel warrant for all the way to Cloughjordan, though it could be Timbuctu for all they knew. Trains ran to Clough only on certain days of the week and even then were not too reliable as the turf on which they ran was sometimes damp, causing unscheduled stops!

Life in Cloughjordan was restricted by the War much as elsewhere in Ireland. Many commodities were scarce or unavailable. Nevertheless, social life continued. I remember one incident when we were observed by the guards driving into a dance in Nenagh when it was illegal to use petrol except for emergencies. We parked at the back of Hodgin's (key rural business people and solicitors in the town) house on the outskirts of the town, but on our return from the dance the guards were waiting at the gate to nab us as we came back out on to the road. Quick thinking saved the day. We pushed the car down several fields and then out through a gap on to the road. I'm sure the guards are still waiting for us.

On our trips we brought with us goods that were scarce on the other side — tea, etc. to Ireland, hairgrips, eggs, etc. to England. I wasn't particularly aware of Ireland's neutrality, although we didn't wear our uniforms on leave — the Irish were in fact the only members allowed to keep civilian clothes. Molly as an ex-plotter remembers an incident where neutrality played a part. An aircraft was shot down near the Wexford coast and they were absolutely at high doh because they couldn't send a naval vessel to effect a rescue, nor could they persuade the Irish, because of neutrality, to go and pick them up. Eventually it was a fishing boat that heard a radio message and went and picked them up.

It was through the RAF that I met my husband, John, a Scot and an RAF pilot. I remember flying with him in a single-engine plane to an Ireland-Scotland Rugby match shortly after the War — and also to meet his mother. I got sick all over my uniform!

Anyway, the War ended and we settled to a more normal life. Eventually, in 1961, we returned to Ireland where we both enjoyed new careers. Ireland was always home to me and although my father's generation would have seen themselves as Unionists, we saw things somewhat differently being aware of the way that Irish people had been mistreated historically. I must say that one difficulty that we encountered growing up in the new state was that of the Irish language; later a better knowledge of it would have been very useful for me. But that is all a story for another day.

BARNEY'S TEA

Kathleen Deegan (b 1932)

Drumcondra, Dublin

My mother always added the milk and two spoons of sugar to my father's tea. When we were older we used to rib her about this asking 'Why don't you stir and drink it for him as well?'

We had a dog called Barney. Barney loved tea and as it was war time and tea was rationed and very precious, he had to make do with the dregs from our cups. These were poured into the slop bowl and saved for the dog's dish.

One evening my father was late for tea so we carried on without him. As usual, the dregs were kept for Barney, but on this occasion, the slop bowl was missing so we poured the dregs into the spare cup.

Father duly arrived and took his place at the table, reached straight away for his cup and drank thirstily. I can still see his expression of pure horror as he gasped, 'That's the WORST tea I EVER tasted'.

A chorus of 'That's Barney's tea' went up from his four giggling daughters.

THE CIGARETTE SITUATION

Jeremiah Desmond (b 1916) Bandon, County Cork, 1945

The following poem was written in late 1945 just after the end
of the War by Jeremiah Desmond, Innishannon:

I walked out one morning and the horse I did yoke
And I drove into Bandon being short of a smoke.
There were none in the village but I must tell the truth
That the cigarette situation was very acute.

At 'The Maid of Erin' I stepped on the flags
To ask Maurice Riordan where would I get fags.
He said 'They're in Deasys by hook or by crook
But you know what to do — not a word to the cook'

So in to J.P. Deasy's I softly did steal
And I got every attention from Eilish O'Neill
But 'twas 'No Cigarettes' to my utmost surprise
As she looked me right through with her beautiful eyes

So I walked away out in a kind of a dream
Praying for Maurice Riordan and the Carnival Queen.
I went up to Flor Begleys and there I met 'LALL'
'Twas a cure for sore eyes I got a box of Pall Mall

But in Market Street they all refused me quite calm
And 'twas likewise with Peter and Mary Keohane
I went in to Victor Farrell my vexation to smother
And he says to me, 'Jerry how is your mother?'

I mentioned a smoke and he said 'They're a curse
If you come back again, you'll get 20 White Horse'
I crossed into Jones's and though times they were lean
I thought I'd be fixed up by Mercy Dineen

But inside in Jones's I clearly could see
The clerk they called Mercy showed no mercy to me.
'Twas at Mrs McCarthy's I made my last call
And out walked her daughter both graceful and tall

After slight hesitation she handed me five
But she said I'd get more when the van would arrive.
Now the war is all over and Peace in each Nation
But we'll always remember The Cigarette Situation.

A NIGHT OF TERROR

Elizabeth Clancy

Ballywire, County Tipperary, 1945

It was a beautiful summer's night on the 5th August 1945 at 11p.m. Irish time. I was cycling along the Kilross road. There was a long stretch of straight road from Ballywire to our road. I suddenly had an eerie feeling as if something terrible was about to happen. Then this girl I knew from my school days came along from the opposite direction. She jumped off her bike and she seemed very frightened. Now at this stage there was no visible reason for her to be afraid. She asked me to pump her bike. When I examined her wheel, I saw it did not need to be pumped. As I raised my head, looking towards the east, I saw what I thought was the whole town of Tipperary going up in a blaze of fire. It was very frightening and I whispered a prayer to God to have mercy on anyone who might have lost their life in that ball of fire. I could not tell her what I saw, as if I told her, I knew I'd have to convey her to Galbally. As I have already said she seemed to have sensed some sort of holocaust was about to happen. As for myself I was very shaken. I kept all this sight to myself as I was sure to hear on the radio next morning about Tipp town being blown up. There was not a word on radio or paper. I put it out of my mind and one year I saw on a paper a letter written by a Dublin man to Dunsink Observatory. He said he was walking along the Hill of Howth on August 5th at 11p.m. and he saw this raging fire going up to the sky. He went on to ask if it was possible he saw the atomic bomb that was dropped on Hiroshima. They replied it was quite possible with the latitude and longitude of the place. It was quite possible he saw it. Just imagine the shock I got when I realised I had seen that awful catastrophe and the date was right as it was 6th August in Japan and 5th August in Ireland. I console myself by thanking the Good Lord for letting me have the presence of mind to say may God have mercy on anyone who may have died in that fire. Deo gratias.

THE PEELERS' PLOTS

Mary Hodge (b 1913)

Waterford City, The Troubles 1910s and 20s

I was born in Waterford City in 1913 and educated at the Presentation Convent School not very far away. On fine days my school companion and I made a short cut to school through the Peelers' Plots where the ex-RIC men were busy attending to their drills of potatoes and vegetables. Those plots were separated from our back gardens by a ditch but it was no trouble to us to climb over and the Peelers never objected.

The First, Second and Third Babies' Classes were held in a building called the Tin Shed and I was happy there. We sat on wooden steps which ran the width of the room and a very large trough full of Tramore sand was always in front of us. Our lady teacher (not a nun) filled small tins like cake-tins with the sand, gave one to each of us and we happily drew figures and letters in the soft sand which was easily swept up if spilled. Sometimes we were given small slates and chalk. The first song I learned was 'The Farmer's Doggie in the Yard, Bingo was his Name O' and we spelled B-I-N-G-O four times in the verse.

In Second Babies our nun taught us to draw a daffodil with crayons amongst other things and I can still draw a daffodil exactly like hers. In Third Babies I felt very important when given a pen with a nib and the nun poured ink into the inkwells for us to write the word HORSE. I thought she was a wonderful person when she added 's' to horse and told us it meant more than one horse. How could a little 's' turn it into a whole lot of horses? It puzzled me.

We had to buy green, and later red, catechisms which we learned off by heart. On our First Holy Communion day the nuns invited us to a party at the school and we were given bread and jam, lemonade made by the nuns and a few hard boiled sweets from a gallon tin bought at O'Neills Moneyball shop, the most famous shop in Waterford at that time as you might win a halfpenny if you bought a halfpenny moneyball there.

My mother died the following year and life seemed very different then. My father took me to the pictures now and again, silent movies of course in those days. It was in the 'troubled times' and one night when on our way home from the pictures, our lives were in danger as bullets started whizzing around us. To get to our home we had to pass two Barracks but this particular night we couldn't go near any Barracks and had to go miles out the country and home by a circuitous route. A few nights later there was a tapping at our back door and I knew my father was nervous as he opened it. Apparently he recognised the man who stood there as he invited him in and got clean water to wash a bad gash on one of the man's legs. I was sent to bed but the following day I heard people talking about someone 'on the run' and 'shrapnel'.

A few other events of the troubled times remain in my mind. One was seeing an aeroplane stuck in the roof of a three-storey house which was directly opposite the lower Barracks. I suppose the pilot intended landing in the Barrack square but misjudged the distance when descending and ploughed into the roof of the house. Luckily none of the occupants was badly injured but I don't know what injuries the pilot suffered.

Around that time my uncle was building an extension onto his house and when working on the roof one morning the bullets started whizzing around him so he hurriedly descended. A neighbour around the corner was shaving himself when a bullet came through his open window and struck him on the arm. A nurse living nearby attended him and later helped him to hospital.

Later that day we had to leave our house and make our way out the country for safety with lots of other neighbours, all of us loaded with bread and butter and fresh water for making tea later. One of my cousins got the job of carrying a large kettle of water. When we all felt safe behind a ditch in a field my aunt decided to make tea and asked my cousin to carry the kettle to her to put on the fire she had lit, but unfortunately he tripped over something and spilled every drop of the precious water. When the troubles ended we often laughed over the little incidents that occurred in our lives.

Of course the Peelers' Plots are long gone and houses built on the site. The Upper Barracks went up in flames and I felt sad when I saw it burning as Little Nellie of Holy God lived opposite it when her father was a soldier there.

EMIGRATION FROM DUBLIN TO BELFAST BY BOAT

Matt Camplisson (b 1929)

Dublin and Belfast, 1912

Many years ago, I was a brush maker (a dying trade) and before that my father and grandfather had also been brush makers. This story concerns my grandfather and his family.

My grandfather and his family lived in Rutland Cottages, Rutland Street, in the centre of Dublin, around the year 1900. My grandfather was a brush maker and worked for a brush company called 'Varians' (I believe this company is still in business in Dublin). As the work was very much spell work, with the dread of being off on the dole always hanging over one, my grandfather was glad to get a telegram from a firm in Belfast (R.J. Hall and County, also still in business), offering him a job during one of these many spells of unemployment.

This would have been the year 1912 and my grandfather left his wife and seven children and made his way to Belfast. He had promised my grandmother that he would send for her and the children, as soon as he had accumulated a bit of money and got a house. In those days it was the easiest thing in the world to get a house to rent.

Well, after a few months, he sent my grandmother some money and told her that he had rented a house on the Ormeau Road in south Belfast. (I believe that the rent at that time was about three shillings a week — i.e. fifteen new pence!). Of course his wages would probably be no more than one pound a week.

Anyhow he had sent my grandmother enough money to get her and the children to Belfast. As her children ranged in ages from three years up to twelve years, she would have to pay for most of them on the Great Northern Railway to go from Amiens Street Station (now Connolly Station), so a friend recommended that she go by boat!! Well, she was astounded, not knowing anything about travelling to Belfast. The friend told her that Kelly's Coal Boat called in Dublin every morning and, made its way by short stages up the East coast, calling at Drogheda, Dundalk, Warrenpoint, Newry, etc. en route to Belfast, and that the Master of the 'ship' would take her and the children to Belfast for a small sum of money, so although the journey would be a bit long, it would be a big saving for her in comparison to the railway fares. I can't remember what my father had told me was the exact amount but I believe it was under ten shillings (about fifty pence). The journey was long indeed, but the children were delighted, and my father who was nine years old at the time said they had never had such an enjoyable journey on a boat. My grandmother finally arrived in Belfast docks, with her seven children, one daughter and six sons. It is the only instance I have ever heard of, where a family emigrated from Dublin to Belfast by BOAT.

My father's sister subsequently went to live in London, but my father and his brothers all remained in Belfast. One of the brothers did not marry but the other five did and their children are now carrying our unusual name here in Belfast, so the Camplissons are more prolific here in Belfast although we have one cousin who went back to Dublin, and married a Dublin girl, but that is another story.

NOBLETTS FOR TOFFEE

Sarah O'Carroll (b 1908)

Dun Laoghaire, County Dublin, 1916 and after

M y father, mother, and some cousins and their parents were in our parlour. I was about six at the time. We were sitting on the floor playing but the grown-ups were very silent and seemed to be listening for something which was unusual as they were very fond of music and singing. We heard noise from time to time and our parents would look terrible and bless themselves. We were too young then to know about war. But we knew in after years it was Easter Week 1916.

Those same cousins and their parents, in the summer, each Sunday, would come and take us all out for a picnic in their brake (a long trap with four horses) usually to Glendalough or the Scalps which was our delight, as we loved climbing up the rocks which was great fun, or to the Meeting of the Waters and many other places. We had a great time when we were young. In the weekdays, together with other children, we would go to Salthill and play in the sea. It was always nice and warm. On other days we would go to the beach at Dun Laoghaire and play shops and houses. We would use broken delft as money. I always used the steps for my house, as I liked having a big house.

One day on the beach we were playing jumping from the bandstand (it is broken up now). It used to be high and I jumped the highest but I couldn't get up and I was brought home in a go-car. I spent six weeks in hospital and it was there I heard about the North of Ireland as an old woman told the other woman about her whole family having to run out of the North because of the Troubles around the 12th July (then the children's beds were in the women's wards).

There were days we would spend the whole day walking to Killiney Strand and play on the beach, or to Killiney Hill. We never had any money but (we never thought about it like the children now) we had plenty to eat and that was all we wanted. When my father would get his holidays (a week) he would bring us somewhere every day and the last day he would bring us to Stephen's Green where we would play and then go to Woolworths for our lunch. But best of all, to Nobletts for toffee. Beautiful hard toffee with nuts. We always loved Nobletts for toffee. It was at the corner of Stephen's Green. He would also bring us on the last day of each holiday to get our photo taken.

Life long ago was so different from now. We only got small things at Christmas and we certainly didn't get Easter eggs, at least if we did, I don't remember, but we were never short of anything at least not while my father was alive. When he died while we were still young, then it was a different matter.

When he died my mother had to go out to work to feed and clothe us and me being one of the older ones had to mind the smaller ones. One day I was minding the children, my brother kicking the ball, kicked it to the top of the dresser, he climbed to get the ball and pulled the dresser with all our cups, saucers and plates down and not a thing escaped. When my poor mother came home from work there was nothing left in the way of delft. She was the most patient woman I know.

TWO STRANGERS IN BALLYMUN

Eamon D. Dunne (b 1919)

Drumcondra, Dublin, 1930s

As a native of Drumcondra, Dublin, and a person who knew many areas of the city and particularly the north urban area as a youth, I am still amazed at the development that has taken place over the years. Where there was once green fields and small farms, these lands are now occupied by schemes of houses, shopping centres, parks, churches and schools. I remember playing in fields we called 'Watson's' and seeing the construction later on of a wonderful avenue from Malahide Road to Glasnevin, Griffith Avenue, right across our former playgrounds. I also saw the former Puckstown Lane, which ran from Donnycarney to Whitehall, become the grand straight road known as 'Collins Avenue' today. So many roads and avenues and hundreds of houses were built. What a sight it would be for somebody living in the last century to be able to return to his native place of north city Dublin today. To them it would be like seeing another planet.

Ballymun was a rural area in my youth and to tell you how rural it was at the time, I will relate the following true incident. Early one Sunday morning I went with my brother Emmet to collect mushrooms in the fields around Ballymun. It was a nice easy cycle ride from our home in Drumcondra to our favourite fields. As we passed St Pappin's Church in Ballymun we saw the congregation going into early morning Mass. We decided to attend Mass before going on to look for mushrooms. Like all rural churches the congregation was pretty small, less than a hundred people. After Mass we continued on our quest for the elusive mushrooms and having collected the required quota we cycled home to a belated breakfast and then to the other activities of the day.

The next morning my father was chatting with a colleague in work named Dick Manifold. Dick lived with his wife and family on the main Dublin to Belfast Road, about a mile beyond Santry and perhaps two miles from Ballymun. During the course of their conversation my father mentioned to Dick that his two sons had attended Mass in St Pappin's Church the previous morning. 'Yes', said Dick, 'my daughter was at that Mass and she mentioned that she saw two strangers in the church'. The strangers of course were us, all the way from Drumcondra.

To me, this story illustrates how rural Ballymun was at that time, when two 'strangers' could be recognised in the congregation, particularly by a person who lived two miles away from the church. How much different Ballymun is today, with the massive tower blocks, hundreds of dwellings, shopping centre, etc. and of course a huge population. St Pappin's Church is still there with, I'm sure, lots of strangers attending the many Masses, but the mushroom fields are gone forever. As a footnote, the young lady who saw us in the church that morning long ago only saw two handsome youths and was much too shy to describe them to her family other than as 'strangers'.

THE FLIGHT OF 'THE SOUTHERN CROSS'
Portmarnock Beach, Dublin, 1930

It would be hard to convince the youth of this generation that nearly ten thousand people (as reported in the press) rose at an unearthly hour one morning to watch an aeroplane take off. Yet it is true. The event is commemorated on a plaque at the steps leading down to the beach at Portmarnock, County Dublin, where the flight took place on the 24th June 1930 just as dawn was breaking. An aeroplane which was aptly named 'The Southern Cross' had come from Australia to Ireland to attempt an East to West crossing of the Atlantic. The pilot and owner of the 'plane was an Australian named Charles Kingsford-Smith, familiarly known even then to the world as Smithy on account of his many long-distance flights in the 'Southern Cross', including a flight across the Pacific from America to Australia. The other members of the proposed flight were an Irishman, Captain Saul, an Englishman and a Dutchman. None of these people had flown in the 'plane before this proposed flight from Portmarnock. The reason why Ireland was chosen as the taking-off point was the saving of a few hundred miles travel in distance and fuel across the Atlantic to America. The strand at Portmarnock was chosen as it had a long stretch of firm sand which gave plenty of room to the plane, with its cargo of a huge quantity of fuel, the maximum length in which to take off.

The proposed flight of 'The Southern Cross' caused tremendous excitement not only in Dublin and Ireland but overseas as well. This was helped by the great newspaper publicity and in the human interest about the crew and the obvious dangers in crossing the long stretch of the Atlantic Ocean in those early days of aviation. In common with the rest of the population our family were caught up in the excitement of the occasion. I was then almost eleven years of age, so with my younger brother, Emmet, we got up in the middle of the night and cycled from our home in Drumcondra to Portmarnock. As we arrived we were amazed to see the huge crowd that had gathered and the array of vehicles, motor cars, motor bikes, bicycles, horse-drawn and even ass drawn carts that blocked the road. The army and Gardai were out in force trying to control the vast crowd. As it was still dark the whole scene was lit up with the many bon-fires which had been lit by the early arrivers. All around us was a great hubbub of excitement and with the crowd we were borne to a position high up on the sand dunes overlooking the beach. As the dawn light came into the sky we got a great view of the preparations below us at the 'plane. It was being fuelled up with individual cans of fuel which took a lot of man-power. Other men were walking along the two-mile stretch of beach to check for any foreign objects that might hinder the take-off. After a while we could see the crew climb into the 'plane to the cheers of the vast crowd. By today's standards you would hardly trust such a small aircraft to cross the Irish Sea, never mind the vast Atlantic Ocean. Shortly afterwards the engines started up and to us small boys sounded very healthy. It was nearly 5 a.m. when to the tremendous clapping and cheering from the vast crowd the 'plane moved slowly along the sands. It gathered speed and seemed to run on and on and then at last to a great cheer, 'The Southern Cross' took off and we all let out a great sigh of relief as it started on its long journey to the New World. For a while it seemed to fly towards Howth Head and then while still only a few hundred feet up it turned a half-circle and flew straight over the crowd who had come to wish them 'bon voyage' and silently prayed for their safety. The buzz of excitement was still in the air as we left to cycle home. The rest of the family were still in bed when we arrived; later we gave them a first-hand account of the take-off of 'The Southern Cross'.

To tell you the happy result of this famous flight, after thirty-six hours in the air, 'The Southern Cross' landed in a place called Grace Harbour, Newfoundland, Canada, without mishap. What a story the crew had to tell after that successful flight.

'The Southern Cross' is today in a museum in Eagle Farm Airport, Brisbane. Our son Maurice and his wife Vivienne visited this museum to see the 'plane when they lived in that city. Their visit was nearly sixty years after his father and uncle and half of North Dublin had stood and cheered the successful take-off that morning of June 1930. How proud we were to witness such a great event in the history of famous flights.

YORK STREET FLATS

Ann Leahy

Dublin, 1930s

As I sit here in my nice comfortable home wondering what to buy for my grandchildren for Christmas they have so much I feel sorry for them as they know nothing of the great joy of getting a new toy.

I think back to when I was a child and we lived in one room in York Street which my lovely loving mother kept like a palace. My sister and brother and myself were always nicely dressed and we never thought we were poor even though at one stage my doll's pram had to be sold to buy a new pair of shoes for school. I got great pleasure out of a new copy or maybe if things were good a brand new pencil case.

I loved to make clothes for my little plastic doll, but its legs or arms did not move. One day my father brought me into town and we were walking past the dolls hospital in Mary Street and I saw this little doll about four inches long and its legs and arms could be moved to get clothes on.

I didn't expect to get this doll as I knew we didn't have that much money so we walked on to Capel Street and my father said, 'Ann would you like that little doll?' I was speechless. We turned round and back to the shop and sure as eggs are eggs he bought the doll. I was sick with excitement and thought I would never get home to show my mother and start making clothes and a bed out of an old box for my doll. But Christmas was great, we were allowed to go round to the Baby Carriage on the Green and choose a toy in the window for Santy to bring. I always chose a cotton wool house which would be filled with all sorts of surprises, but one year there was this lovely tea set and a table which could be folded up and the lid was a tray so I asked my parents if it would be too much to ask Santy for, so they suggested I write and ask, and if he couldn't bring that I could have a surprise so Christmas morning came and would you believe I got my table and tea set. Christmas was really great. My Granny couldn't buy presents for us as she had too many grandchildren. I really loved my Granny. When I got pocket money I used to save up my pennies and when I would go down to Abbeyleix for my holidays I would bring her a little present. She loved that, and it gave me great pleasure. When I got bigger I was able to buy tobacco for my Granda (St Bruno). He always gave me a shilling when I was coming home from my holidays. When my granny died I was fourteen, it was my first experience of sadness and heartache. I suppose that was when I started to grow up.

My childhood was so happy I would not change it for anything. I would love to give my grandchildren this kind of happiness for Christmas.

MEMORIES OF DUBLIN

Rita Hussey (b 1930)

Inchicore, Dublin, 1930s and 1940s

Talking about old times in Ireland, I went to Golden Bridge School in Inchicore with the Sisters of Mercy. I was there till I left at sixteen years when I got a job in the Mater Hospital. I remember as a child my poor mother taking me through Chapelizod. It was a big park which led you to Cabra Road where my Auntie lived. I loved to go and see her, she was very good to my mother giving her potatoes and cabbage out of the garden. She was so kind to my Mum and me. I looked forward to going. I loved the long walk.

Mother lived in Keogh Square, Inchicore. I had two brothers, George and Tommy Hussey, I don't know where they went to. My sister Maureen worked in Ardwick, Manchester in a Presbytery and brought me over to England which I found very depressing and the people were very hard. I worked in the cotton mill in Oldham, never forgiving my step sister for inviting me to England. I would never have left Ireland only for her.

My Auntie and Uncle are dead now and I've no relations in Ireland now but I still go and see lovely Ireland now and again. I find it a very expensive place when I go over there but I love to go and see Dublin again. We stayed in Dun Laoghaire last time we went. St Michael's church in Dun Laoghaire was on TV lately. I loved the service, it's a lovely church.

I love Ireland. My heart is there all the time. I love to go to Howth as well. I think of Gay Byrne when I go to Howth. Someone told me and my husband that Gay Byrne lives at the top of Howth Head and walks his dog there.

THE NEW CURTAINS

Peggy Crofton (b 1924)

Bray, County Wicklow, 1930s

While growing up in the thirties, our house was built on the side of Bray Head and it seemed to sit in the middle of a field. Our boundary was just wooden stakes with two strands of wire joining them.

We children just crept through the wire and Bray Head was our playground with cows grazing. Mr Quinn was the farmer who owned the land and the cows ambled down every evening for milking just beside our house.

I recall my mother doing a spring clean and she had lots of washing. She ran out of clothes line space and hung her best living-room curtains on the wire.

Later in the day my young brothers called out that a cow was eating the curtains and when we all ran to investigate, my brothers were pulling a curtain that seemed to come from the cow's stomach. The more they pulled the cow pulled the opposite way and the curtain came away in pieces.

Thinking the curtains would be replaced my mother told Mr Quinn about her loss, but he replied, 'Sorry about that Ma-aam. Show me which cow it was. I'll have to give her a dose of medicine in the morning'. So much for the new curtains.

GAMES WE PLAYED

Billy French

Crumlin Village, County Dublin, 1930s – 40s

Do children today get as much fun out of their many varied, sophisticated, highly-complicated, computerised toys as we did from the games we played when I was a boy growing up in Crumlin Village? I doubt it!

Aside from football, games played a most important part in our lives. Games like Spin the Top, Marbles, Hoop the Hoop, Hop Scotch, Conkers, Kick the Can, Scut the Whip, Jackstones, and Box the Fox. Hop Scotch has survived to some extent, but only among girls.

With games and occupations that spanned the four seasons, we never had a thought for such phrases as 'I'm bored', 'I've nothing to do'. For we hadn't enough hours in the day for all we had to do.

Even when the dark evenings closed in, we enjoyed such games as 'Battle In, Battle Out' and 'Jack, Jack, Show the Light'. 'Battle In, Battle Out' was also known as 'Relieve-Eh-Oh' and had a den, which was always strategically placed under the village lamp. The games consisted of two teams — the pursued and the pursuers. If one of the pursued was unfortunate enough to be captured he was dragged somewhat ungraciously into the den where he waited for one of his team to come charging in from the darkness with the cry 'Relieve-Eh-Oh'.

'Jack, Jack, Show the Light' also engaged two teams, only this time the chase took place through the fields that surrounded the village. The object of the game was for Team B to capture Team A. Team A had a lamp, or a candle in a jam jar, and Team B had three chances to call on Team A by shouting, 'Jack, Jack, Show the Light'.

It's only fair to say that Team A usually went undetected, for after slipping into dirty ditches and cow's droppings their dark and brown figures blended into the surrounding darkness.

In springtime we went tree climbing and bird nesting. It was a great thrill to go every day and watch the nest, at the same time being careful never to go too close, for we were always told that if the birds suspected that they were being observed they would forsake the nest. In all my life in the village I never remember any boy vandalising or destroying a nest.

Summer brought rambles through fields of cowslips and buttercups, turning white runners yellow. Fishing for pinkeens and tadpoles on the commons or just lying on your back in Mooney's Meadow, watching the airplanes from nearby Baldonnel Aerodrome loop-the-loop, while listening to the corncrake utter its off-key cry which always sounded like 'Jack Mac, Ate'in Bacon'.

Harvest time brought mushrooms and blackberry picking, chestnuts and rides on the bogies as the men gathered the haycocks in the barns from the surrounding fields.

Winter brought its slides and snowball fights and when the cold winter winds did blow, as the poet said, we would retire to our Shangri-La. It was only a hut in Reilly's back garden, but we had built it ourselves, block by block. It even boasted its own fireplace that could and did consume a wet sod of turf or a wellington boot with equal ease.

In my mind's eye I can still see apprehensive young faces caught in the shadows of flickering flames, listening in awe to

eerie ghost stories which none of us really believed, while the
wind and Jack Dark played hide and seek outside. Sometimes we
would play 'Twenty Questions' and such like, finishing off the
night listening to one of the Brophy Brothers belting out jigs and
reels on their Button accordions. Pat and John Brophy have long
gone to their rest, but their music lives on.

   With all this high power tech of today, we have lost something
on the way. This was brought home to me recently by a remark
my twelve year-old grandson made to me after I had spent some
time telling him about the games we played when we were his
age. Looking at me with all the wisdom of his computerised years,
he blurted out, 'Grandad, you had more fun than I'm having!'

BESIDE NELSON'S PILLAR

Frances O'Brien (b 1919)

Dublin, 1930s

   I was born in Tipperary seventy five years ago. I lived on a
farm until I came into Dublin at the age of seventeen to work in
business for my Aunt. I worked in Earl Street and O'Connell
Street for many years. I could see the Pillar from my place of employment, The Kylemore Café. It was a great meeting place for
couples, you would see three or four fellows standing there, we
had great fun looking to see if their girl friends would turn up.
There was also great characters such as Forty Coats and Bang
Bang. Johny Fortycoats was a small man with a long white beard
and about six overcoats, hat etc. He was a quiet man, didn't speak
much just looked for alms to keep himself. Then Bang Bang was a
young man. He would swing onto a tram and shout 'Bang Bang'.
Most people knew him but if you didn't you would get a fright. I
often saw people very frightened. They would think he was going
to shoot them, but then people in the tram would tell them it was
a toy gun. He was harmless.

   People hadn't much money but times were good. You could
dress up and carry your handbag up O'Connell Street and not feel
frightened. We spent all our nights around Christmas or Easter
out window shopping. There were no shutters, drink or drugs
then. Shop windows were lovely. Fur back gloves were very
popular then and a great Christmas Box from a boy friend. People

enjoyed the simple things in life, the smallest gift was treasured.

Then at night you had all the neon signs. I often spent half an hour looking at the large neon sign on Butt Bridge. It would change from red to gold and then green. We thought it was great. Then you had the 'Stop Press'. When any thing special happened you had all the young lads with bells ringing and shouting 'Stop Press' and every one stopped to hear what the news was. The city was very lively. Everyone was out walking day and night and police were at every corner. You never felt afraid at night.

I would walk down the street coming from a dance at twelve everywhere to look after you. You might meet a couple of lads with knuckle-dusters on and they might hit a window with their knuckles and make a noise but they never broke a window.

There was terrible poverty in Dublin when I first came up. Children had no shoes or socks in winter and the children looked very thin and small compared to the children of today.

Then the businessmen got together and formed 'The Herald Boot Fund' and gave all the poor children a pair of boots and socks for Christmas. That was a wonderful thing in those years. People were talking about it for a year. Wages were very small in those days; 14s a week with your keep. Very few had £1 unless they were outdoor workers.

Married men had from £3 to £10 per week. Then most homes were rented. There were no private cars then, only businessmen could afford a car. We all had bicycles. On a Sunday we would cycle to Bray and spend the day there, take sandwiches with us, climb up the Head and have a great time, then cycle home again very tired after our long day out. Most girls were quite slim, about eight stone. They didn't need 'Unislim' then. Work was hard for some. I worked in a shop. I was on my feet all day. We were very busy. I also worked every second Sunday and we never minded how long we had to work. I loved meeting the public and not having much money. We preferred to work. I got two weeks holiday every year. That was the only time you went home to the country and after five years we hired a car with friends and went home for Christmas. We thought that a great treat. There was such a difference then in city and country, not like now. The country is just private living now. They have every thing we have here.

One other thing stands out in my mind. The night the bombs fell in North Strand. I lived in Store Street, not far away opposite the Custom House. There was an air raid shelter there and all the people came over trying to get into the shelter, but the police assured them it was a once-off thing and it was. There were no more air raids. We had to use our blackout curtains every night and let no light out. Then peace came and everything was free and easy again. These are all my recollections of my youth in Dublin.

DANCING WITH OUR COATS ON

Mary and Edward Balfe

Dublin, 1940s

I went to a girls' club called St Dominic's when I was in my teens. There were no drugs at that time. No young girls would ever go into a pub. There were no cars around, only horses. We used to go to places like Dun Laoghaire and Blackrock on a tram. It was small and went along a track. People used to come around the roads with a handcart selling ice-cream and fruit. We used to go dancing every Tuesday and we would get a free ticket for Thursday's dance. The women always danced with their coats on — they never took them off. There used to be candle grease on the floors so everyone could slide as they danced, or if we didn't go out and had nothing else to do some nights we would sit on our doorsteps and talk or tell stories.

I used to go to a concert at the back of a basement. We used to dress up in coloured crêpe paper and all the neighbours paid two pence to see us.

In those days things were very poor, so we used to go to the Pawn every Monday and pawn in sheets. When we got our pay at the end of the week we went back and got our sheets back. If you had nothing to pawn in your friends or neighbours would give you something because in those days everybody helped each other. For sheets we sewed up flour bags together. In most houses there would be a family of fourteen. They would have had to live in one room. There was no carpets only a bit of lino. People had to use newspapers as toilet rolls because there was none. For table-cloths they used newspapers too.

There was no electricity so we had no washing machine. We had to go to a small bath in a yard. We used paraffin lights. There were no fridges so it was very hard to keep things fresh. Newspapers were hard to sell. They were sold for one penny. There used to be a man giving balloons on sticks away to people if they gave him rags. He would say, 'Rags for balloons'. Or he would take empty bottles or jam jars.

On Christmas if you couldn't get a turkey you would have to settle for a goose. Nobody ate meat on Wednesday or Friday. They still kept the fast. Stew was everyone's favourite. Some people would call it Blind Man's Stew because no one could afford meat to put in it.

Edward: I started work when I was fifteen. I got one pound four pence. My other job was in a butcher's. I got two pound odd weekly. People used to work five-and-a-half days Monday to Saturday. They had no choice about it. They were known as 'the good old days'.

SPECIAL NOVENAS

Betty McDermott (b 1930)

Mark Street off Pearse Street / Theatre Royal, Dublin, 1940s

I recall my teenage years in the 1940s and the visits of screen stars who performed on the Theatre Royal. One such star was Gene Autrey the singing cowboy, because he would come to a side window in Poolbeg Street and sing for the crowd who waited there to get a glimpse of him. These poor sods could not afford the price of a ticket to see him on stage. I was one of them. Could you imagine the pop stars of today doing this without the aid of the sound effects.

Another memory was of Holy Thursday nights; it was a must to do the rounds of seven churches in our locality to gain a Plenary Indulgence, but that was not the only reason, as all the entertainment was closed for Holy Week. Everyone would be on the march from church to church and this made for some fun. Many a romance started through meeting this way.

I also remember the local grocer shops. There were five in our area where people were known by their first name and they could get credit until pay day when the need arose and all the local gossip could be picked up. With the coming of the supermarkets all these shops disappeared. I am glad to say since I moved house to Navan three years ago I have found three such grocers and it reminds me of days long gone. The multi-nationals did the same thing to the small business firms but I think there is a move on to encourage people to work for themselves because I feel there will never be full employment again.

I also recall when my husband and I were saving to get married we would spend our meetings going to Novenas, the miraculous medal on Monday nights and Tuesdays was St Anthony and all couples did this. Another memory is of all the young men playing football on the roads with a ball made of newspaper held together with twine, and the scatter when the bobby would come round the corner, they were like Houdini disappearing down nearby lanes, up hall doors or where ever else they could find. If anyone of them was unlucky to be caught the policeman would summons him. When you think of it the Police had very little to do then. God be with those days of peace.

I remember too the night Dublin was bombed during the Second World War. My mother RIP awakened us to get dressed and every-one in the house spent the rest of the night on the street. The bombs were dropped on the North Strand which was not too far from where we lived. I heard my mother tell how she had just retired for the night when she heard the plane, which was very unusual as she was looking out the window. The sky was lit up by the explo-sion and our house shook. It was the Whit weekend and the whole country was stunned by what happened and no one knew who was responsible as we were not involved in the War. That weekend very few people in our area went to bed in case they would come back.

FIREWOOD

Kathleen Moore (b 1915)

Donaghmede, County Dublin, Second World War

During the Second World War, it was known as the Emer-gency here, we were on stricter rations than they were in England. You were only allowed two ounces of butter, one ounce of sugar and one ounce of tea per person per week. There was only black flour and black bread. Tea was a pound a pound on the black market.

There was no coal and we had to go out and collect firewood, not only for heating but for cooking in the black stove which we called a range. As the men were out working it was often us women that had to go out to find firewood. I remember doing this in ditches that were full of snow. On one such occasion I was collecting firewood with my neighbour, Mrs Shanley, who was very superstitious. We heard a cock crow three times and Mrs Shanley wondered what terrible thing had happened. We were still in the ditch when we heard her brother calling to tell her her sister Madge had been knocked down and killed by a train at Howth junction railway station.

The farmers were never pleased with us collecting for firewood on their land. One old lady who had nothing better to do would sit in her wheelchair by the window and as soon as she saw the children picking up sticks she would phone the guards who would come and make the children leave the rotten wood back on the ground where it was no use to anyone.

One night my sister-in-law and my neighbour took a railway sleeper that was used as a gate-post on the farm where Donagh-mede Estate is now. We cut it up and shared it out the next day while the men were at work. My sister-in-law's husband worked on the farm and that evening he was angry at whoever took the sleeper. He complained about the disregard that cattle could escape and roam wherever they liked. He was sitting by the range where I had my share of the sleeper in the press. Of course I couldn't take it out to cook the dinner and I went into Mrs Shanley who luckily had other sticks that she loaned to me. While this was happening, and her husband was giving full vent to his anger, my sister-in-law was in our big bedroom laughing her head off.

We cut down a young sapling tree on the farm where Newgrove Estate is. The guards were sent out looking for this tree and one came around the cottages with a branch of the tree in his hand. He came to our house where my husband, who was a mechanic, was working on a car outside.

'I didn't know this was where you lived Luke,' the guard said to my husband, who was well-known as the proverbial begging ass around Howth, Baldoyle, Raheny, Malahide and that general area.

The guard explained to my husband that he was calling into all the houses and that he couldn't be seen to pass by him because he knew him. He stayed out in the yard talking to my husband for a time where he wasn't seen from the road, but did not come into the house. As the guard was making friendly conversation in my yard I was in our big bedroom sitting on the young tree which by now had been cut up for firewood to be shared among the neigh-bours. I was crying with fear. The other neighbours were braver than I was but there was more room in our house than anyone else's at the time.

I was cooking later that evening with the wood from this young tree when the foreman from the farm came to visit. He sat down by the range and was angry about whoever cut down the tree. He didn't know that he was warming himself with what remained of the tree. When his anger had died down somewhat and the conversation had gone on to other things he commented that nothing burned as well as a bit of ash.

DEAD AND ALIVE IN THE RICHMOND

Patrick Boland (b 1920)

The Richmond Hospital, Dublin, 1940s

I worked as a porter in the Richmond Hospital in the 1940s. My job was to bring the dead over to the morgue and other general duties. It was shift work of twelve hourly shifts, six days a week, hail, rain or snow.

At first you would feel a bit squeamish bringing down the dead and a hell of a lot scarier when you were on the nightshift. Anyway after a few years of doing the work it became just another chore. I am going to tell you about two nights that were to change my life forever. After the second event I had to leave and change careers.

It was in the dead of winter and I was on the night-shift when I was called up to take a body over to the deadhouse (that's what we used to call it), nothing new you would say just another poor soul passed over. When I got to the ward the body was already on the trolley. The night nurse told me that it was a young woman who had just passed away. She was feeling sad that the young lady had died.

I wheeled the body over to the deadhouse that was on the other side of the grounds. It was raining and the sheet got wet and the shape of the body was clearly formed in it. It looked real scary and I got a bit of a fright, so much so that when I got to the morgue I just rolled the trolley in and fled. My job was to remove the body onto the slab and bring the trolley back to the ward.

About an hour after I had gotten back to my hut I was called up to the ward again to take another body down. It was my job so I had to be brave and carry out my duties. When I got to the morgue I started to whistle and pushed the trolley through the swing doors. I would have to slab the two bodies now as the room was small and two trolleys would cause trouble. I switched on the light still whistling. But I stopped dead in my tracks when I saw the other trolley was empty. The hair stood up on the back of my neck and everywhere else as well. I was about to run when someone's hand grabbed my shoulders. 'Help me', the voice said. I did run, I ran like I had never run before, right into the ward where the nurse was having a cup of tea. She got such a fright that she spilled the tea all over herself. She tried in vain to calm me but I was gone beyond that by then. A doctor was called and I was given a relaxing injection to calm my nerves. A few minutes later I was able to tell them what had happened and they went to investigate. It turned out that the rain had revived the young lady who they thought had passed away and she was too confused and frightened to leave the deadhouse.

She was cured and was able to leave the hospital a few days later. She came down to see me before she left to say sorry and to thank me. I was glad to see her well and able to leave the hospital but I had put in for a transfer and I was now the boiler man. And it was as the boilerman that I was to have my second and last fright as an employee in the Richmond Hospital.

It was almost a year after my encounter with the live dead person and I had settled down as the boilerman when I was having my midnight lunch. Now it was very warm in the boilerhouse and when I sat to have my lunch I used to open the door to cool down. The boilerhouse overlooked the courtyard and one could see everything when the moon was full, as it was on that night. I was half way through my sandwich when I saw the figure of a nurse walk across the yard to the deadhouse. This was unusual because the nurses were told never to walk the grounds at night alone. I put it down to something or another and decided to stay and watch until she came back as I was going to warn her of the rule and the danger. I sat there for a whole hour but she never returned and return she would have to as there was no way back only across the courtyard. I let it go so as not to cause any trouble for anyone but I wish I had told someone because the next night at the same time as I was eating my lunch looking out at the yard to my horror the very same nurse passed by the boilerhouse on the same path to the deadhouse.I was scared but decided to follow her to see where she was going. She was heading to the morgue alright and I in hot pursuit only she didn't stop to open the door! She walked right through it.

I was a little bit doubtful of what I had seen so I went up just to see if the door may have been left open or something but it was

padlocked from the outside like it always had been. I did not wait
till my shift was over. I couldn't. I ran all the way home and became a chef. Not ever to work in a hospital again.

THE DUBLIN FLOOD

Catherine Murray (b 1934)

Fairview, Dublin, 7/8 Dec 1954

Back in the 1950s before decimalisation, decentralisation and
retail innovation, i.e. shopping centres, the 8th December
was the BIG yearly shopping day. Families from all over Ireland
converged on the Capital City to do their Christmas shopping
and to bring the children to see Santa. As it was a Holy Day all the
schools were closed so Dublin families also took the opportunity
to come to town and bring the children to Santa. All of the big
Dublin stores had a Santa in those days.

The retail trade had a five-and-a-half day week. The more 'up-
market' stores closing at 1 o'clock on Saturdays and the remainder at 1 o'clock on Wednesdays. In the year 1954 the 8th
December fell on a Wednesday, if the usual trading rules were to
apply the 'Wednesday Houses' would lose a great deal of money.
An agreement between the management and unions was arrived
at and all the stores were to remain open that day.

I worked in the cash office of one of the big 'Saturday' houses
and on the Tuesday we geared ourselves for the next day's 'invasion'. That same was wet and cold. In fact it rained continuously
all day. I lived on Fairview Strand on the North side of the city.
When I arrived home from work my Aunt was lamenting the fact
that she had seen swans sheltering under the bridge at Ballybough and (she felt) they must be hungry. Nothing would do her
but after tea we should go down to the bridge and feed them. I
can still see us leaning over Ballybough (now Luke Kelly) bridge
feeding those swans. Even at that time in the evening (7.30 or 8
o'clock) I remember the water being exceptionally high.

Back home we settled ourselves down for a night by the fire listening to the radio. Some time later one of my uncles who had
been walking his dog called and told us we should move my
grandfather, who was a semi-invalid, from his downstairs bedroom to a safer room upstairs as the Tolka was in danger of flood-

ing. More to pacify him than anything else (the idea of the Tolka flooding and entering our house was we thought very unlikely) we moved my grandfather upstairs.

As we were doing so a small trickle of water had appeared on the road outside our house but we didn't give it much thought. We made a cup of tea and as we were opening the door to let my uncle out to go home we were suddenly met by a torrent of water which gushed in the door and was in no time covering the entire downstairs portion of the house. He managed to get out and make his way over the railings of the other houses to his own home six doors up. We were left with the water swirling around our legs and covering as high as the fourth step of the stairs.

That night was spent watching the shop opposite to see if the water would rise any further. We had marked out a spot on the opposite wall and if the water rose any higher we felt we would then be in real danger. Thankfully that didn't happen as the expected high tide never materialised.

We learned later that the prime reason for the flood was the collapse of the railway bridge which spanned the Tolka near Fairview Park, forcing the water back up Ballybough and down Fairview Strand. Just minutes before that happened a train had crossed the bridge, the passengers in that train had someone's prayers!

Every situation has a funny side if you care to look for it. While we were sitting watching through the night for fear the water would rise, the same swans which we had fed hours before came gliding majestically up the road in front of our house. Needless to say I did not report for work THAT 8th December. I was in fact up to my ankles in very cold, very muddy, Tolka water. No doubt the store got on very well without me.

All the while the water was rising my grandfather whom we had managed to move upstairs slept peacefully. Early next morning when he awoke to find himself in (for him) a strange room he enquired of my aunt what had happened. When she told him the house downstairs was flooded he calmly asked her if she should not get a brush and sweep it out. It would be prudent not to give my aunt's response to that, suffice to say she mumbled it under her breath.

Late the next day when we were able to assess the damage we discovered every piece of floor covering downstairs was sodden and had in fact to be destroyed. Some furniture too was ruined. That night soldiers came round with coal and blankets. I remember there was some quibble with the insurance. In the end we received something in the region of thirty pounds. To this day I can still remember the intense cold and the smell of the horrible gunge left on the floor after the water had gone. Some months ago a friend and I decided to do a course in UCD in Earlsfort Terrace. The title of the course was 'What's Under Dublin?' One lecture was all about the engineering works that kept the city going. The lecturer spoke about the flood and how as a young engineer he had witnessed the results.

When we were leaving the building we got into conversation with the security man on the gate who enquired as to what we had learned that night. We told him we had been learning about the flooding on the 8th December. He said he knew more about it than anyone. I said he couldn't know more than I as I had been actually in it. Then he said, 'Well if you were, I was one of the soldiers who brought you blankets that night.' What a small city we live in. It was lovely to be able to thank that man face to face after all these years.

PRIMROSES

Catherine Murray (b 1934)

Fairview to Fairyhouse, Dublin, 1940s

My lasting memories of Easter are not of Easter eggs, but of primroses, those beautiful little yellow flowers that grow in abundance on road banks and under trees. Not that I come from a rural background, I don't, unless you consider the North side of Dublin in the 40s the countryside (which in fact it was) before the city spread out like the octopus it is today. I lived with my extended family, grandparents, uncles, aunts and cousins just four miles from the city centre. It was a great time and a great place to grow up in. We could walk to town and cars were a scarcity. Those that could afford to own one could not run it because of petrol rationing, the Emergency had us all captives. The majority of Dubliners and country folk alike either walked or if they were lucky and owned a bike, cycled. Those were the days of The Glimmer Man, food rationing and silk stockings. Nylons didn't arrive on the scene till after the war, not at an affordable price anyway.

Easter in my household meant only one thing and place, Fairyhouse Races. My uncles (and I had five of them) and one or two of my aunts cycled every Easter Monday to the races. As I was the eldest grandchild I was usually taken carried on the cross bar of one or the other of my uncle's bikes. To help to make the journey more comfortable (for me) a cushion was strapped to the bar. Sometimes this proved to be more trouble than it was worth as it would keep slipping and we would have to stop and tighten the strap. This stopping and starting was very irritating as it could have meant missing the first race and that would have been worse than committing a mortal sin. On the way home we would take a more leisurely pace. It was then that my aunt would insist on stopping to pick the primroses. My uncle would keep insisting they (the primroses) would be dead before she got home and true to his word, they were.

After the war cars became more numerous and my uncle Jim was the first of the uncles to own one. But one car can only take a limited number of people no matter how you squashed them in, so my grandfather would hire two funeral cars from the local undertaker and we would all set off. In those halcyon days cars were allowed to park right along the railings of the course. We always parked at the last jump just before the horses entered the 'straight'. In between races the adults drank tea from thermos flasks and the children (my cousins had joined the flotilla by then) had lemonade. All ate ham sandwiches. To this day I always associate ham sandwiches and lemonade with Fairyhouse Races! It was on one of these excursions I was caught smoking. My cousin and I had gone off ostensibly to buy chocolate but in fact had gone off to smoke. We should have been more careful where we decided to position ourselves. We returned to the car to discover we had been on the opposite side of the course to where the cars were parked and had been observed through my uncle's field glasses.

When my uncles acquired cars of their own my grandfather dispensed with the services of the undertaker. When the organisers of the meeting decided that all cars should park outside in a designated car park my aunt Lilly, who was a rather formidable lady, wrote and obtained a permit for my grandfather to be driven in and positioned where we always parked. And of course where my grandfather went so did the rest of the 'tribe'. A Chief goes nowhere without his Braves and Squaws. Although only standing 5ft 5ins my grandfather strode his world like a Colossus.

Coming home on these occasions, my aunt, who had progressed to bringing a small trowel with her, removed the primroses roots and all (conservation was a long way off in those days), but even though she had 'green fingers' and could make an oasis out of a desert the little yellow plants did not thrive when she planted them in her own garden. Somehow these delicate little flowers just did not wish to become urbanised.

All my extended family are gone to their reward, but I never see primroses wild and beautiful that I don't think of them and whisper a little prayer of thanks for the wonderful memories.

MY SWIMMING COMPANION

Patricia Gibson (b 1926)

Rush, County Dublin, 1953

This is a true story which happened to me about the year 1953. A few friends and myself were staying for a weekend in Rush, County Dublin. It was a lovely summer Saturday evening, the water was calm and the tide was receding so the four of us decided to have a swim. No one was on the beach except ourselves; it was about 8.30 p.m. The water was warm as the sun had been shining all day.

Somehow I became detached from my friends after doing a few strokes and I decided to lie on my back, enjoying the peace and gazing at the sun as it sank like a ball of fire on the horizon and enjoying the total relaxation of the moment. Suddenly I felt something hard under my body and with great force fling me into the air. I came down with a splash and needless to remark I was terrified. I knew there was something there in the water and I felt the sooner I got out the better. I struck out for the shore as fast as I could and when I got to the water's edge I shouted to my friends to come in.

Eventually they did and of course they wouldn't believe me. I was furious but managed to control my feelings.

After Mass the following day coming out of church we met some people who asked me if we had been to the beach. Candidly I didn't want to go near the beach at all, until I heard someone say, 'it's only a basking shark, it must have got caught in the receding tide'.

We then went to the beach where a crowd had gathered around a dead shark. It was about fifteen feet in length. A native of Rush had put a plank of wood in its mouth revealing the sharp teeth of this monster. My friends looked at me; then and only then did they believe what I had told them the previous evening. I had actually been hoisted into the air by this shark and to this day believe I am lucky to be alive, even though I've been told over and over again that basking sharks are harmless. Having seen the film 'Jaws' I still regard myself fortunate to be alive to tell this story and that luck was on my side forty years ago.

PS: A picture of the shark on the beach in Rush was in one of the daily newspapers a few days later.

FADED LETTERS

Maureen Browne Mahony (b 1901)

Dublin, 1920s

In a drawer where someone knows
Tucked away in tiny rows
Are faded letters tied with blue
That speak of tender words and true.

And oh somebody fondles these
For they recall dear memories
Mem'ries that will always last
Of a wondrous past.

And they'll be treasured day by day
E'en when their owner's old and grey
These faded letters tied with blue
Dear memories of a loved one true.

A CHILD'S EYE VIEW

Brendan Cantwell (b 1919)

(Extract from an autobiography), Lonford Terrace, Monkstown,
County Dublin, 1920s and after

The very earliest recollection of my childhood gives me a very warm and comfortable feeling. I am pushing open a very large and heavy door, having just turned a gold-coloured round knob. Behind the door a heavy dark coloured curtain hangs from gold rings on a bar attached to the back of the door. The curtain drags on the floor, making it difficult to open the door. As I put my head around it I am fascinated by a warm flickering light from a fireplace which makes shadows of the fireguard dance on the walls and high ceiling. Gradually, as my eyes adjust to the warm glow, I can see a large screen or partition partially hiding a very large bed which seems to be very high up. From the depths of the bed a gentle and familiar voice greets me.

I have come to see my granny and to ask her, from mother, if there is anything she wants. I do this every day except when I am sick or when mother takes me in a pram with my twin sister perhaps to Seapoint for a picnic on the sand. Granny is propped up on pillows, partly hidden by her silver hair hanging in loose folds about her kind and somehow young looking face, although lined with age. She asks me if I have been good for my mother. When I whisper — yes — she tells me that last night the angels left some sweets under her pillow for me and she puts a little brown paper bag in my hand as I try, excitedly, to reach up to hug and kiss her.

Understandably I absolutely believed everything my granny and my parents told me and therefore I was quite certain that granny had a very special relationship with the angels. She could see and hear them. She could speak to them quite naturally. She could ask them to appeal to Jesus or his mother and daddy for special favours. I know, she told me so.

My mother told me that I had my own special angel who watched over me constantly to ensure that I came to no harm. But if I ignored my angel and failed to take his advice I could get into trouble. I believed my mother then and still do.

Granny tells me that one day I shall be big enough to open the window shutters for her, let up the blinds and let in the light. I remember wishing for the day when I would be able to do this.

All the windows in the house were fitted with storm shutters. It would become a veritable fortress if all the windows were shuttered up. These timber shutters folded back into recesses on either side of the windows when not in use and shut out the outside world completely when used and secured with a great flat iron bar which spanned the windows.

I also remember almost every detail of the house — Number 1, Longford Terrace, Monkstown, County Dublin — in which my twin sister and I were born and my brother some two years later, and which was to be my home for about twenty years.

Today the exterior appearance of the house and the rest of Longford Terrace remains almost as it was fifty years ago. It is the first of an imposing set of thirty houses, three stories high, stretching some four-hundred yards and overlooking the sea at Monkstown. There is also a fourth floor — the basement, which had more of a fascination for me than any of the other floors.

Spiked wrought-iron railings protect a small front garden with a long walled garden terminated by stables at the rear.

Because it was the house at the end of the terrace our hall door led directly on to a side road. It was a very heavy door. A draught proof curtain hung from its back. Having negotiated this door one was confronted with yet another. This was of solid mahogany construction which opened in two halves onto a wide hall, the coloured stone floor of which was strewn with heavy oriental carpets. Against the opposite wall stood a long hall table over which hung a large oil painting of a harbour scene in a heavily moulded frame. On either side white plaster-cast figures of uncertain origin stood sentinel. In the centre of the table two cavaliers were to be seen fencing; their cloaks flying; their broad-brimmed feathered hats awry. This beautiful bronze piece was to fascinate me for years.

To the right of the hallway a wide carpeted staircase led to a landing and then to the first floor. To the left of this staircase more steps led to a lower landing, to the garden and ultimately to the basement, seen through my childhood eyes as a world of dungeons, treasure troves and stone flagged passages from which bells rang and hurried footsteps resounded.

To the left of the hall there were two large mahogany doors, one leading into the drawing room and the other the diningroom. The characteristics of these rooms and the atmosphere they — and those in the basement and first and second floors — created, may, perhaps become evident in the course of highlighting some of the things I remember about my childhood and teenage life in Longford Terrace.

There was, of course, the servants' entrance! A door in the wall separating the back garden from the road led down some steps into the garden and across stone flags to the back door of the house. This led into a small conservatory with an opaque glass roof and sides. Part of this 'back entrance' was partitioned to accommodate what was known as the outside lavatory and with it the proverbial chain which we loved to pull at every available opportunity because it made such a fascinating noise in the process of flushing the system!

The people who came through the "servants' entrance" regularly provided much excitement for me and my brother, but were avoided by my sister. Among them was the milkman. He always came with a large and shiny metal container full of milk. Julia, our maid, her unruly black hair partly captured in a white lace headband tied with black ribbon at the back, would ask for four pints and the milkman would pour four beakerfuls of milk from this container or small milk churn into the vessel she held out for him. Julia in her rich Kerry accent would look suspiciously at him and say, 'Are ye saying ye have given me four full pints there, boy?!', and with a wry smile the milkman would again dip into his milk churn, take out a sizeable measure and top up Julia's four pints! This extra quantity of milk was known as a 'tilly' and Julia more often than not got her 'tilly'!

Then there was the bread-man who daily delivered fresh bread still hot from the bakery, Johnston, Mooney and O'Brien; which reminds me of the rhyme we used to sing:

> Johnston, Mooney and O'Brien
> bought a horse for one pound nine
> When the horse began to kick
> Johnston, Mooney bought a stick
> When the stick began to break
> Johnston, Mooney bought a rake
> When the rake began to . . .

The coal-man always fascinated us with his blackness and white eyes. He would come stumbling down the steps on the stone flags with a huge black sack on his back which he would proceed to unload over his shoulder into a hole in the ground and down into the cellar beneath followed by a clattering roar and a cloud of coal dust.

The pictures I have seen in the family photographic albums are locked into my memory and it is all too easy to confuse this artificial memory source with a genuine recollection generated from within the memory banks. One such deception is evident, my recollection of the pram in which the 'twins' were enthroned and wheeled into the garden for 'airings'.

The perambulator was a large navy blue box-shaped affair supported on elegantly-curved and ornately decorated leaf springs attached to four very large diameter spoked wheels. Two fold-down hoods at each end and two swan necked chrome bars supporting a bone handled push bar completed the construction.

Inside, supported by frilled pink and blue pillows the twins faced each other. Between them lay a light blue and pink eider-down on the centre of which reposed a freshly picked rose or other seasonal flowers.

My mother's whole life centred around the twins; nothing else in the universe existed. We were handled as if we were made of Dresden china. We were the objects of her unrelenting attention to our every need. We were adored. We were loved.

I have two images of the mother of my childhood, one from a photograph taken by my father of my mother in Kilkee just before they were married; the other as seen through the eyes of an eight to ten year old son.

On the wall overlooking the beach with the West End Hotel in the background sits the young woman who was destined to be my mother. Her tiny waist and straight back; her high necked blouse and bow tie; her miniature face and large twinkling eyes, set beneath a mass of wavy black hair; her neat limbs and hands holding a book. This was the mother of my infancy.

My fondest recollections of my mother stem from the years when as a family, we were probably at our happiest. I was somewhere between eight and twelve years old.

We were in Castlecove, County Kerry, for many summers. My mother was the driving force, the vital spark that fused our little family together. Shooting stick in hand — a commander in charge of her troops — my mother would lead us triumphantly up every mountain, down every valley, across every stream, along every beach, in all weathers. She was at the centre of everything that happened in my little ten-year-old world. And so was my father. But it was my mother who took the sea urchins out of the soles of my feet; who scrubbed me down and wrapped me up when I was cold after a swim. She chased me along the beach and swathed me in seaweed for fun. She threw buckets of water at my father and sang and danced in the sun and the rain. She was the very embodiment of love and of happiness.

They were made for each other, my mother and father. They seemed to love each other just as much as they loved us. They tumbled about with each other just as they tumbled about with us. They had pillow fights with us and with each other. They threw buckets of sea water over each other and over us on the beaches and swathed each other in oily seaweed.

My mother loved teasing my father and because he was so very shy she took a roguish delight in embarrassing, taunting and challenging him at every opportunity when we were alone as a family in Kerry with only the mountains, rivers, beaches and sea for company. Come to think of it, my mother and father's personalities were complementary. They were as different from each other as the sun and the moon. My mother possessed a dynamism, a vitality that bubbled over. My father was of a quiet and tentative disposition but the sparkle in his keen blue eyes betrayed a wonderful sense of humour and perceptive and inquiring mind. He had the ability to respond sympathetically and eagerly to other people's feelings and other people's sense of fun.

Being a good listener and having an inquiring mind, coupled with an excellent brain he was able to indulge his passion for all things technical to the exclusion of the more trivial pursuits. Electrical engineering was his profession. He had the rare ability to excite all with whom he came in contact with his ideas for putting the electrical sciences to practical use.

The many wonderful summer holidays that I enjoyed with my family in Kerry — and later there as a young man with my uncle — stemmed from my father's pioneering work in rural electrification — the subject of a later and proud chapter in my reminiscences of things past.

MY IDEAL MAN

Maureen Browne Mahony (b 1901)

Dublin, January 1928

Men indeed are not much use
But if a choice I make
T'will be a man — not an excuse
My tender heart will break.

He must be rather tall and square
And not be easily led
He should have clouds of nice
  brown hair
For freckles go with red.

My man should have a kindly face
For beauty reigns therein,
But hope he never dares disgrace
It, with a double chin.

I'd wish my loved one to be neat
In every kind of way
Well cut clothes and tidy feet
With linen clean each day.

Chamois gloves he should not wear
A bowler hat I'd like
And it would be just simply rare
If he rode a motor bike.

The man I get must NEVER drink
(In that I think I'm right)
For if he did there'd be no chink
To keep the home fires bright.

Preserve me from a man that's
  mean
(I hope this is not crude)
There is no doubt I would get lean
By being bereft of food.

Sense bids me not expect a lot
But please do what you can
To help me find, and tie the knot
With my dear ideal man.

THE MISSION

Molly McDermott (b 1921)

Ballinaheglish, County Roscommon, 1920s

Missions have been preached over the years by the different Orders of Priests — Jesuits, Redemptorists and others in the Parish churches and in the towns around the country.

Everybody had to attend Mass each morning and the sermon in the evening. The Mission usually lasted for a week or two in each place, depending on the size of the parish or town or if there were two or three churches in each area. This still takes place every four years or thereabouts. Thankfully the Mission nowadays is far removed from that of my young days. The Sermons preached then put the fear of God in the hearts and souls of the young and old alike. All left the church each night thinking that there was no hope whatsoever for them of ever reaching Heaven but that they would surely be damned in the fires of Hell. People kept putting off going to Confessions — they were in all honesty afraid to go after listening to some of the sermons preached which took in all aspects of religion and life as it should be lived. Special time was given to the Sacraments, Penance, the Blessed Eucharist, the importance of Mass and daily prayer, and the occasions of sin which always got a great airing.

One particular sermon stands out vividly in my mind — 'Company Keeping' was the subject discussed by the Missioner. Silence reigned supreme. Everybody listened attentively. A story was told later of a couple whom we all knew and who had been going out together for years and were present on that night. On the way home as they jogged along the lady in question got a brain-wave. This surely was her chance to speak up, so she plucked up her courage. 'What a wonderful sermon that was', she said to her companion. As no reply was forthcoming she continued by asking if he was listening to the sermon or what he thought of it, more or less confident that he would 'pop the question'. 'Come to think of it', she added, 'isn't it about time we would consider getting married?' 'Ah', replied her life-long boyfriend, 'who would bother with either of us now?'

This story is true.

HAFNERS' SAUSAGES

Elizabeth Mooney

Rathgar, Dublin, 1930s

I was an only girl with five brothers living in Rathgar. My father worked in the Evening Mail Office and being the day and age it was he rode a bicycle to and from work from Rathgar, through Rathmines, down Georges Street and into Dame Street. He was a great family man, liked to bring us out walking Sunday mornings after Mass while my mother got the lunch. When he got older of course we all got bicycles and were on cycle runs as far as the Phoenix Park and many more places. One of my most cherished memories is of Saturday nights, having had our weekly baths, sitting around the big range in the living room, a big pan of sausages cooking and my father reading Hans Andersons or Grimms Fairy Tales to us. Every Saturday he bought the sausages in Hafners of Georges Street on his way home from work. It was our weekly treat and how we looked forward to the winter Saturday nights, sitting in front of a blazing fire, eating our Hafners' sausages, bread and butter and a glass of milk.

MY DAUGHTER'S BIRTH

John James McManus (b 1915)

Blacklion, County Cavan, 1963

My name is John James McManus and I have lived on our small family farm in County Cavan all my life. I would like to tell you the story of when my youngest daughter was born. She was our eighth child so you would think we would have been very calm and relaxed about the whole event but it wasn't to turn out that way.

It was two days before the Christmas of 1963 and the ground was white with snow and frost and it held all the promise of a white Christmas. It was just getting dark when my wife said she thought it was time to go to the hospital. I walked to my brother's house as we did not have a car and he said he would drive her the twelve miles to the hospital, despite the snow.

By the time he arrived I was in a bit of a pucker (panic). My wife said to pour a glass of whiskey for myself and my brother. I went to the press and got out the bottle and when my brother saw it he said you'd better make mine a very small one, thanks — poteen. My wife who was calmer than either of us looked at the bottle and said you can have as much as you like — that's Holy Water! We put two shovels in the car just in case we got stuck on the way and proceeded to the hospital. It was the next morning when I got the call that we had a new baby girl.

Now while all this was happening my oldest daughter was in charge of the house. On Christmas Eve I set off on my bicycle to visit my wife and our new baby. I came home after a delightful visit to find the table set for supper and all the children excitedly talking about the new baby, missing their mammy and looking forward to Santa coming.

When we all had our supper eaten, myself and my daughter put the little ones to bed. Before going to bed each child had left their wellies out for Santa to put their present on or in them. My daughter opened the locked press and took out each present and carefully laid it beside the appropriate wellies. I watched with great delight and amusement as she then went and got out her own wellies and laid her own present beside them.

The next morning after the excitement had died down we walked almost two miles to our chapel for Christmas Morning Mass.

This Christmas will always stand out in my memory. It is young children that really bring out the real meaning of Christmas.

OUR HOUSE IN GLENCREE

Mona Smyth (née Conway b 1925)

Dublin / County Wicklow, 1920s – 30s

We were a family of nine children — three boys and six girls — the youngest twins. I was the middle one. Father was a Bank Manager and we lived in the North side of Dublin in a large bank house with a small garden.

Imagine our delight on returning from school to find three gleaming bicycles and to be told that Father had rented a house in the Wicklow hills and we were going to spend all summers there for the next eight to ten years. Father, Mother, and the twins set off for the journey by taxi. We children followed by bicycle, headed by the eldest of the family, Desmond. It seemed to take us all day to get there, though it was only approximately twenty-five miles. We went through the town of Bray and then on to Enniskerry and on up to Glencree, and then we came upon the house known as Ballyreigh. What a sight that met our eyes. It nestled in a valley overlooked by the Sugar Loaf. We city children had never seen such scenery. We had a large garden with potatoes, carrots and onions and never to be forgotten Victoria Plum Trees.

Every morning Father would wander off with my brothers and they would catch fish and shoot wild rabbits. How we loved Mother's rabbit stew and griddle cake and buns cooked over an open fire.

We were allowed to bring friends and one of my brother's friends is now my husband. It was the summer of 1938. We made our own amusement. We had a gramophone and we learnt to dance. My brother's friend taught me.

I returned to Glencree just a month ago after many, many years to find the house still intact and no new buildings anywhere. A very nice young woman was walking her two large dogs and making for 'our' house. I walked over to her and mentioned that we had spent all our summer holidays there all those years ago. She seemed very interested and asked my husband and me in for a coffee. How the memories flooded back. The house is beautiful and the present owners have added on some extra rooms. It is very tastefully decorated and a haven from the hurly burly of life.

Long may it last.

SPRINGS, SCREWS AND CLIPPINGS

Rosaleen Cotton Wynne

(Chapter from Autobiography) Keenagh, County Longford, about 1920

Our father could turn his hand to almost anything that needed to be done around the farm and home. He could make a gate and do a bit of thatching and shoe a horse. He made the stools which we children sat on and he made a set of crates for the cart and built a turf house. He could fell a tree and clip the horses and shear the sheep. He was an expert at mending our shoes and preparing the horses' harness. When the clock stopped he repaired it and for good measure he oiled it with a hen's feather dipped in sewing-machine oil.

It was no surprise to us when he said that he was going to take his big pocket watch apart and put it together again on that bright Sunday morning so long ago. Not that it needed attention, as it was keeping perfect time but his idea was that if one wants to learn one had to find out by getting down to the root of things. As he pointed out, somebody with less brains than he had, probably made it in the first instance. Our big sister, Mary Ann, was setting about the business of cooking the Sunday dinner. She worked at the table at the back of the big kitchen so our father laid out the things he needed on the front table while Kathleen and myself stood on each side of him, looking on.

Our father was wonderful, we thought as we watched in awe as he took off the back of the watch. Then, carefully, he unscrewed each part and laid them in an orderly line on the dish cloth which he had spread on the table for that purpose. Then without warning disaster struck. Mary Ann had the dinner well under way and now turned her attention to the job of washing up. She looked around for a dish cloth and saw it on the front table. Of cause she had no idea of the sacred use it was being put to. With one swift movement it was caught up in her industrious hands and every wheel and spring and screw of the watch scattered over the floor and some rolled out of sight into the turf fire.

We wanted to say words of comfort but nothing suitable came to mind. Our father put his arms down on the table and laid his head on them. Words of sympathy can come in different forms and at last little Kathleen thought of something. She said softly 'Daddy, let me trim your hair'. Our father lifted his head and looked at the child. 'Yes, you can cut off the ends', he told her.

Overjoyed she set about her labour of love. She got the scissors and brought the little 'Creepy' stool to stand on while he laid his head on his arms again. The child's little dimpled hands moved softly over his head and the scissors made a gently clipping sound. Warm sunlight flowed in through the window. The kitchen was full of lovely smells from the cooking. Our father fell asleep. Mary Ann was steeped in the business of looking after the cooking food. I wandered out to watch for our mother's and Christina's return from the eleven o'clock Mass (the rest of us had been at the earlier Mass). Our father slept on, there, beside the clippings of his brown hair and the skeleton of his watch. Kathleen went on with the task of cutting the ends of his hair but now the ends had got very near his scalp. Noiselessly, she moved into a new position so as not to miss any of the ends. Our father awoke when he heard the crunch of the wheels outside as our mother returned home. He had a habit of running his hands through his hair after he had a nap. This time he had no hair to run his hands through! He was shorn like a convict.

Our mother had a very hearty laugh. It was a joyous sound which rang out full and clear.

She laughed a lot on that Sunday long ago.

WHISKEY (a short story)

Winifred O'Driscoll

Cork City

One morning a lovely black kitten with a round white face and two large green eyes walked into our garden. When Mammy picked her up she tried to crawl up on her shoulder, and began purring with contentment. She patted her back and head and kept calling 'Puss, Puss'! After a little while Mammy handed her to me while she went into the kitchen to heat some milk for the little creature who was both cold and hungry.

I was thinking if we could keep her I would surely think of a nice name for her. Near the kitchen door was a rubbish bin and lying on top was an empty bottle which Daddy used to keep distilled water for putting in the battery of the car, and being empty and unused, he had thrown in this bin. The label had 'Black and White' and the word 'Whiskey' written on it, so I thought Whiskey would be a lovely name for puss.

When Mammy returned she put a container of milk on the ground and poor Whiskey, as she was now christened, nearly jumped from my arms and in seconds she was licking her lips and had lapped up all the milk. In no time she was rolling on the grass, then got up in a flash and was purring and circling around my feet, almost asking to be picked up in my arms again.

Mammy decided she would prepare a bed for her, so she got a large box, lined it with plenty of old newspapers and an old blanket, and when she was put in she appeared very pleased with herself in her newly found home.

Every evening Daddy, Mammy and myself would sit looking

at television. When there would be a break for commercials Daddy would go to the kitchen and bring in a small glass of water for Mammy and two glasses of Lucozade, one big one for me and a small one for himself. The one extra thing on the tray was a plate of my favourite biscuits. Now and then I would pay a secret visit to the cupboard and raid the tin and steal a few and sometimes I would hear footsteps and be forced to make a hurried exit and leave the tin uncovered. The post mortem on the uncovered tin very often put me in a spot.

One day as I was rummaging in the cupboard to get some biscuits I saw a bottle of Lucozade among others. One of the others was marked Black and White and had the same word Whiskey written on it. Curiosity got the better of me and I sampled the two bottles. Good Lord! I spat them out and nearly choked as the taste was terrible and burning.

My birthday was on the following day and a few of my school friends were invited for tea, after which we were sitting in the drawing room chatting and awaiting their parents to collect them, when Daddy brought in a tray of drinks and biscuits and the remnants of my birthday cake. This time there were a few large glasses of Lucozade and Mammy's glass of water. One of my friends remarked that her Daddy and Mammy always had a glass of whiskey and vodka every night. She turned to me and said 'Don't ever taste them! They are awful and you would get very sick'. I wondered if I made a mistake in calling pussy the awful name of Whiskey.

Later I told Mammy where I got the name for pussy. Her face paled and I knew she was thinking deeply but said nothing. When Daddy arrived home that evening they had a little whisper in the kitchen, and after the evening meal was over out came a chisel and screwdriver and in the toolbox he found a cupboard lock, and after many years of postponement the lock was eventually affixed with the utterances of a few curses and gripes, but, my excursions to the cupboard were finished. Should I have kept my mouth shut and not taken part in the christening? I'll know better the next time drink and biscuits are mentioned!

THE BAY TREES — a true story

Maeve Bolger (b 1934)

Clonskeagh, Dublin

The love they had for each other had always been unique, and somehow the bay trees became the symbol of that love, their growth in love, a representation of their very beings.

At first there was a childlike delight in each other's company, the joy of sharing common interests, the wonder and surprise of discovery. Time stood still as they explored the tenderness and passion of their private world of romance.

As the years passed their family grew; likewise, their love expanded to embrace the God-given fruits of their union. The earlier years saw good fortune and prosperity; the sun shone endlessly and whatever clouds there may have been were soon dispelled by the joyful buoyancy of spirit which was his, infectiously transmitted to her. He could always make her laugh; this ability and his selfless love were the greatest gifts she could receive. She loved him deeply, admiring his generous nature and noble character, and although tending to be self-centred, she learned to be less so from the ongoing contact of their lives together.

With the advent of world recession, their circumstances started to change. The clouds that loomed on the horizon of their idyllic situation troubled him, but loving her so tenderly, he was careful to shield her from the full knowledge of the seriousness of their situation. Harbouring these worries to himself without any outlet or sharing caused him further anxiety which, with an instinct born from an intimate knowledge of her man, she very quickly recognised. There then ensued a long time of coaxing and cajoling before she could persuade him to offload on her the enormity of the problems he was facing; his was the old-fashioned approach that the man of the house must deal alone, with the problems which attach to providing for his family; she was his 'brown-skinned-girl' who would 'stay home and mind baby'; in their most tender moments he called her 'sweet baby wife of mine'; these sentiments provided the underlying essence of his firm conviction that he must shoulder the burdens of life alone, but his health inevitably suffered.

Realising that shielding her from reality was only creating for her an anxiety of the unknown, he eventually unfolded all his overpowering business and financial problems. He found in her a new sort of strength of which he was not previously aware; there was an instant lightening of his load. He had always been proud of the ease with which she gave birth and reared their extensive family. Now with a new awareness of the untapped potential of this partner who, heretofore, had been but the sleeping one, he found his burden shared. They were to enter the final phase of their lives together.

For six wonderful years they were to work, unfold their problems, find solutions and deal with them accordingly. Although they were tough times, full of all sorts of deprivations and adversity, they were rewarding and fulfilling for two people whose love had deepened and matured with the buffeting of life. There were many disappointments, but to balance these, there were days when things looked a little rosier. Sometimes, the whole business scene was so depressing as to be almost unendurable; then when things were at their lowest ebb the tide would turn and something exciting and uplifting would occur which once more would inspire a little hope. Throughout it all he never lost his sense of humour; he had a true sense of the ridiculous which sustained the spirits of the whole family.

To lighten the grimness of their existence, he adopted the role of court jester, but beneath the surface of levity there was a broken and bleeding heart. His heart bled for the woman and family he loved. He saw them working and struggling in comparative hardship. He longed to relieve the situation, to be able to afford to give them small treats and some luxuries, adequate heat in the home and perhaps an occasional break from the work routine. As none of this was possible he began to consider himself a failure and, having voiced the sentiment, caused her anger to flare. She could never agree that he had either failed her or the children. What had happened to alter their circumstances, she said, was fate and the world recession and many people were experiencing similar hardship. She was fierce in her rejection of his denigration of self. She loved him too much to allow him lose his self-esteem.

To hear him express such negative thinking was indeed a rare occurrence; but although, he did hold negative views concerning his own performance he never subsequently indulged in verbal remorse. Instead they went on to have happy days and evenings together in spite of their general difficulties.

Mid-way through these rather special six years their twenty-fifth wedding anniversary took place. Leading up to the date both he and she became increasingly anxious concerning some way to mark this important milestone in their lives. They were always aware that as a last resort they could sell their home to ease their financial problems and bearing this factor in mind, she thought of the ideal exchange of gifts for their anniversary. Through general pressure of work their garden had become rather neglected, but they both loved trees. Due to their feelings of impermanence there was no sense in planting a tree, but the notion of neatly-clipped bay trees in pots seemed to make great sense. It was discussed and agreed that it would be a delightful and most appropriate gift for their anniversary; the bay trees would be most ornamental in their present home, and if and when they sold and moved to a smaller house, they could either maintain the trees in the pots or plant them out in the garden.

The anniversary duly arrived and, early in the morning he came home with two of the most perfect bay trees standing proud and trim in magnificent earthenware pots. The trees were identical. Overall, they stood about four feet off the ground and conjured up images of Dickensian or Christmas stories. Behind the iron gates, they were placed like two sentinels at either side of the entrance to the conservatory (where the children played) and were visible from the kitchen window. The kitchen was where the family spent most time, due to the heat from the range. There was great excitement about the trees; it was a happy day ending with a simple family celebration.

During the following months one of the trees grew taller than the other. Its rich leaves were glossy and healthy looking. He would look out the kitchen window and say to her with a wry smile, 'that one is me; see how much taller than you I am'. Looking at the rather scrawny second tree, she would answer, 'small is beautiful; see how dainty and neat I am'. And so the joke would continue as the trees continued to give pleasure. Life went on with the usual ups and downs, but through it all there was a deepening contentment in their lives as they enjoyed working and being together. They were now working from their home and when he was out on business for the day, she would eagerly await the familiar crunch of tyres on the gravel outside to herald his return. She could gauge, to the last second, the time it took him to lock up the van, put the key in the hall door, and call out a cheery 'hello'. Then he would come though the hall and down to the kitchen where she would immediately feel the strength of his embrace and wallow in the delightful familiarity of his person. He loved these moments, the bustle of her around the cooker, recounting the day's events, children coming in from their work or studies, helping with the chores and, finally, sitting down to their meal. He never forgot to inspect the trees outside to see how much he had grown that day!

Then one September morning (after an arduous week of business) he stood up from the breakfast table, laughed lovingly over some incident which concerned one of the children, gave a huge shout and fell to the floor. For a split second, she thought he was joking as usual, but then she realised he was dead. They were alone, and as in the early days of their marriage, time stood still. It seemed to be someone else who attempted to resuscitate him, who automatically called the doctor and the ambulance. There was an unearthly stillness. Ambulance men and the doctor arrived and took over; people were weeping but she was calm and remote and confident that he would be there for her always; there was no need to worry; everything would be fine. She went to bed, slept for a few minutes but woke with a start to a sickening void in the pit of her stomach. Something was definitely wrong; she knew he must be dead. He had been taken away by the ambulance men; later the doctor returned to say that they had done everything possible but it was too late; tears streamed down his face as he told her how sorry he was. One of her older children brought her to the hospital to identify him. He looked so peaceful. He was no longer 'tossed by storm and tempest' but had 'passed to an unknown and blissful calm'.

His body was removed to the church. The Mass and funeral took place the following day. The church was packed to its limits; he was a much-loved man; his saintly but very human character was an inspiration to many in their striving for personal salvation. The boys' choir sang with a joy which soared up to the heavens through the rafters of the church. When the burial was over and friends and relatives were offering comfort she still had not shed a single tear. Somehow it all seemed unreal to her; she was outside these events, as if it were happening to someone else.

During the following days she went about her work as though nothing had happened. Like a sleep-walker she tended to the business, answered calls, filled orders. Six days after he died a violent storm gathered. Torrential rain and gale-force winds whipped around the house where she had spent all her time since his death. The rain lashed and the wind whistled and howled all day and through the night. The following morning all was calm in contrast to the turbulence of the night before. This was a week from the time of his death. When she came down to breakfast she looked out the kitchen window and immediately saw that his tree, the taller of the two, had blown over in the storm and the earthenware pot was smashed into many pieces. With lack lustre attitude she went out to examine the damage, but she had no motivation to do anything about saving the tree. Instead she left it there exposed to the elements, with its roots surrounded by a certain amount of soil which eventually fell away leaving it to dry up and die. It was after this that she began to cry. But once the floodgates were opened she realised that there was a sea of despair in which she could very easily drown, so she tried desperately to board up the chinks in the dam and get on with her life. She knew that she must maintain her buoyancy of spirit; this, his legacy, would sustain her. He never wished to wallow in woe even in the midst of enormous adversity and his 'joie de vivre' must live on in her.

Later on she transferred his tree, sadly wilted, into another pot but it never recovered its vitality although she clung onto it for a very long time. The 'small, neat' tree began to thicken and expand and when, four years later, she sold the large house and moved her family to a smaller one, she took the tree out of its pot and planted it in the new, very bare garden, where it went from strength to strength.

She sometimes felt herself bursting with creativity and thought that she should write down all her feelings and emotions. Although constantly tired and worn out, nevertheless there was always within her a driving force, an endless goal, a never-defined purpose. What was it that kept her forging ahead, always trying a new challenge? It would have been more sensible if she were to calm down and grow old peacefully, but then she was never sensible! She thought of him constantly, longed for him, ached for him. His absence was the kernel of her whole problem existence. But the bay tree thrived in its new setting; it grew and grew, its branches increased and strengthened just as her family grew up, qualified in various professions, married and had their own children.

Dedicated to the memory of John F. Bolger (1930 – 1983)

BRIGIE ROGERS' STORY

Brigie Rogers (b 1910)

Dunderry / Navan, County Meath

Here I am Brigie Rogers née King. I was born in the Parish of Dunderry in 1910. I was baptised, got my first Holy Communion, Confirmation, and was married sixty-two years ago to the nicest young man you ever saw RIP.

I had a very happy childhood. I was one of six sisters and one brother RIP. Thank God all the rest of us are alive still, my eldest sister is ninety-one years. I attended Tullaghanstown school till I was almost sixteen years in 1926. Mrs McCabe and Miss Brennan were sisters, they were our teachers and good teachers they were. My first day at school was when I was only three years old, the reason was Fr Brennan visited the school to give his Blessing. He was brother of the teachers and he was newly ordained. At that time there were fifty pupils so I was put on the Roll Books to get as many as they could for a two-teacher school. Before that there was only one teacher. Now the school is gone and replaced with one in Dunderry. Two of our children went to that school, before it was demolished.

We had great fun at school, it was not all lessons and no play. At playtime the boys had one half of the yard and the girls the other half. The pump was outside the wall, it's still there, we had leave to go out and get a drink. I remember one day I was going out the school gate and one of the boys followed me out and I banged the gate and got him. He had a lump on his head. I thought I'd be killed for what I'd done to him, but lucky enough the teacher only laughed. We were a fairly well behaved lot. The school was about a mile from our house and we had to cross fields to get to the road, we were like goats eating blackberries and haws along the way and even pulling turnips and peeling them with our teeth and oh how sweet they tasted. Those were the days. All the schooling I got was in the same school. I left in 1926. I remember the Troubles in '21 and '22. Mrs McCabe crying, telling us about Kevin Barry being hanged in Mountjoy and we praying for him, it was a terrible time. I remember we running to hide when the Tans passed by, there was such fear in us.

Then came happier days when the Irish classes started in the school. The night classes in Irish were fun and Irish dancing, the teachers were Ciaran O'Connell for the language and Mick Gaynor for the dancing. What a time we had. The music was great. Bobbie Mullen and Tommy Donnelly on the fiddles (all of them gone RIP).

My teenage years were very happy. Plenty of work and no money. Myself and my sister Agnes had to help on the bog, we were good workers and everyone around our place would be wanting us to help with the weeding. Picking the potatoes on a cold November day was no joke, the funny side of it was great. I remember we being on the bog and a young lad we knew had two donkeys one in the cart and the other with a spare shaft attached to the cart but when he tried to get across the Kesh it was too narrow and down into the drain he went and no-one around to help because everyone at six o'clock flew off the bog. Instead of having sympathy for him we laughed and laughed, we didn't see the serious side of it, but he got out safe.

When we got our summer holidays we'd have to get home the turf. It was great fun coming and going, the pony we had sometimes he'd go well for us and sometimes not. Anyway we got it home and what a fire would be put down in the long winter's night, the form in the corner and we under the paraffin lamp knitting for anyone that would ask us. When we got something to do in a hurry Mother would say put two stitches into one and Agnes said 'well mother, if we did that we wouldn't be long getting the jumper finished'. She took a fit of laughing. Mother had a great sense of humour. She played the melodeon and she taught us how to dance a half set, we had lots of fun, all our cousins would be there.

Then came the time as my mother used to say we were on the lookout. We got plenty of dancing. We were fairly choosey who we'd get up with, some were great dancers and others hadn't a leg to put under them. Now came the best days of my life when I met my husband. I was eighteen and he was twenty-three. It was on a loft, above all places. There was a send off as it was called for four young men and three girls who were going to America and one of them was my sister. She is home now and is 91 years. They had a band from Navan playing and my husband was one of them. He came into the room where they were serving teas and Mrs Newman said to me, 'Now Brigie wouldn't he be a lovely boy for you?' I thought to myself he wouldn't look at me, so there's where it all started.

Matt was a great footballer. What would I give to be sitting on the Hogan stand watching him again march by, his lovely shining fair hair. I could see no-one else in the field only him. He was very kind to me and to our children. God Rest Him.

He had a Hackney car, the only one outside the Chapel on Sundays (some change). He did work for lots of people from driving to fairs, football matches, weddings, funerals, christenings, dogs, races, you name it he was there. He did one funeral, it was sad, it was in the 40s. He was a soldier that was washed up on the strand near Drogheda. The Meath County Council was in charge, he is buried over at Mornington. Matt often showed me the graveyard. I remember the big snow 1933 and he going to a fair with six men. He left the house in the morning and didn't come home till Sunday eve, tired and weary, they took shelter in a house near Kells. I didn't know what to think, his mother was alive at that time, she thought he was with me and I thought he was with her, he often visited her. She was lovely poor soul RIP. That was February

1933. Everything happened that year. My first daughter was born October 1933, the week Meath won their first National League. The last races were in Boyerstown just near where we live.

Dedicated to the memory of Mattie 'Buller' Rogers (1905 – 1991), the renowned Meath footballer, winner of nine county senior medals with Navan Gales between 1924 and 1938; he won a National League Medal with Meath in 1933 (their first ever). He won Railway Cup medals in 1929, '30 and '32. He made his debut for the Meath senior team in 1923 at the age of 18 and played with them until 1938. His final game was with Dunderry in a Junior Tournament Final in 1951 with one of his sons Brendan on the same team.

THERE'S MANY A GOOD TUNE PLAYED

Thomas P. White (b 1930)

Raheny, Dublin

I remember the first girl I loved in my life,
Patricia I think was her name
Or was it young Brenda from Manchester Town
Or was it sweet Katy or Jane.

Perhaps fair Collette was the first girl I loved,
For she was as sweet as the rose
Or was it young Trish with the raven black hair
Or Marie with the cute button nose.

Ah, those days that we shared, I just floated on air
And with happiness I nearly burst,
And each I love still, in that same special way,
For each in my heart was the first.

Now in life's golden years, I remember each one,
As I stroll in the sun or the rain,
And the thought comes to mind, if my life I'd relive
Sure I'd love them all over again.

Well that's my wee story, but still I'm not sad
For my heart is still young and quite spry,
And now I must go, for a Goddess just passed
And I swear that she gave me the eye.

VII

REMEMBERED LIVES

Reminiscences and autobiographical fragments

MARTHA REID'S STORY 1904-1995

Martha Reid

Corofin, Donegal

I am now 89 years old. My grandfather's name was John Begley born in Corofin around 1813. He trained as an NT in Cork Street, Dublin, was originally RC but changed to C of I during the Famine not because he was a 'souper' as was common practice then, but because he didn't agree with the Pope's infallibility.

When he changed he was sent as a 'reader' a rank lower than Rector to various parts of the west of Ireland. He was a fluent Irish speaker and is purported to have written speeches for Daniel O'Connell.

During the Famine he was in charge of ticket allotment for soup and one of his catch-phrases went:

'Mary Picket has no ticket

Give her one or she'll kick it.'

He was married twice (his first wife died) and had six children. His second wife was a very learned woman, a great grammarian, a student of Astronomy and read the books of Euclid. Their youngest daughter was Maggie and became a governess in France and while there learned to speak French and Russian fluently. She returned to where her parents were then living, Errislannon, a peninsula outside Clifden, and one day answered an advertisement for a governess in the UK. She was interviewed by the Duchess of Marlborough, and got the job which was governess to the Churchill girls.

My father was Alexander Reid. He was orphaned quite young and was fostered to the Mongomerys in Donegal (where he met his wife in later years); this was paid for by the Church of Ireland

Orphan Society. Later he was apprenticed to tailoring but did not like the trade so he joined the British army — my mother used to say he took the 'Queen's Shilling'.

They had eight children. I am the youngest in the family and am myself a retired N.T.

A BLACK PIG

Maggie Cummins (née Caulfield, b 1908)

County Galway

I am 85.5 years. Our family was one of seven children, my Dad and Mam were very kind and never slapped us. I and two other sisters got married, Martin also got married. I had twin sisters, one died. Her bag was packed to go with her sisters to a Franciscan Convent. Her nun sister lived to be sixty years, came home after twenty-one years in USA, Baltimore. During that time, she was allowed home for a visit only three times — that was very sad. But Ellie that died sang the Hymn to Sacred Heart before she died at nineteen years. I never went to High school but I was in 6th class and I was sixteen years then. I am the last of the family living now. But this is a funny one, my brother and his wife used to go to England to visit my sister who was a nurse and my brother went to visit a farm in England, so what if he didn't purchase a Black Pig, so the man on the farm sent the young sow pig home and when Martin went with his horse and crib to Athenry to take it home all the neighbours flocked around the cart, so it was like a circus. Poor man enjoyed telling that story. Mart is dead RIP.

I played hurling, also my sister. Went in the bus, the boys were very nice, we did not have much training then, won a few matches.

We went to the Galway Races in the side car, with our Dad, he gave us 2s 6d. The sun would be shining and we would try to have the thinning of the turnips all done before going. We all did our bit on the farm. I was not as good as my sister, she looked after the sheep, but enjoyed it. And the four of us settled on the farm.

Neither my husband nor my Dad had a tractor or motor car.

'SUNNYSIDE'

Ruth Wheatley (b 1920)

(Extract from Autobiography), Ringsend / Sunnyside, Dublin, 1920s

My first memories are of sailors and seamen coming to our house in St Patrick's Villas, Ringsend. My mother's father had his own fishing boat called the 'Irene' and his sons were the crew. Nearly all my uncles lived and earned their living by the sea. Most of my relations were connected in some way with the sea, even my father's family, ship builders or connected with shipbuilding. Two of my brothers were sailors too, the youngest served right through World War Two. Even the women were involved as they knitted the big heavy navy jerseys worn by nearly every sailor.

Because we were Protestants there was a great deal of inter-marrying, which meant we had plenty of relations and could drop into so many homes. Mother never worried about us as we were sure to be in some relatives' home and would come home at bedtime or when we got hungry. My father's parents died young and most of his family were fostered, my father went to live with a family named Bowden in Belfast, he went to serve his time in Harland & Wolff, Shipbuilders, Belfast. Mother joined him up north and they were married. My two eldest brothers were born there, then they came back to Ringsend. The British Army were recruiting men to fight in the Great War, they were each given a shilling when they joined up, this was called 'The King's Shilling'. It was during this time that my father got his training as a boiler-maker.

When he came back from the war, he got his own business after working for some years in the Liffey Dockyard. Many of the men who came back after the war had to emigrate to Canada and other places. I remember the sadness when families we knew had to emigrate.

We are now eight in family, I am six years old, a brother and sister were born later on.

I can remember the big bath full of heavy clothes on the open range, they seemed to take hours to get clean, no washing machines and very few people even had gas, the clothes were rubbed on a washing-board and wrung out by a mangle in the yard, it took all day.

At this time there was an organisation called 'The Protestant Orphan Society' in Molesworth Street. So many of the men were killed in the Great War and their wives had no income, this was a Society and was a great help to my mother, when father died at the age of fifty. We had to go to Molesworth Street once a month to get help. The amount was 2s 6d per month for each child. We hated going as they made us undress and inspect our heads for lice, but mother needed the money, so we had to put up with the terrible feelings, they kept telling her that she would be better off if we went to the orphanage in Kilternan, called Sunnyside. She would get so upset, however we soon cheered her up after a visit to the Natural Museum and a treat. They must have worn her down, because when I was nearly twelve years old I was sent to Sunnyside as the orphanage was called. So for a few weeks before the end of August, I was being 'rigged out'. I got new underwear and pyjamas, what a thrill, I had only had outgrown nighties up to this, so when mother gave me a new school case as well, I felt on top of the world. Being the fifth girl in the family I was fed up with old clothes.

We met another girl who was going on the Enniskerry bus that Saturday afternoon and we liked each other and got on very well on the bus, our mothers liked each other too, so every month on visiting day they met and became great friends. I settled in very well and enjoyed myself very much.

That first Saturday still stays in my mind. Miss Cox, the Matron, told Margaret to take us up the hills to the farm of Mrs Hicks. She supplied Sunnyside with buttermilk for our bread-making. We got over the stile and just then we saw a big bull in the same field. He was quiet, but I wasn't to know that, I don't think I ever ran so quickly. This was Miss Cox's (the Matron) way of keeping me occupied, so that I would not miss my mother when she and Nora's mother went for the bus. She need not have worried, as I settled in very well. We joined the Girl Guides in Kilternan and loved going camping to Rush for two weeks each year, before going home, until September. Some of the girls had no families and had to stay in Sunnyside. I stayed there until I was 16 years of age and loved every minute of it.

LIVING WITH CHARITY

Seamus Byrne (b 1931)

Dublin, 1930s – 40s

Seamus is my name born 31st March 1931 in the old Coombe hospital. The family lived in one of the railway houses, Murray's Cottages, Inchicore Dublin. My father was a train driver, the old steam trains. One of my brothers who would be the oldest in the family was killed by a tram in Dolphin's Barn. My mother watched him being dragged along the road, which created a form of insanity in my mother. My mother also had another son who died of pneumonia, all of this grief did not help her sanity. My mother ended up in a mental hospital called Grange Gorman.

I knew nothing of all of this for the first sixteen years of my life.

There are four of us still alive, two sisters and two brothers. I am the youngest of the four – sister in Bournemouth in England, (Eileen), sister in Drimnagh, Dublin eldest of the four; brother in Coventry in England and myself in Cork. We are all in touch for a number of years now. The four of us married and have raised our own families.

What I have done before I acquired all of this information makes my life interesting. The first sixteen years of my life were hell.

Writing a factual story of part of your own life does not come easy, when I am casting my memory back to the age of four years old, as I was born on the 31st March 1931 which makes me 64 years old this coming March 31st.

St Philomena's Home in Stillorgan, County Dublin was to be my home from age four. It has been a time of my life that has remained in my memories throughout my lifetime. The home was controlled and run by The Sisters of Charity. They wore long white habits and a very large white head-dress shaped like a white dove with two large wings which flapped on their heads when they walked.

Sister Mary was one of the sisters I will never forget as she was the Sister who had kept me under her wing for the next six years. Sister Mary was in charge of the altar boys and it was her duty to teach Latin and the serving of Mass. Her way of teaching was sadistic and very cruel. There was an average of twenty altar boys out of approximately three hundred boys. There were as many girls whom we did not see or have anything to do with. The Latin mass was very difficult to learn for young boys though I became very good at it. Sister Mary was very cruel to boys who were unable to make the grade. One of Sister Mary's ways of punishment for making a mistake while you were serving mass was filling a bath of cold water and, with four or five other boys who served mass all standing around the bath, the boy who made the mistake was made strip naked and get into the bath. Then Sr Mary would push his head under the water and repeat this for twenty minutes or more. The boy would be screaming when he got out of the bath. She was using this boy as an example to myself and other boys who made a mistake when serving mass.

We all slept in two large dormitorys, the sisters worked on different shifts looking after us. We were called every morning at 6 a.m. and we had to jump out fast or a cane came down on you in the bed which made you jump. You dressed and went to the washroom. The big boys dressed and helped the small boys to wash. We were then taken to the refectory for our breakfast, the time would be seven o'clock. Breakfast consisted of porridge, two slices of bread and treacle and a mug of cocoa.

The one thing wrong with all the boys at all times was hunger, we never got enough to eat, and that went on throughout my six years.

After breakfast we were all taken into a very large play hall also called the Drill Hall where we were lined up for drill. Guess who was doing the drilling? Yes, you're right, Sr Mary. She was armed with her walking stick cane that was unbreakable. She also carried a clicker that she clicked when she wanted us to change positions when we were drilling. If our hands were not straight she hit us on the backs of our fingers with all her might. This was Sr Mary's way of putting the greatest fear into the boys, a fear they will always remember.

For lunch everyday, we had stew and for supper we had two slices of bread and treacle and mug of cocoa. One morning at mass one of my friends was serving mass and he made a mistake. His mistake was during the Consecration of the Eucharist. The priest puts his two hands over the pall on the chalice and you should ring one bell. My friend forgot to ring that bell and Sr Mary, when punishing the boy in a bath of cold water very nearly drowned him and he had to be taken to a hospital. She said he slipped in the bath.

Our education was very harsh and strict. We had three class rooms 1, 2, 3. A nun in each class and corporal punishment was very harsh. There were beatings every day in each class.

One day in class I was sent for by the Sr Superior whom we never did see. When I got to the Superior there was a small girl with her. The Superior said, 'This is your sister, Eileen'. I was dumbfounded, yet very happy. Eileen said to me, 'Our uncle has come to see us'. I said 'What's an Uncle?' and she said she would tell me about it. However, we went to see this Uncle together holding hands and full of joy. I had a sister Eileen. When we got to the front hall, our Uncle and another young man stood there. Shaking hands with us, they were complete strangers to me as I did not know them. I was six years old and Eileen was eight. This was the beginning of my family I never knew existed and I learned a lot more about my family as the years went on, and more sisters and brothers. After the visit of my Uncle, Eileen took me back to the boys and she went back to the girls. We both shed tears on our parting.

The next four years while I was at St Philomenas Home were becoming routine. I served mass every morning. I rarely saw a Priest visiting the boys; the only time was when I was serving mass. I knew the Latin mass off by heart and it came easy to me. It was routine.

We never heard of Santa. Christmas meant nothing. There was nothing changed at Christmas to indicate it was a special time of the year. We went to Mass seven days a week. We had religion around the clock every day and the weeks and years came and went.

When we reached the age of ten years, nine boys and myself were put into an ambulance and driven from St Philomena's Home to Upton Industrial School for another six years of torment. That is another story.

MEMORIES OF YOUTH

Jenny Kehoe (b 1921)

Wexford Town, 1920s – 30s

Memories live longer than dreams — and I agree whole-heartedly with that song. At the early age of fourteen months I became an orphan and as was very usual in those days, I automatically 'melted' into my Aunt's household of ten children, a grandmother and a grandfather. Whenever she was asked, 'How many children have you?', she would say 'ten plus one'. Reflecting now on her answer, I maintain she should have answered 'one plus ten'. You see, I was always treated as the 'special' one in that very big and 'not too well-off' household and I know at many times during that very, very happy childhood I demanded that VIP status! That 'house of memories' still stands and every time I pass it I relive every day of my young life there. I think winter was my favourite season for the days were short and the nights wet and windy. We usually sat round a big rosy fire that had earlier been brought to life by my mother with a bellows, and she loved to sing as she blew it.

Tea time was a special time and we looked forward to endless pancakes, griddle cakes or apple or rhubarb tarts, with the juice just oozing out of them. My old grandmother preferred a boiled egg, which she patiently awaited the hen to lay, but it had to be a brown egg. She kept a few hens 'for herself' at the end of the yard, so that she would never be hungry!! The month of May was lovely for we had our own May altar up in our bedroom at the top of the house, where the girls slept in two kingsize beds. Benediction was celebrated each night and of course I always claimed the honour of priest, reciting the Divine praises and burning papers in the thurible instead of incense. The Tantum Ergo and the Adoramus was sung by my sisters kneeling behind. Very often this ceremony got out of hand and was quickly ended by my Mother's footsteps coming up the stairs to see what was burning.

I can still see all our shoes as we came down each morning for breakfast lined up at the fireplace shining bright; they had all been polished by my grandfather the night before. We lived next door to a 'big house' owned by very wealthy people, who were very generous with supplying flowers for the May procession. As a rule I won the toss to go in and collect the flowers. The butler answered the door and before long the lady of the house would appear with a glass of milk and a slice of chocolate cake while she went to pick the flowers. I used to spend hours looking at that big house and wondering why we didn't have one like it. In 1932 they were the only people who owned a radio in our area, so you can imagine the enjoyment the neighbours got when they brought the radio out on the lawn and we heard John McCormack sing at the Eucharistic Congress in Dublin. That house also stands today but it is no longer the house of sweet smelling flowers and chocolate cake. I feel I could write books on the very special memories of my young life but pangs of sadness overshadow most of them now for the people who made them no longer exist and will never know how grateful I am for the loving and unselfish life they afforded me, when times were pretty hard but their hearts were full of love.

A TRIP TO THE MILL

Mary Walsh (b 1925)

Ballygriffin, Waterford, 1935

I grew up on the banks of the River Suir, three miles outside Waterford City. Although it was a country area we did not have a farm as my father worked in a local brewery. Each Autumn after harvesting my father purchased a sack of oats from a local farmer. This sack of oats would be brought to the nearest mill and ground into the sack of oatmeal that would last our family, of seven, until the next Autumn.

1935 was a special year for me because at ten years of age my father decided I was old enough to go on that special trip to the mill. The night before the trip I could hardly sleep with anticipation and fear that I may not wake up in time as we would have to start out very early. My brother harnessed the pony to the trap and my mother and I prepared the lunch, a flask of hot sweet tea and a cake of homemade brown bread and butter. Off we set on the journey, I felt very important as I waved goodbye to my mother. It was a bright crisp Autumn morning and somehow that morning seemed more beautiful and more golden than any other morning I could remember. Although the journey, from our home in Ballygriffin to the Clogga Mill in the parish of Mooncoin, County Kilkenny, is only twelve miles it seemed like a marathon to me. We had to travel slowly as the pony was old and we did not want to tire him. When we came to the village at Silversprings we stopped to rest the pony and it was there we had our lunch.

Eventually we reached the mill and my brother asked for Mr MacDonald the miller who told us we would have to wait for half an hour. I enjoyed the wait, watching the farmers coming and going with their grain and churns. It was only that day I discovered it wasn't only a mill but also a creamery. Our turn came, almost too soon for me, and my brother loaded our sack of oats into the mill. Mr MacDonald, a large jovial man, told us to come back one week later to collect the oatmeal. The journey home was as exciting for me as the journey out. My brother and I chatted and told each other jokes and on that day I felt very grown up indeed.

A week later we went back to collect the oatmeal and paid Mr MacDonald the pricey sum of five shillings. For the next year from that one sack of oatmeal my mother baked oaten cakes on the griddle and made hot porridge each morning for us. Having paid fifteen shillings to the farmer, the total cost was one pound!

I made many such trips to the mill after that day. Sometimes we would vary the journey by visiting my grandparents who lived in Kilnaspic, two miles from the mill. Although I always enjoyed those days, my first trip to the mill is one of the fondest memories of my childhood days.

TWO FOR THE PRICE OF ONE

Mary McEnroy (b 1928)

Glenade, Kinlough, County Leitrim, 1930s – 40s

The big thing about the 1993 Leitrim final of the Irish Country-women's Association competition in Kinlough, was that it made me zoom in on the long defunct shenanigans in Glenade hall. Gleefully, I flattered myself that, likely enough, I was the only person in the auditorium getting double value from the afternoon. Deriving great mileage from the medley of song, dance, drama, recitation and what have you in artistic endeavour portraying the lifestyle of bygone years, I simultaneously indulged in the most pleasant memories of my happy childhood. Then Annie, my contemporary and co-parishioner, leaning over a few bodies whispered that it reminded her of Glenade in its heyday. I was no longer in a category of one.

'If only', I said to Annie, indicating the way producers of the next item were switching the lights on and off with gay abandon, 'if only Glenade, in its glory, had half the mod-cons.'

We reminisced about the paraffin oil lamps, with their graceful curving globes, strung along the stage-front, facing the actors, and the way they fulfilled the role of footlights, then considered essential. We shivered to recall the heavy curtain falling within a whisker of the blazing wicks. We marvelled at the zero accident incidence and enough flammable fuel in them thar things to ignite Fort Knox. We quaked afresh at the memory of more of their kind suspended precariously from nails on precariously balanced props, and of others similarly distributed to supply the house illuminations, and of prompters holding candles an inch from conflagration.

It was a thousand pities too, we agreed, that we hadn't seating like this, with reference to the chairs around us which, though no Parker Knolls, were light years ahead of the forms. They were a tough and wiry race, we pursed our lips in assent, to sit for hours on those long, thick, wooden planks, planed but unvarnished, polished and shining from abrasive contact with a decade of frieze and tweed and flannel — and they with nothing behind them to prop them up if they tried to lean back.

And, we wagged our fingers at each other, there was no running in and out of toilets; indeed the word may not have been invented at the time and as far as our place went, the contraption ALMOST mightn't have been either.

Well Annie may have remembered the lamps and the backless forms, the excitement for months before the great night, the free show for the children the Friday before, but she didn't even *know* half the things I could remember. I didn't ask her if she were allowed back to the adult paying 'concert', as they persisted in calling the event. But even if she had been I still held the five, Jack and ace.

Annie *couldn't* know about the months of preparations, chiefly in my grandmother's home, only a field away from the hall, where heat, comfort, refreshments and an air of undying hospitality were always on tap. There was the choosing of the play, a Summit decision. There was the scrounging to provide the royalties, especially during the Economic War years. There was the posting of the order for the play scripts to some mystic Aladdin's Cave named Duffy's in a faraway place called Dublin. There was the laborious memorising of the text by weary men and women after a hard day's work. There was the nailing of props and the painting of scenery by the artist of the group. There was the fabrication of costumes; for instance the making of the scarlet tunics for the Red Coats from cheap slippery artificial silk that wouldn't stay in place on table or sewing machine. There was the 'language' that this frustration gave rise to and which I ignored, reasoning that that was the way men spoke when they hit their thumbs with a hammer or otherwise injured themselves. I remembered my grandmother cutting the pattern of the jackets from old newspapers held against the torso of the men chosen to be English soldiers. There was the hunt through the dump at the back of the house for a not too thoroughly smashed-to-pieces drinking vessel when a cup or mug had to be broken on stage.

There was the search for worn-out jumper or sock, visibly patched or darned in non-matching material. And, when acts of violence were perpetrated on stage I recall informing all around that the person wasn't really dead at all and that he or she would get up again when the curtain was lowered.

An ICA lady was reciting a humorous, interesting and

entertaining parody about falling in love in London and being carried back to her husband's home in Leitrim. 'Excellent Ma'am', I applauded with the rest. 'But, ma'am', I'd love to have challenged her, 'have you spoken to Helen my friend, four score years and three at present, who migrated from the relative civilisation of the Gorbals and at the then tender age of twenty or so was set down in the North Leitrim mountain fastnesses and required to have a go at the everyday tasks? She had never beheld a turf fire and failed to kindle same. She had not been in close communion with cows and didn't know which end of the beast the milk came from. She had never gone to the well for water, never witnessed hay or turf being harvested. But most of all she feared the churning.

Yet, she in time not only became adept at all these and more but turned out a champion boxty maker.'

CELLULOID REMINISCENCE

Fr Pat Deighan (b 1931)

Castletown / Kilpatrick, Navan, County Meath, 1940s

My reminiscence has to do with a series of experiences during the early forties in my home. The scene was a little room — a sort of attic — upstairs. This I had converted into a picture-house, and, with the means at my disposal in those halcyon days, the only resemblance to a cinema proper was, apart from a rusty cinematograph, an old bed-sheet pinned to the wall, which served as a curtainless screen. The film projector, of which I was very proud, was, if you like, a magic-lantern powered by one flat (i.e. in shape, though often enough, in another sense as well!) battery. The energy was restricted to the light factor, as the film had to be cranked by hand. As a child of its age, to use the phrase, the device was faultless, and, apart from a cracked lens, which showed up in no uncertain fashion on the bed sheet, it afforded countless hours of entertainment, not only to ourselves, but — and this was part of the thrills of growing up, and graduating to long trousers — to all and sundry who might come, sometimes on formal invitation — to see the show!

You could call it the 'Battery Age!' Oddly neither of us could remember when the rural electrification dawned on our country. We were privileged, though, to possess what was called a 'windcharger' — i.e. a wind-driven propeller with dynamo, attached to the top of a sixty-foot high mast, securely fastened by wires to mother-earth, providing us with light as long as the wind Gods were propitious! Anyway, this particular room in our house was sacrosanct. It had a mystique of its own — experienced only by those who belonged to that age of time, never to be tasted by anyone in quite the same way again. Not even retrospectively by the most emotionally sensitive souls today, who lived out their young lives then! The room was something akin to a tree-house and, indeed, we had one of these too — a sort of secret magic place, that offered an almost perennial enchantment to a young heart, hypnotising it at each encounter. In 'playing cinema' we conformed to the norms of the picture world of the day in so far as we could, announcing the times of showing, titles, providing refreshments in the form of 'conversation sweets', 'bon bons' — the equivalent of today's popcorn!

The picture-show itself varied from time to time, except for one item, which was part and parcel of each performance. It had to be so, because it was the only piece of celluloid in our repertoire that could be cranked through the cinematograph, to give a fairly decent impression of movement. It was, like the room itself, a hallowed thing, even though its duration was but three minutes or so, and monotonous to boot! In fact, my brother and I took infinite delight in turning the knobbed handle of the machine, to project the celluloid's contents on the wall-screen. It showed a burly man, stripped to the waist, stoking the furnace of a ship — just that! Whether it was a Cunard liner, or a humble craft, we never knew — and we never will! Anyway, great the wonder grew, as they say, at each showing in that upstairs room. Indeed, I can still feel the bony knees of a neighbouring parish priest, whom we invited on one occasion, who acted as a chair for me as my brother operated the projector, thus giving my own arm a rest. As well as the film-clip, which was the centrepiece of each performance, we experimented in home-made cartoons in the form of static images of characters such as Mutt and Jeff, Desperate Dan, Korky the Cat, Keyhole Kate, Donald Duck, etc., which we transcribed onto butter paper. Come to think of it, it must be aeons since I saw such paper — gone into oblivion like so many other things we knew then. Delicate commodities have long since been wrapped in more durable and protective material!

GRANNY'S ORDEAL

Maureen Mahony (b 1901)

Dublin to Castlebar, 1950s

My daughter, who lives in the West, asked me if I would go down for a short holiday. There is nothing out of the ordinary in that, but it was winter time and I was undecided whether to accept, particularly as I had never travelled to that part of the country. However I felt it was up to me and I agreed to go, but not without trepidation. I have often travelled on trains, of course, but then I knew the line well and recognised the different stations, but on this particular journey, I might as well be taking a trip to the moon. [Now to start off with, I happen to be a granny — there are young grannies and old ones and I came under the latter category, therefore thinking is a bit slowed down.] However the day came and I boarded the train and carried myself and my luggage. I felt all-right steaming out of the station and I recognised the various landmarks for a while but after that I felt completely at sea.

The family told me when starting off that it would take me about four hours to reach Castlebar — where my daughter resides — but to my horror I found that I had forgotten my watch which would have saved me a lot of mental stress and I could not judge four hours. It was winter, as I have said, and there was hardly anyone on the train and I was in a compartment to myself. It did not stop at any station earlier on, but flew past them, which left me completely bewildered! I was bothered by the thought that the porter had directed me to the wrong platform and I was, maybe, on my way to Cork, where I knew not a soul.

I had been travelling for what seemed ages when I decided to walk down the train and enquire from someone where I was. A man a few carriages away glared at me from behind his newspaper, and on my enquiry just scarcely said — 'Next stop Athlone'. He looked odd, or so I thought. I had read numerous stories of people being murdered on trains and I hastily withdrew and literally flew back to my compartment.

There was a long wait at Athlone, and I wondered should I get out, as I had been told that I might have to change to another train there. I asked a porter who said 'no change'. On and on we went, until suddenly I saw a large expanse of water just after leaving Castlerea station. Now I never could get out of my mind — ever since schooldays — that Castlerea was in Galway — and I nearly had a seizure thinking I was on the line to Galway and knowing no-one there either. I was afraid to enquire from the man I had asked before. I just suffer in silence — and suffered I did. Luckily a ticket collector appeared and informed me that Claremorris was the station before Castlebar. It was like manna from Heaven to know I was on the right line. I started to gather up my luggage, but it seemed a very long time before I actually reached Castlebar. At last the train slowed down and stopped. Then I actually got into a panic when I could not open the door of the carriage, and feared I would be brought to the next station. The only consolation about that was, it being the end of the line the train could not go any further — unless into the sea.

The family met me and realising I was in difficulty with the door released me. It took me days to get back to normal, and I made a solemn resolution that never again would I take a long train journey by myself in the winter on a strange train. On relating my experiences to the family they just thought it all very amusing. At least I have the consolation of feeling after my great ordeal, that my heart must be strong and (remembering the odd individual on the train) that I apparently was not worth murdering. May I say I was in my fifties when all this happened — I am now in my ninety-third year, and remember it well.

MAGGIE

Thomas P. White (b 1930)

Raheny, Dublin

Behind forbidding walls you grew
And many tears you cried,
And in the silence of the night
At birth you wished you'd died,
For love is what you needed most
But love you never got,
For you were but a bastard
And your mother just a slut.

O Maggie, hold your head up high,
Walk tall, and proud, and strong,
For you are worth a million more
Than those who did this wrong,

And Ireland on her bended knees
Should hang her head in shame
To leave you in that living hell
When you were free from blame.

But in your wee, poor battered soul
Forgiveness try to find,
For those to whom Christ's message
Were ignorant and blind,
And all your pain and sorrow
Behind you try to put,
For *you* were not the bastard
And your *mother* not the slut.

For the ex-inmates of the Magdalen homes, who were known as 'Maggies'.

BRIDGET WHO?

Johnny Bond(b 1928)

Foyle Hill, Derry, 1960s

It is ironic that one of the most central figures working tirelessly to bring about change in Derry is unsung and unmentioned in her native city. Bridget's name however, is there to be seen if looked for. She unveiled the Bloody Sunday memorial, her name is on it. Her name is entered in the book of visitors as the squatter who took over the Council Chambers on behalf of the homeless people of Derry.

Bridget (1929-1990) was a founder member of the Derry Housing Action Committee (DHAC) and worked diligently on behalf of the homeless within that committee, leading sit-ins of housing offices and blocking roads and bridges to highlight the plight of the homeless. On the occasion of the first civil rights march, held in Coalisland, Bridget organised buses for all who wanted to attend (the march was held in protest at biased and unfair allocation of housing in that area).

In the aftermath of that march Bridget was the prime mover to have DHAC affiliated to NICRA (Northern Ireland Civil Rights Association). The infamous 5th of October march was by the invitation of the DHAC to the NICRA to hold their next march in

Derry which was also suffering from having a biased and gerry-mandered council. Although my memory is not too clear about whose idea this was , one thing is certain and that was Bridget's enthusiasm for the idea.

Who was Bridget Bond then? Well, she was a loving and caring mother of four fine boys, and a devoted wife of Johnny. She was a housewife, but as things developed, no ordinary housewife. She was born and bred in Derry, and had a well developed sense of justice, and a strength and drive to bring about justice for all, that never flagged. People of all creeds and political beliefs came to Bridget with their problems, no one was turned away and every request for help was treated on equal terms.

In the process of negotiating on behalf of others and their families, Bridget earned the respect, grudging sometimes, of most of the officials that she came in contact with: army, police, housing and civil authorities, some of whom no doubt considered her a thorn in their side. Was Bridget a political person? I feel not. I think she would be described by a political person as apolitical. Perhaps it is not so ironic that few know of her, she shunned the limelight and did not seek reward for her labours on behalf of the homeless and those in trouble.

The driving force for Bridget was her fight against injustice from wherever it came, and her sincere belief in the equality of man or woman, wherever they came from.

FOOTBALL, MY DAD, AND ME

Brian O'Brien (1914 – 91)

Rossa Ave., Close to The Markets Field, Limerick

It was one of those rare mild Sunday afternoons in January, 1991, that I took myself off to see a League of Ireland soccer game between Limerick and Shamrock Rovers, not because either side were setting the competition alight by previous displays or were playing in a cup semi-final, but to celebrate what was to me a kind of anniversary. It was fifty years almost to the day that my dad (Brian O'Brien snr 1898 – 1971) had brought me to the Markets Field to see my first match with the same opposition in action on that day also. We both had this passionate love for the game of football but we never even bordered on the fanatical and in the words of a poet whose name immediately escapes me, we treated those impostors victory and defeat in the same manner.

Media coverage at that time must have been relayed by pony express or the trusty carrier pigeon because I never knew when a game was to take place until two days before the kick-off when three double demy posters were plastered horizontally on various walls advertising the match on the street where I lived just around the corner from the venue. The great names of Rovers, Drums, Bohs and Shels, The Gate and Brideville were complemented by the pride of the provinces, Cork United, Dundalk, Waterford, Sligo and of course, our favourites, Limerick.

The happiest of memories used to flood back as we both sat around the fireside without even a radio to listen to, but I didn't care a whit because he reminisced about football until the cows came home or the fire went out, whichever came first. I had the feeling that he secretly hoped that I would make the big time and if love and ambition for the game of football could be exchanged for talent and skill then Stanley Matthews would only be trottin' after me. But it was not to be, and in hindsight maybe for the best as nothing could equal the total enjoyment we received from this code.

Night after night he went through the same ritual recalling the stars he had seen. Oh what players as he began to reel them off — Alf Peachey, Tom Priestly, Jimmy Dunne, Joey Donnelly, Charlie Tizzard, Gerry Matier, Bob Fullam, Freddie Horlacher, Paddy Bradshaw, Peadar Gaskins, Davy Cochrane, Dicky Lunn, Timothy 'Jim' O'Keefe, Owenie Madden, Paddy Coad, Joe O'Reilly and that list was endless. He left the local lads until last, maybe like good wine, the Ahernes, Harterys, Keanes and O'Mahonys, Billy Harrington, Jimmy McCann, Billy Nash, Paddy Cronin, Richie and Eugene Noonan, Mick McKenna, Davy Walsh, Paddy O'Leary and a legion of other fine players.

Now, to modern day sportsmen these names must make as much sense as one reading the passenger list of the Titanic, but to me they were everything and when I had the pleasure of meeting one of these players some time ago it was like something that jumped out of a Charles Dickens novel.

I have stated in the past that life is a circle, and as I prepare this article the Rugby World Cup is at its zenith and one All Blacks player has opted out of Sunday football on religious beliefs. This was a contentious issue back in those far off days also and I cannot recall whether my dad said it was Alf Peachey or Tom Priestly that chose a similar role. It was an unusual experience for the spectators to see that said player wear a small cap on the back of his head during matches.

He could recall team after team like poetry in motion and the reason being the composition changed very little over the years and after a while I knew them better than my school lessons.

Rovers beat Cork the year you were born he would add, and inevitably he would recite the team — Behan, Williams, Gaskins, Glen, Blake, Kinsella, Byrne, Moore, Reid, Ward and 'Dinger' Dunne. One evening while preparing the tea, or as it is referred to now, the evening meal, my mam rattled off the Shelbourne team — Tapkin, Wall, McGonigle, Johnston, Kinsella, Keeley, Hanson, Laing, Lester, Maloe and Peelo. She had heard these names so often it had become second nature and there and then I knew she was hooked also.

Any player worth his salt has a 'nickname' he would add, and I secretly hoped that someone would call me something like 'Rocky', 'Butch' or 'Tiger' but that didn't materialise either. Just to include a few of his favourites — 'Sacky' Glen, 'Kruger' Fagan, 'Babby' Byrne, 'Sally' Connolly, 'Fox' Foley, 'Diller' Delaney, 'Fatty' Phelan, 'Wagger' Byrne, 'Tol' Daly, 'Mungo' Patterson, 'Juicy' Farrell, 'Barreler' Cassidy, 'Podge' Gregg, and to round off with a few that were very popular in my own era — 'Rosey' Henderon, 'Robin' Lawlor, 'Bunny' Fullam, 'Maxie' McCann, 'Longo' White, and one could not leave out our own 'Togsie' Cunneen and 'Beaver' Cronin.

As the years rolled on we continued to go to the matches until I got my independence. As a compositor by trade he was involved from the beginning with the preparation of the match programme and it was a natural progression that I should become one of the sellers before a game. Priced at one old penny I could dispose of fifteen dozen (no problem) as a better man than I once said, before kick-off time, and with free entry and a commission I thought all my birthdays had arrived together. Like many a schoolboy he encouraged me to secure a scrapbook and collect the match reports and pictures from the daily newspaper which we were privileged to get, to have for posterity.

Sunday after Sunday with a religious fervour whether in hail, rain, snow, wind or fog he made his way to the popular side and took up a position at the very end of the 'Stand' stand. You could set the watch (if you had one) and he would be there in readiness fifteen minutes before the teams made their entry. Success in the early years was limited; to be frankly honest it was non-existent and except for a runners-up spot in the league championship there was little to be enthusiastic about, trophy-wise anyway.

No matter how lowly the team's position was, individual players kept the flag flying and on many an occasion they had representatives on the international, inter-league and amateur teams. He was fully convinced that winning a trophy every ten years would keep the supporters happy and in hindsight he wasn't too far wrong. He seldom showed emotion during a game and when a goal was scored or the goalkeeper made a spectacular save he was jostled and pushed about by all the excited fans and often lost his hat in the bargain, but never took offence and put it all down to high spirits and in the final analysis it was well worth it anyway.

The big break-through came in 1953 with the winning of the Shield, the first real trophy. He was visibly excited at this great feat and forecast it would unlock the door to even greater success. His judgement was vindicated but not at the rate he had first anticipated. More achievements followed at intervals but his one dream was to see the locals lift the FAI or Free State Cup as he used to call it. The League title came and he beamed with delight as another milestone was reached, but the cup was still the elusive dream.

He had a philosophy which is worth recalling: 'Give your loyalty with a will and expect neither award nor reward for something that gives you the greatest of pleasure.' I only hope that I lived up to his expectations.

So in 1971, another sort of anniversary, the cup campaign got under way. This could be the year, he would add, with more hope than confidence. As the rounds went by and Limerick still well in there with a shout, comments like 'we will not count our chickens yet' were very much in vogue. After a testing time the team deservedly reached the final and he was fully convinced the glory hour had arrived. I travelled up to Dalymount Park for the big day, but he did not. The game ended in stalemate and so to a replay in mid-week. I must confess for one reason or another I did not make that game but we listened to the match on the radio, though not together.

The longer the game went on the more it became evident that this was going to be Limerick's year and as the final seconds ticked away even Philip Greene was jubilant in his efforts to describe the euphoria that was about to unfold. The final whistle blew, Limerick lifted the cup and the rest is history.

Even though it was very late that evening and the weather was miserable I decided to go down 'home' to get his reaction and have a chat about the game. He was sitting there again by the fireside, just like before, with a smile on his face like a Cheshire cat that had lapped the cream. He was, as we all say today, 'over the moon'. I sat by his side, drank some tea, and we played the game all over again. Then the ritual of all the previous years was again unfolded and we reminisced well past the midnight hour. As I rose to leave he made one of those off the cuff expressions, 'I could die happy now', and sadly enough just two weeks later, he did die, and I am so sure he was happy.

I hope that this short sentimental story of a special relationship between a father and son could somehow be your story, or in years to come be that of the thousand of boys and girls who love the game of football, or any other sporting activity.

'A TRAVELLER'S STORY'

John Ward, (b 1927)

I was born in James Street Hospital Dublin May 16, 1927. At that time, travellers lived in tents, lying on straw with an open-out stick fire at the door of the tent. Mother would be baking bread on the griddle and boiling potatoes outside in a pot.

You stopped wherever the night fell on you. It could be 3 or 4 a.m. in the morning when the police and farmers would come to get us off — walk with childer, put on horse and car, clothes wringing wet from the rain and off you go. We'd keep going 'til night would fall again. The women had to beg for flour, tea, sugar in the houses (farm houses) and then pull in again for the night.

If left, we'd stay there for a week or so and would be moved on again.

My grandmother was a settled woman who came from the Coombe - Margaret Fitzgibbons. When she married my grandfather, also John Ward (known as 'The King'), then settled in Blackbanks, Raheny and stayed there in a thatched cottage for thirty years. When grandmother died, he went back on the road again. They half reared me, I lived in the cottage in Blackbanks.

My father, Patrick Ward, came from Oranmore, County Galway. He was a traveller and went to fight in Dunkirk in World War I. He returned because his father and two brothers were killed in front of his eyes. His commanding officer sent him home.

My mother was also born in the Coombe hospital - Bridget Ward (and she married a Ward!) My father was shot in 1942 in Mount Temple outside Athlone by a farmer over rabbits. My brother went out snaring rabbits (they'd boil them and then roast them in a pot of grease). Brother snared rabbits in a farmer's field. The farmer came up to the caravan with a double-barrell shot gun and said 'You stole my rabbits'.

'I never hunted a rabbit in my life' said my father and he hadn't. 'Move on your caravan' the farmer replied. 'I work for farmers around her, mending pots, kettles and so on'. 'Doesn't matter who you know - you're moving'.

My father stood up, not to attack him but to pacify him and send him away; the farmer pulled the trigger and blew the side of his face off. My father fell on the fire (it was outside), grabbing my mother by the cardigan as he fell (there were holes in the cardigan after from the intensity of his pull). The priest came out andthey brought my father's body to a shed in a farm house. The Doctor held the post mortem in the shed - they didn't bring him to the hospital. I saw the shed not so long ago. It's still there.

This was December 2, 1942. The farmer walked into the Guards in Mount Temple and said 'Help me Sergeant, I've just shot a tinker'. 'I hope its not Mr. Ward' the guard said. 'The very man' was the farmer's response. The farmer was arrested and locked up. He was in Mountjoy for three months. Then there was a trial and he got twelve months in jail. You'd get that now for driving a car without insurance. After seven months they released him and turned him loose. He had a wife with the greatest principle I've ever seen. When he came to her door, she said 'No way under my roof will a murderer live. You did it once. You'll do it again'. He kept arguing and she got the guards who sent him off. About six to twelve months later, they found him dead from exposure in a ditch – you see the conscience was killing him. That happened in '42 and he not long back from the war with bravery medals – don't know where they are now, some in Belfast and London, there are five altogether.

I came down to my mother and we moved caravan (horse-drawn) from Athlone to Dublin and moved into a flat in Summerhill. We sold the horse and caravan. We got in with lovely neighbours, beautiful people, they wouldn't know what to do for you. They had all the sympathy in the world for my mother.

I travelled County Carlow, Limerick, Cork, Kerry, Galway – all over. You name it, I've been there in the horse drawn caravan. I used to love the Corkscrew Hill. I'd love to stand on top of that mountain and watch the herds of goats. All day, I'd run after goats but would never catch one of them. My father would run after me with a whip saying 'Come back, you'll fall over the cliff'.

I used to go down the Corkscrew into Kinvara – never cycle down a hill like that in case the brakes fail. Away up into Clarenbridge and down to Oranmore where me father came from. We used to camp in Brian Hill outside the Racecourse and used to stay there for months. When the local people got to know us, they got nicer – they couldn't live without the traveller then because we made buckets, kettles, saucepans etc. for them, so they'd leave the travellers beside them for months and months. When plastic buckets started to come to the shops, the tinsmith died out slowly but surely.

I thought travelling was a lovely life. In the evenings, we'd jump on horses backs and go off to the hills of Clare or Galway.

My mother moved to Belfast in '64. She died in her caravan one night. After we buried her in Dundalk I burned her caravan.There's some comical people going who'd say it was haunted so I threw a gallon of petrol on it and let it off. That was the end of my mother's career.

I was in 'Glenroe' in one episode before Christmas '92. My grandson Michael is Blackie Connors' son in 'Glenroe'. They're all really nice people there – Miley, Biddy – they wouldn't know what to do for you.

Next summer, I'm off to Knock and Innisfree. I'm looking forward to that.

ROBERT TWEEDY'S STORY

(b 1909)

Dublin / Wicklow

I was born in Dalkey, County Dublin, in 1909. My mother, a parson's daughter, was a Marsh before marriage, her family claiming kinship with Narcissus Marsh, Archbishop of Dublin, who in 1703 founded and bequeathed Marsh's Library to Dublin.

My father claimed he was Cornish, in no way to be considered English. His family had lived in Cornwall for six generations, the original member, a Scot from the cradle of the Tweedys in Drumelzier near Peebles on the Lowlands border. The very name speaks of their origin. My father came to Ireland in 1903 to take up a post with a Belfast company of electrical engineers and all his life was involved in the development of electricity in Ireland, widening that interest to include the Peat Bogs and the Canals, serving on the respective commissions. My early life was a part of a liberal and constructively radical family, where individualism could develop, conditional always on a refusal to accept the dictation of organisations, whether clerical or political, and the acceptance of responsibility for one's own actions.

With that background it may be understood why Owen Sheehy Skeffington was my closest friend from school days onward, though in some ways we were seemingly direct opposites. Owen and I were foundation members of the newly formed Sandford Park School, under the forward-looking Headmaster, Mr. Le Peton, a wonderfully fertile nursery bed for the likes of us!

From Dalkey the family moved to Killiney, Dundrum and finally to Carrickmines in 1923, so for the whole of my life I have lived under the shadow of the Sugar Loaf. The last two houses had large gardens and a small stream on their boundaries, a perfect setting for a young boy. 'Dun Emer' in Dundrum had been the home of Miss Gleeson and the Dun Emer Guild, with wonderful possibilities for play in its large stable yard and enclosed garden. To all intents I was an only child as my sister, Marion, known for her connections with the Country Shop and Oxfam was five years older than me. It can be understood that such an upbringing nourished an empathy with things of the countryside and the changing seasons of the year and thereby led to, and found an outlet for, my growing awareness, hence much of what was written in verse comes straight from the natural world.

This was the period in which An Óige was founded, when notonly were the hostels rudimentary, but because of that austerity, were the greater fun for the hardy members, such as Terry Trench, Thekla Beere, Heine Petrie, De Brun, Colm O'Loughlin, Owen Skeffington and the members of our Holiday Fellowship walking group who tramped the Dublin and Wicklow mountains in all weathers. In 1927 Hilda appeared on my stage and the emphasis shifted to express those deep feelings made more dominant when she went to Egypt for seven years, where her father was rector of Alexandria, only returning for a couple of months every second year. History was repeated in 1936 when we married for I was following in my father's footsteps, he having married a parson's daughter as had his father before him.

By then I was working as manager of the Court Laundry in Harcourt Street, a position I held for nearly thirty years, covering the Second World War period, on a weekly salary of £8! By the mid 1940s, and a son and two daughters later, we were living in Stillorgan, where we have stayed for almost sixty years. When I left the laundry business in 1960 we 'invented' and ran 'Nimble Fingers', a toyshop with a difference, for another twenty years before retiring. Whether through work pressure, or changes in that unfathomable inner chemistry, there was a period of complete absence of versification, only to reappear in the late 50s. The old themes of countryside and searching remained, but with a more mature understanding.

Much water's flowed from Liffey Head,
Much snow has lain on Djouce,
Since you and I tramped Feather Bed
Or heard the cluck of grouse.
The water's spread round Humphreystown

And all that vale is dead.
Many a bell of heather's blown
Since Glendoo felt our tread,
Yet those were days and nights that live
And in our memories stay;
And who of us would not retrieve
That past had we the way?

(Written for the 21st Anniversary of the Holiday Fellowship.)
16th February 1951

ALL OUR SUMMERS WERE IRISH ONES

Anne English

(Extract from a full length autobiography) Liverpool / Mayo, 1940s

Because it is a land whose — sometimes heart-breaking — beauty cries out to be put down on paper, there must be hundreds of books about Ireland, but I promise you, hand on heart, that this one is rather different.

It doesn't even pretend to compare with those well-informed, scrupulously researched above mentioned tomes and I should make it clear here and now that if your aim is to learn substantially more about the country's history, the statistics of the tourist trade, the commerce, or the poignant political 'troubles' of Ireland, then this is not for you.

This is above all else a simple unacademic tribute to Ireland intended for all age groups as seen through the eyes of the child I was long, long ago in the 'dear dead days beyond recall'.

In particular it is for other England-based second generation Irish youngsters like us who, Summer after Summer, went or were taken on sentimental journeys 'home' to Ireland and who grew to love it with a fervour that was to endure — like mine — undiminished down the years.

It seeks — perhaps vainly — to recapture that halcyon time when Ireland meant pure joy to me, when I, my brother and my two sisters embarked with our mother on that wonderful journey across the sea from our birthplace, Liverpool, to our maternal grandmother's small farm mid-way between Foxford and Ballina in County Mayo. Dublin was merely a 'half-way' landmark which we glimpsed in the cab which carried us — to the clip-clop rhythm of the horse's hoofs — away from the North Wall after we'd sailed all night on the British and Irish Steampacket Company Steamer from Liverpool. It deposited us at what used to be then known as Broadstone Station where we caught a corridorless steam train which took five or six hours to each its destination.

We loved everything about the sea crossing from the minute we climbed the gangplank and stepped aboard at the Princess Dock and took in the familiar scene. The Purser's Office on the right, the Dining Saloon on the left, the Gift Shop in between, and drifting overall was the heady pot pourri compounded of tar, coffee, ocean breezes and rich cigar smoke.

The elderly Stewardess recognised us immediately and she would usher us along one of the narrow side corridors to our cabin, murmuring to Mama en route: 'Get their heads down before the boat sets sail Ma'am and they won't be seasick'.

There was always terrific competition as to which of us would occupy the upper berth with the porthole.

It was thrilling to wake in the middle of the night and sit up to observe the dark mysterious ocean shifting and surging down below. Once when it was my turn I looked out and there, floating in lonely isolation on the glinting surface of the sea, was a big scarlet ball. How it had come to be there, and to whom had it once belonged, I wondered as our ship ploughed majestically on leaving it far behind. The Stewardess's advice was right except for one voyage when we had a horrendous stormy crossing which made a casualty of poor Nell.

In the morning, however, Mary and myself were conducted up to the bearded Captain's cabin where our Stewardess told him proudly, 'These two little girls were the only children aboard who weren't seasick'.

He patted our heads, presented each of us with a two shilling piece (untold wealth to us) and assured us that he'd take us on as stewardesses when we grew up. He became one of our heroes.

Once settled into our carriage in the train we looked for some of the things that confirmed we really were heading West. First of all was the somewhat baffling sign secured to the wall of a squat building on our left proclaiming 'McHUGH HIMSELF'. 'Who?', we asked each other 'could 'McHUGH' possibly be except himself?'

Next we looked for the name of every station spelt out in royal blue letters on a shiny white background. We knew them all by heart and ticked them off as we got nearer and nearer to Ballina — or Foxford where we knew our Uncle Walter would be waiting to greet us.

One year on the return journey to Dublin when we were already down in the dumps because our holiday was over we were further saddened by an incident we never forgot.

A young man stood on the platform of a little station called Ballyvary. It was obvious that like so many of his compatriots he was emigrating. His parents and family clustered around him tearfully bidding him farewell. He stepped up into our carriage and stood at the open window, waving to them when in a heartbroken voice his mother wailed 'Goodbye my son, goodbye for ever'.

Sadly all too often at that time emigrants never did return to Ireland either because they couldn't afford the fare, or because of other inescapable circumstances. Mama took the poor boy under her wing for the rest of the journey and told him that she too had gone to America when she was a girl and that she *had* come back and so would he, please God. By the time we parted in Dublin she'd coaxed him into a more cheerful mood.

It's a well-known fact that as we get older our memories of bygone days become infinitely more vivid than recent happenings and according to Radio psychiatrist Dr. Anthony Clare the Irish, as a nation over and above all others, tend to go drifting off into 'Once upon a time land' at the drop of a hat.

Being Irish himself he should know — and any reader of my out-pourings will find out how true his statement is of me.

Looking back from 1992 over all those years it wouldn't seem unreasonable to expect that by now Ireland should have reached the stage when it could guarantee jobs to well-qualified youngsters, but no.Is it any wonder that I still remember the anguish in the voice of that Ballyvary mother when she cried, 'Goodbye my son, goodbye for ever'.

VIII

THE RAMBLING HOUSE

With some pishogues and other sayings

THE RAMBLING HOUSE

Molly McDermott (b 1921)

Four Mile House, County Roscommon, 1920s

God be with the old days and the Rambling House where at night-time, especially in winter time, all the neighbours gathered in for a good hearty chat, after their hard day's work. Old stories were told which included tales of their youth, their school days, teenage pranks and of course a night never ended without a ghost story or two that would put the fear of God in your heart and the hair standing on your head. Nowadays the TV has completely taken over and more is the pity. A person dare not utter a word once the programme has started, whether they are interested in it or not. As a child our house was the rambling house of our village. We had a large open turf fire in our kitchen. After nightfall one by one the neighbouring men came in. Before too long we had to resort to the Parlour for more chairs to accommodate the visitors and the circle around the glowing fire grew bigger.

Oh, what a happy atmosphere prevailed as each person in turn chimed in with an item of news or a yarn. It gave more enjoyment than the best film ever seen or best TV programme produced.

There was one neighbour in particular whose visit we all looked forward to eagerly. The reason being that he worked away during the week and therefore had some strange events to describe or story to relate. To us it was as if he were in America, although he worked only twenty miles away, which to us seemed such a long distance in those far-off days. He was a very tall, strong, robust man. Naturally he had to stay in lodgings near his work as it would be impossible for him to travel to and from daily. When he returned he had a story to relate about his first night away from home. 'Tired and weary', he commenced, 'I rolled into bed, cuddled up and eventually fell asleep. Around midnight a mighty thud awoke me from my deep slumber, only to find that my bed had broken down in the middle'. I can still hear the laughter ringing in my ears as he told of his ordeal. Somebody interrupted him to ask how he managed for the remainder of the night after the bed break-down. Humorously and in his usual calm, slow voice, he answered: 'I lay there with me head and feet up and me bottom (not the word used, as you can well guess) down until morning'. P.S. To hear him tell it himself was much better than my poor effort. Go dheanaigh Dia trocaire ar a anam dhílis.

ROUND THE FIRE

Edward McNerney (b 1924)

Corclara, Edgesworthstown, County Longford 1930s – 40s

It's hard to imagine that a group of eight or ten men could sit around a big turf fire for two and a half hours every night of winter during the Second World War and have non-stop conversation. News at this time was spread through conversation when people would meet after Sunday Mass, and on fair days and market days. When you think that there was no television or wireless at the time, young people of today might wonder what did they talk about.

Well in the course of the day everyone would be in a different place doing some job or other in their field. One fellow might be dragging a drain to let the water away, and wouldn't he see an eel as long as the handle of the shovel, and as he was about to grab him didn't he slide away through the muck and weeds. Another fellow might be throwing in hintins in the hill field and a shower of hailstones as big as marbles fell there and no one else in the area saw any such happening. Then a fellow who was breasting a hedge would see a blackbird that was almost white, and a fellow that was dagging rushes in the bottoms would rise several hares. A fellow that yoked the mare and went into the town three miles away was sure to meet a few people on the way. After meeting someone in the town who had a wireless he would be full of news coming back. Someone would give him twopence on the way in to bring back a newspaper and on the way home he would see the terror stories about the War and look at the pictures; some other fellow might be at a cattle fair in another town and he would have a story or two also. The events and stories of the day would be released around the fire.

An old man would clear his throat when he heard about the almost white blackbird. 'It's a sign', he would say. 'It was predicted that before the end of the world that the blackbirds would turn white'. He would adjust his cap to indicate how serious his words were meant to be. With words of gloom the peak was pulled down well over his eyes. With a more lighthearted comment the cap would be pushed well back off the forehead.

The hares that the fellow saw in the bottoms was a sign of a storm, they had come down from the high bog to shelter and the big hailstones that fell on the other fellow could be part of it. And sure you only have to look at them blue flames in the fire to know that there is something strange up there. And there was a fellow that would swear he heard a thrush singing in the middle of the night. The eel that the fellow nearly caught was only a small one compared with the ones that had been seen in that area from time to time and he wasn't alone. They took that route on their way to the Shannon and were known to rest in drains around there.

Facts like this mixed with the possibility that the Germans could land at any time and overrun our country made non-stop conversation — sometimes the night wasn't long enough and some topics were carried over to the next night.

In those days conversation was a very important part of our make up. Story-telling was a natural art that most people had. Today it is becoming a lost art. It was around the turf fires in the years that are long past that many beautiful stories were passed on. With facts and fiction tastefully laced together by the story teller the younger generation didn't know the treasure that was being handed to them.

DELIA FLANAGAN REMEMBERS

Delia Flanagan (b 1912)

Cummer, County Galway, 1910s – 20s

I grew up in a small village in the West of Ireland named Cummer, 'Comor na Trian Uisge' (in English 'the Meeting of the Waters'), where three rivers meet and join the Diocese of Achonry, the Diocese of Tuam and the Diocese of Elphin. These rivers flow into

Urlaur Lake where I fished and bathed in summer time.

My memory goes back to the years of the First World War, when my uncle Paddy returned home, wounded. He had lost a leg, hence, he had to live for years walking around with a wooden leg. When he came to visit us, I remember our neighbours coming in to see his wonderful wooden leg, with all the straps and buckles. He used to sing 'Over the Top and the Best of Luck' and 'Hinkey Dinkey parlez vous', he seemed happy and always cheerful.

During my school days the Civil War took place. I remember a Derrylackan Ambush, the shots echoing across the lake, houses being searched, ours included, many sad happenings took place where an only son was shot, and houses burned to the ground. It was a dangerous worrying time for everyone especially for the elderly people.

There were happy times too, there were no dancehalls at that time, so the Céilide dances were very popular; the half-sets, the stack of barley, also step dancing, and ballads were sung. Refreshments were dished up in the parlour. Another popular event was the races, horse racing was held annually near the local towns, where we bought ice-cream, delish, and sweets in the street stalls. Another memory was the Mission my sisters and I would walk to on moonlight nights. We would have to go early to get a seat. When the Mission was a long way off, we would go off in the side car. A lovely custom held up to the present day is the Station where the priest comes to celebrate Mass in each house in the village.

On long winter nights the elderly people told ghost stories, they had some deep-rooted superstitions. For instance, no milk given to a neighbour on May Day. It was considered bad luck to meet a red-haired woman, or to build to the west. If it happened that a neighbour or anybody came into a house when the people were churning, if that person didn't take the 'dash' and churn for a while there wouldn't be any butter in the churn. The people firmly believed in the 'Banshee', a sort of keening cry was heard in the village or in the sky near to the house where a person had died or after the funeral was over. When visiting a friend's house, the elderly people said, 'God save all here!' 'A lovely day, thank God'. When seeing men in the fields working, we said 'God Bless the work'. They answered 'and you too my friends', and there was the Rosary and all the trimmings.

Living through the years of the disastrous Civil War and First World War, the War of Independence, the Second World War, I'm old now, but somehow I don't feel old living in a small farm. I keep busy with my garden, flowers and books. My motto is, Be active, Be alive, and never lose your peace of mind.

POEMS AND SAYINGS
Susan McCarthy(b 1911)
Ballingarry, County Limerick

I am eighty-two years of age and over the years have been interested in gathering different pieces of lore, some of them passed on to me by my mother, Bridget Gilbourne, born 1869.

THE WASP AND THE BEE

A wasp met a bee that was once
  buzzing by.
Said he, little cousin, can you tell me
  why
You are loved so much better by people
  than I.
My back shines as bright and as yellow
  as gold
And my shape is most elegant too to
  behold.
Yet, nobody likes me for that I am told.
The bee replied:
You have a fine shape and a delicate
  wing.
I own you are handsome but there is
  one thing
They cannot put up with and that is
  your sting.

My coat is quite homely and plain as
  you see
Yet, nobody ever is angry with me
Because I'm a harmless and diligent bee.
From this little story, let people beware,
Because like the wasp if ill-natured you
  are,
You'll never be loved be you ever so
  fair.

LEARNING AND MANNERS

Learning and manners are
  charming companions
Pray lassie, why do you hate them?
From the King on his throne to the
  beggar alone
They are useful in every station.

PROVERBS

It is not the house that counts, it's the folks who live in it.
Step lightly on the edges of time, like dew on the tip of a leaf.
Sun before seven, rain before eleven.
For age and want, save while you may.
No morning sun lasts a whole day.
Your mind is your kingdom.
Experience is the best school, for fools will learn in no other.
He who builds the church for God and not for fame,
will never mark the marble with his name.

A fellow feeling makes us wondrous kind,
But I think the poet would have changed his mind
If standing in a crowd he chanced to find
A fellow feeling on his coat behind.
When the wine is in the wit is out.

A BOY WHO HAD NO LOVE FOR SCHOOL

A little boy said to his mother at
school time that he was not
feeling well.
The mother replied:
Your cheek is red,
Your eye is bright,
Your hand is cool,
Your step is light,
At breakfast time,
You ate your fill,
How can it be
That you are ill?

The boy said:
Ah, Mammy I would not miss
much for one day.
The mother replied:
A bee gains little from a flower,
A stone a day
would raise a tower,
Yet, hives are filled
and towers are done
And steadily the work goes on.

BELIEVING IN PISHOGUES
WAS NEVER TABOO

Frank Harte (b 1913)

Tuam, County Galway

Now and again some incident or remark causes me to think
back on some of the weird beliefs, pishogues and taboos
which were in vogue when I was a young lad — and that wasn't
fifteen or twenty years ago. Most of those, thinking back on them,
were rather harmless, and indeed childish to a large degree. At
worst, some of them bordered on witchery. Most sensible people
paid little or no attention to them, but many of the older people
regarded some of them very seriously, and would not risk breaking certain old rules or taboos on any account, in case some mis-
fortune would befall them. Of course we all knew about the old
saying that seeing one magpie was for bad luck; often on our way
to school if we happened to see a single magpie it boded ill for the
rest of the day and we looked anxiously around for a second one.
I think three was for a letter, four for a wedding and five meant a
death.

A cock crowing during the night was a bad omen, and if he
persisted with his nocturnal breaches of the peace he very soon
ended up in the pot. A hen crowing was even worse. Yes, I've
known hens to crow! What a poor old hen would have to crow
about I would not know, unless it was some idea of equality or
'Hen's Lib'. Anyway, if she was recognised she also provided a

meal for the family in due course.

My own parents (God be good to them) never had much time for a lot of the more rubbishy stuff. Having spent some time in the USA must have weaned them somewhat off many silly superstitions, though I often heard them speak of certain dos and don'ts that were observed by many of the older generation.

Women, on occasion, were regarded as less than lucky. If a woman was the first person met when taking a cow on a certain journey the chances were you would be off again with the same cow in due time. A red-haired woman was real 'bad news' more often than not. I was told a story about my grandfather (on my father's side), who was a coachman at one time in the local 'Big House' where the RM for the area resided at that particular time. He was a Scotsman, a non-Catholic and to all intents and purposes, an educated man. However, as he set out one particular morning in a coach with my grandfather driving two horses, on the way to attend court in a local town, the RM espied a red-haired woman coming towards them and he immediately ordered his driver to turn the horses round and face the other way, telling him that it was unlucky to meet a red-haired woman. I shudder to think what his verdict might be had that poor woman ever appeared before him for the slightest offence.

The unfortunate person, man or woman, who may, for one reason or another, be branded as having the 'Evil Eye' would not be a great favourite in the area. Certain days and dates, apart from Friday the 13th, one had to be careful about. The 1st of May, 'May Day' had quite a list of pishogues attached to it. If, as was often the case, a neighbour was giving a bottle or jug of milk to another neighbour whose cow would be dry, a double supply would be given if possible, on May eve as it was the practice not to give anything away on May Day.

I heard a certain woman who was noted for always having lashings of milk and butter at all times of the year. It was said that before sunrise on May morning she went to a spring well on a neighbour's land and skimmed the water off the surface of the well and took it home, and also went to another farm and at a gateway or gap where their cows passed through, took mud or soil from the little ridge raised up by the cleft in a cow's hoof. She must have a fine collection of mud and water, whatever about milk and butter, as the years went by. New Year's Eve was another date to watch out for, and I knew of people who wouldn't put out the ashes or throw out their floor sweepings on that day, especially if it had been a lucky year for them.

When visiting a house going out the same door by which you

came in was important. There was something about bringing the luck out with you. Opening an umbrella indoors was also frowned upon, being considered unlucky. The phases of the moon played no small part in certain operations. It was believed that if a clutch of eggs — hen eggs that is — were put to hatch when the moon was full there would be more cockerels than pullets. Likewise, if small seeds like cabbage or swede seeds were set at full moon, most of them would be 'bolters'.

Lá na Leanbh, or the Feast of the Holy Innocents, was a date on which certain operations on the farm were avoided. There was a multitude of cures and charms. One supposed cure for whooping cough was to ask a person you might meet with a white horse what he would recommend and whatever he prescribed was expected to do the trick.

HOCUS-POCUS

There was an amount of hocus-pocus when churning, especially if for some unknown reason the butter failed to materialise. Cows calving brought on some strange rituals with some folk. I heard of an old grandmother, steeped in pishogues and charms, who, when a young cow delivered her first calf, would put a florin, or half-crown, in the bottom of a bucket for the first milking, which would mean that she would bring wealth to the house.

OTHER PISHOGUES

Nearly everybody knows about the 'lone bush' and most people even nowadays would be reluctant to cut down a lone hawthorn bush. Indeed, I myself, although on the verge of eighty-years and having outgrown most of my childhood fears, would be slow to cut down any old bush or tree unless for a very good reason, apart from the risk of upsetting the fairies. Many people still hesitate about walking under a ladder. The belief was that if you walked under it on the way back, assuming it was still there of course, no harm would come of it. Killing hares was considered very unlucky and if the 'man of the house' persisted in catching and killing hares it wouldn't be surprising if in due time a child of his would be born with a hare-lip. On the other hand, as with the ladder, the bad luck could be warded off somewhat by pulling off the hare's 'scut' or little tail and sticking it in a hole in a wall or some such place before taking the hare home. Of course there were lots of creepy stories of hares being able to turn into old witches — or vice-versa.

There were good and bad omens with regard to getting married or getting buried. An old saying went like this: 'Happy is the bride that the sun shines on. Happy is the corpse that the rain pours on.' Older farmers would try and plant some seed on Good Friday. They would also take a half-burned sod of turf from the bonfire on St. John's Eve and throw it into a field of corn or potatoes to ward off disease and ensure a bountiful harvest.

If Candlemas Day was bright and sunny it didn't augur well for the weather to follow. It was believed that if a hedgehog (Graineóg) came out of hibernation on that day and there was sun enough to throw his own shadow, he went back in again for another six weeks.

When churning a man would not be allowed to take out a coal of fire in his pipe, or any kind of metal object such as a hammer. If there was difficulty in getting the butter to form some people tried putting a metal object such as an old axe under the rim of the churn (the old dash type churn) or a small dead ember from the fire, or a sprinkle of salt, usually three.

Getting a haircut involved certain precautions in the old days. It was usually got in a neighbour's house and given by some fellow who had a reputation for being handy with a scissors. Some men would gather up their hair and take it home with them, but on no account should you burn it as you could end up with a splitting headache. Which is what I'll end up with if I don't finish this quickly.

Those were some of the Pishogues I learned about as I grew up in my area. There may be a different variety and possibly more weird in other places. Slán.

CHRISTMAS 1922

Kathleen Treanor (b 1911)

Emyvale, County Monaghan

Christmas Eve the feast began,
  it was a lovely sight,
To see the cosy country homes
  lit up by candle light.
To hear the voices loud and shrill
  as folks passed on their way,
Wishing each and everyone
  A happy Christmas Day.
Their hearts were light
  their pockets too,
They did not seem to care,
  They lived their simple Irish lives
with faith in God and prayer.
We children hung our stockings up
  beside the big turf fire,
In hopes that Santa Claus would
  come
  and grant our heart's desire.
Then off to bed but not to sleep
  if I could stay awake,
To listen to the noises that
  Santa Claus would make.
But sleep it came unknown to me,
  so much to my regret,
And it was early morning
  when down the stairs I crept.
There was my stocking on the nail

just as the night before,
And it was brimming to the top
  with toys and sweets galore.
Then off to Mass each family went
  beneath the stars so bright,
Those hobnailed boots on frosty
  roads
  would any heart delight.
The church just looked like heaven
  and it still sticks in my mind;
The oil lamps lit around the walls
  the arch across the aisle,
This trellis arch, with candle light
  and berried holly too,
I thought it was the nicest thing
  that human hands could do.
The church is packed, the priest
  comes out
  to celebrate the Mass,
With heads bent down in silent
  prayer,
  that hour would quickly pass.
Back home on foot we started
  as the dawn was breaking clear,
When I think those happy memories
  oftimes brings a silent tear.
A chat with friends and neighbours

as they pass along the way,
Calling out that well-known
  greeting
  for a Happy Christmas Day.
Then as evening stars appeared
  the shades of night would fall,
The livestock were attended to
  and silences over all.
Some friends or neighbours then
  call in
  which children love to see,
Tonight no call to go to bed,
  this night we would be free.So
  round the hearth we gathered
  close,
  one word we never spoke,
As we listened to the stories
  now being told by older folk.
They talked of fairies in the forts

and how some heard them play;
Their music in the midnight hour
  until the dawn of day.
Twas then the glasses were
  produced
  filled up and raised on high,
Then one man would propose a
  toast
  and all would then comply.
We children got some lemonade
  which then was very rare,
So we enjoyed it all the more
  this special Christmas fare.
Those are my childhood memories
  of Christmases of old
And like all who shared those
  happy days
  more precious now than gold.

WHITE-WASHED WALLS

Annie Dunne (b 1919)

Rathcoole, County Dublin, 1920s

In the 1920s when I was a little girl Christmas was a lot different for us children than it is for the children of today. We got no expensive toys. Actually if our parents had the money that some of today's .toys cost they would consider themselves very rich indeed. Nevertheless we were very happy and very excited about Christmas. In fact we'd be counting the weeks and days for months beforehand.

A few days before Christmas the grocery boy would arrive in a horse and cart or dray as a horse cart was called at that time. Before he came into the house he would hang a little bag of oats on the horse's head to keep him quiet while he was coming into the house. He would then carry a large box in and put it on the table. There was always a huge big coloured candle in it. There would also be currants and raisins, spice and candied peel. All the ingredients for the pudding and cake. Next day my mother made a big fire in the grate and hung on the pot-oven, then she made the cake and put it in the pot. The lid would be put on then and lots of red hot embers piled on top of it. I always loved the smell of the cake baking in the pot-oven and I can still remember the raisins bursting up through the top of the cake when she raised the lid. We usually gathered sticks in the woods for the baking. During the previous week my mother would have white-washed the kitchen walls. On Christmas Eve my mother or father would go out to the woods and bring in great bundles of holly and ivy. This my mother would put up behind the pictures and on top of the dresser.

Before Christmas too an old man often came, he carried a bag on his back. We called Martin McCann the Rabbit Skin Man. We called him that because he collected dried out rabbit skins and my parents kept some for him if they had any. We were always very excited to see him. He would reach down into his bag and bring out Christmas decorations and pictures called Mottos. The pictures usually had a black shiny background. Some had a picture of Santa Claus with lots of holly and berries and the words 'A Merry Christmas'. There was one I'll always remember. It was a picture of a beautiful woman with lovely children around her and the words 'What is Home without a Mother?' As it was always near night when the old man arrived, my parents would let him stay overnight, sitting by the fire in a big chair. He would start off again on the road next morning after he had something to eat and a cup of tea. My mother would then tack up the new pictures on the clean white wall.

Well, all was ready for Christmas and Santa Claus which made us very excited. We always went to bed early on Christmas Eve and after we were tucked in, our Mammy came in and gave us a small drop of sherry out of an egg cup, I'm sure she thought it would put us off to sleep quickly. One time one of my sisters, who was always thinking of food, said 'Thanks Mammy and I wish you a Happy Christmas Dinner'. On one occasion I couldn't go to sleep for a while so I was still awake when my mother tiptoed into the room and rummaged in the press for a few minutes. I didn't let her see that I was awake so I saw her putting a Christmas stocking on my bed and the same on my sister's bed.

It was then I remembered that I had seen her hurrying into the room with something out of the grocery man's box under her apron. I didn't tell my sisters about my secret. But it made me love and appreciate my mother a lot more because I noticed how tired she looked. It was also out of the box she got the sherry. There was also a small bottle of whiskey and some bottles of stout and a Christmas Brack in it. They were presents from the Grocer. They were called 'The Christmas Box'.

On Christmas morning itself we all had to be up early as the first Mass was at seven o'clock and it was four miles to the chapel. It was a novelty having the oil lamp lighting in the morning time as it was usually only lit at night but it was still so dark at six o'clock in the morning. For dinner we seemed to have a lot of food on our plates, and my father would have a bottle of stout with his dinner as a special treat. We'd have fowl and stuffing and bacon or ham and H.P. sauce. I always remember how hot it tasted.

By the evening of Christmas Day all the little toys out of the Christmas stocking would be broken and thrown about. There would be a bugle and a tiny weighing scales, a few sweets and lots of coloured paper. Next day St Stephen's Day my father would be out working and Christmas would be over for another year.

AN EAST CORK CHRISTMAS

Sr Consiglio Murphy (b 1920)

(From a full-length autobiography), Clonpriest, Youghal, County Cork, 1920s

Christmas as I remember it nearly sixty years ago, was very different from what it is today. The Christmas spirit began with the making of the plum pudding about six weeks before Christmas. All the family gave a stir to the pudding so that nobody would die within the year! The pudding was tied up in a greased and floured white cloth and cooked for hours, then it was hung from a crook in the ceiling to season.

On the last day of school we got currants and sugar buns, sweets, apples and we sang Christmas carols. Next day we wrote our Christmas cards, and posted them for a halfpenny stamp.

A week before Christmas, Father killed three turkeys and a goose. He nailed pieces of wood together and made two strong boxes into which he placed the turkeys 'feathers and all'. The lids were nailed down, labels nailed on and the addresses of our cousins in Dublin written. Father then took them to the station to post. In return we got a huge brack about the size of a motor car wheel which was made to order by the famous Johnston Mooney and O'Brien bakers.

A few days before Christmas Mother and Father went to town in the pony and trap 'to bring home the Christmas' as the saying goes in the country. They decided whose turn it was to go with them. What a joy it was to be chosen because it meant new style

— a coat or shoes perhaps for Christmas morning Mass. Father would drive the pony and trap up one side of the street and down the other, stopping at all the shops where they usually dealt. How eyes would glisten at the dazzle and glitter, the tinsel and the lights, the cakes and sweets. In every shop we got a present, a barm brack from the baker, a cake and candles from the grocer. A large tin of bulls-eyes from the tobacconist, meat from the butcher, a calendar from the chemist, and so on. We were left sitting in the trap while Mother and Father bought Santa's presents. When time permitted we went into a tea shop for tea and hot crumpets. All of this time the pony stood still outside the shops — no parking signs or fines to push him on, and no car horns to startle him. By the time our shopping ended all the gas lamps were lit. What a fairyland of gold and glitter to feast the eyes of a country child, who only had an oil lamp and candles at home. Then homeward we would trot, tired but happy. The whole family would be out to meet us and to carry in the spoils. Mother would grab Santa's presents and hide them, as eight lively children unwrapped all the parcels.

A few days before Christmas decorations were put up. Sprigs of red berry holly were put into every crevice in the woodwork of the dresser. Ivy was draped over the pictures. The crib with the infant in it was set up in the hall, decorated with holly, tinsel and cotton wool.

On Christmas Eve the kitchen was a hive of activity. All helped Mother to stuff the turkey and goose. Father took the best home cured ham from the crook on the ceiling. Mother cooked and skinned it, covered it with breadcrumbs and toasted it in front of the open fire. Ned our workman got his week's wages which amounted to 8s 6d, but Mother secretly added to it that day without telling Father. Ned dressed for town, promising to bring us presents. He arrived home that night — merry or 'maic go leor' and true to his word with a Christmas stocking and sweets bulging out of his pockets.

The Christmas candle was placed in a hollowed out turnip, decorated with tinsel and holly and placed on the window facing the road, the door was left unlocked and food left on the table, to welcome the Holy Family and to light them on their way. After nightfall Mother would fill a basket with fruit, brack, tea and sugar and take it to a poor neighbour down the road. All would sit round the open fire telling stories, Father would read the paper and Mother would air the clothes. The Rosary was said and before going to bed the grown-ups would drink hot punch and the children a little wine and rich cakes. Stockings were hung up on the crane near the fire and sixpence left for Santa.

On Christmas morning all were up before dawn. Father tackled the pony, Mother huddled us into the trap and off to Mass we went fasting. On the way as we passed the neighbours on foot, Father would shout, 'Happy Christmas', and they would shout back, 'the same to you and many of them'. The church glittered in candle and lamp light. The singing was heavenly and as we streamed out of the church after Mass all greeted each other.

Home again the fun began. Santa's presents were opened. Father cut the famous ham. Mother made the tea. The ham was delicious, the likes of it have never been reproduced by any factory. While dinner was prepared we played 'tig' around the hay sheds. Dinner was always in the parlour that day. Wine and cake were served after dinner. The postman came in at dinner time. He joined us for a glass of whiskey, a tip and a chat. If he brought the 'American parcel' we could not wait for him to go — to open it. The silks, the satins, the necklaces, the brooches, the high heeled shoes with the peaky toes! There was a fashion parade and much laughter as the boys fitted on the lady's style and modeled them to the amusement of our parents. Ludo or draughts were played that night, Father read the Cork 'Holly Bough' and records newly bought by Mother were played on the gramophone. Nobody went visiting that day and no visitors came. It was a day for the family.

On St Stephen's Day all the family slept late, often it was the singing of the wren boys that aroused us. They sang 'the wren, the wren' over and over, they were lucky to get a penny or twopence each and be on their way. The local coursing was the attraction that day. Once dinner was over the whole family went to it.

Two events stand out in my memory of Christmas time. Mother would send us with gallons of milk to the neighbours nearby where there were many children and bottled milk was not ever heard of at that time. In return they gave us slices of rich cake or plum pudding. Mother would chide us saying, 'you took more from those good people than you gave!' The second memory I have is that there were no dance halls as such near home at that time. We had our own dances, the neighbours gathered in, someone played the melodeon and we danced half sets, jigs and reels until morning. Tea, wine and spirits were served to all. The Hunt Ball dance was held in Monatrae Hotel, Youghal on New Year's Eve. Our older sisters went, we curled their hair with a hair tongs — heated in the fire, they wore full length silk or satin frocks and as we watched them go we felt like Cinderellas.

Visiting the neighbours went on all during Christmas and anyone who called got a glass of whiskey or wine and before drinking it, he always said, 'Sláinte', and having drunk it he said, 'Go mbeirimíd beó ar an am seo arís'.

As the lights of our streets and Christmas candles glitter once more may the light and peace of Jesus light up our hearts, with love for all, but especially for the poor, the old and the lonely. The gifts of Christmas are merry and beautiful and of them all, the sweetest the finest and the most precious is truly the gift of LOVE.

TAWS AND MEBS

Gerry Fehily (1916 – 94)

Donnybrook Village, Dublin

In the weeks before Christmas we were always taken to town to visit the shops, wonder at all the marvellous toys, and of course, tell Santa what we wanted! After tea on Christmas Eve, the youngest child in the family lit the Christmas Candle, which was placed in the window or the porch. Every house had a candle, and it was a beautiful sight to walk along the road after dark and see all the little flames shining so brightly and so welcomingly. We children went to bed early, and hung our stockings at the ends of our beds. Next morning, there was always an orange, an apple and two bright pennies in each stocking!

The sort of toys we got were a lot different too. There were paint books, and paints of all colours in a lovely metal box; Meccano sets which you put together yourself; Hornby train sets with clockwork engines, carriages and tracks; storybooks; jigsaws, and transfers which we stuck onto paper, or into albums. We swopped transfers too if we had two of the same kind — sometimes you could get two for one of yours if you had specially good ones!

What did we do on Christmas Day? Well if the weather was fine we went for a walk before dinner. Usually our relations came to visit in the afternoon, and we played musical chairs with our cousins, while somebody played the piano. We also played games like Ludo or Snakes & Ladders, and sometimes Hide and Seek all over the house.

On St Stephen's Day, the Wren Boys always came round and entertained us, and got rewarded for their trouble! During the

Christmas holidays we were always treated to the Pantomime, and to the pictures. The pictures were silent in those days, and a pianist played all during the showing. The words came up on the screen and everybody read them out loud. We really took part in the whole performance.

As there was no television, or even radio, we played a lot with our toys during the holiday, and made our own fun. On fine days, we had plenty to do outside. Our games included spinning tops, which you kept spinning by using a little whip; hoops, which were old bicycle wheels without spokes which you rolled along the road with a small stick. If you had a wheel with a tyre, you were *very* posh! There were always marbles too; the large ones were called TAWS and the small ones MEBS, but we only played during the Marble Season. There was a Chestnut Season too (called CONKERS) and that was autumn, of course.

Now that you have read all this, you can see that Christmas in the 1920s was a great time for a child!

'BEST PUDDIN' EVER, MAGGIE'

Billy French

Crumlin Village, Dublin, 1930s – 40s

Christmases today seem to come around with ever-increasing speed and they always stir up memories. My own recollections of growing up in Crumlin village in the late thirties and early forties are varied, but remain fixed in my mind.

I remember the kindness of Frank Gaffney, the head master of our National School, giving each boy in his class, irrespective of merit, a toy or game on the last day in school before the Christmas Holidays. For he knew, more than most, that there were some homes in the village and surrounding district where Santa Claus could not afford a visit.

Festival preparations in our home were launched a week or two beforehand, when my father took down from the bedroom walls the several large pictures which included the 'Mother of Sorrows' and 'Daniel O'Connell' and edged them with gold paint. This was before the invasion of Christmas trees and electricity, yet nothing has ever equalled that reflective glow when the rooms were lit by the fire.

Then there was sitting up with my mother late into the night and early morning, keeping the turf fire going as she boiled the large Christmas pudding in a pot on the black-leaded open range.

Afterwards it was hung up in its cloth, only to be ceremoniously taken down a few days before Christmas, when my father would officially taste it. For a man who had a great command of the English language, his verdict was always the same. 'The best puddin' ever, Maggie', he'd say, washing it down with the customary bottle of stout while we looked on with mouth-watering envy.

My mother, like all the other women in the village, washed the clothes in a galvanised bath complete with scrubbing board and scrubbing brush, in water carried from the village pump. But at Christmas time she allowed herself the luxury of a laundry service, or 'bag-wash', as it was called. This consisted of putting as many articles of clothing as possible in a pillow-case and having them collected and delivered by the 'White Swan Laundry' in their decorative carts with well-groomed horses.

Every Saturday I would go into Thomas Street with my mother to get the weekly shopping. But on the Saturday before Christmas, we were all brought into the 'real town' — that was Henry Street and O'Connell Street — to get a parcel from Santa Claus ... When one considers that there were eight of us at home, that my mother was a full-time housewife, and that my father was only earning £3 10s a week, this surely must have been one of the miracles of Christmas.

Christmas Eve was spent cleansing the soul in confession before cleaning the body in the large bath in front of the fire, hanging up our stockings, then with a last shout up the newly-swept chimney to remind Santa not to forget us, we dragged ourselves to bed, too full of apprehension and excitement to sleep.

As Christmas Eve was a fast day, my father being from the Liberties, would stay up till after midnight to eat the giblets of the turkey, an old Dublin custom, while my mother placed a lighted candle in the window.

Christmas morning brought squeals of delight as we discovered our presents in the early morning light, dolls for the girls and wind-up toys for us boys. After Mass we came home to a large fry.

Then as my mother busied herself in the kitchen my father, after helping to tidy the house, would entertain the visitors, mostly neighbours, friends and relations, all male, who would drink each other's health many times ... Then it was a 'must' for us to go with our father up to the old graveyard of St Mary's before dinner to pray at the grave of my two brothers, who had both died of pneumonia.

At dinnertime the turkey held pride of place on the table, flanked on one side by a Christmas cake and on the other by a bottle of port, compliments of our landlord and village grocer.

Christmas dinner in our house was unique because that was the only time my mother sat down to eat dinner with us and that made our Christmas very special.

St Stephen's Day brought the Wren Boys with their gaily coloured bush, going from door to door singing and dancing and in between lamenting the fate of the 'wren, the wren, the king of all birds, who on St Stephen's Day was caught in the furze ...'. Then we youngsters would congregate outside St Agnes' Church to see the weddings and join in the 'grush' — this was the traditional throwing of money by the best-man. The amount you collected would determine whether you went to the Rialto, Leinster or the Sundrive cinema. For to gain admittance into the first two you needed the princely sum of four-pence, whilst the Sundrive, or 'bower' as we called it, had its 'tuppeny rush' where, when the doors were opened, one was physically carried in on the backs of young screaming demons, who already had forgotten the real message of Christmas.

'HOLLY PUX'

Phyllis McDermott (b 1926)

Longwood, County Meath, 1930s

Enclosed is my real-life story as it was for me and mine of Christmas long ago. I am sixty-five years old now but still long for those happy times and for me, Santy Claus still lives on.

It was magical and full of mystery and though in a way somewhat scary to a young child's mind, Christmas long ago was absolute bliss. Mammies and daddies in those days did not know Santa Claus by his first name nor had they been to school with him, nor did he visit shops in our village in November.

No, Santy came down the chimney on Christmas Eve, filled our stockings with goodies, drank his bottle of stout and ate his slice of cake and was gone again almost in a flash — for another year.

We were good as could be all Christmas week because we were

told 'Holly Pux' Santy's friend would be sitting on the chimney watching us and if you were bold then Santy would not come.

On Christmas Eve from dusk onwards there was this eerie feeling. We were terrified to look out (much less go out) for fear we came face to face with this strange old man. Living in the country as we did — all thirteen of us — made it all the more haunting, there being no street lights and the only indoor lighting was that which shone from an oil lamp hung on the wall.

Having to go out in the yard to get water or turf for the fire was a frightening ordeal because every shadow you saw you imagined it was HIM. We were given our tea early and sent off to bed and when the candle was blown out we used to close our eyes tightly and bury ourselves under the clothes. Not a word would be spoken between us in case Santy might come early — not so much that he would see us — as that we would see him.

We would have written our letters to Santy several months before and put them up the chimney for Santy to collect so as he had plenty of time to sort out for each of us what we asked him for. We did not always get all we had asked for but at least being good proved we deserved something.

Christmas day in our house then started ever so early, and no doubt very, very noisy as well. I can almost still hear the sound of the merry-go-round, the bugles, the tin whistles and all the other 'rattly' toys we got from Santy and then the delight in the new socks, the gloves, and above all the lovely new smell of the three little hankies, each one with its own little rhyme written on it. I remember one rhyme so very well because it used to break my heart when I would read it.

> I had a little pony, his name was Dapple Grey
> I lent him to a lady, to ride a mile away
> She whipped him and she slapped him
> And she drove him in the clay
> I would never lend my pony now
> For all the lady's pay.

I fondly remember too the lovely sweets Santy brought us — you would never see those sweets anywhere else. No, those were Santy sweets and they looked and tasted like Santy sweets and they were wrapped in Santy's tinsel paper and on Christmas morning coming home from Mass you might even find one of Santy's sweets which fell out of his sack as he went on his way.

FINDLATERS' HAMPER

Joan Maguire (b 1931)

Inchicore, Dublin, 1940s

I'm a grandmother of sixty-three years of age. I'd like to share some of my childhood memories of Christmas with you. I can remember going into town with my mother, sister and brother, about four weeks before Christmas to look at the shop windows all dressed up with the Christmas toys. We would pick out the gift we would like from 'Santa'. Mother would say 'if you are good Santa might bring you a surprise too'. We would look forward to meeting 'Santa' at our Christmas Party in the Army Barracks as our Dad was a soldier and cook there. Dad never sat at our Christmas dinner table at home as he was always working on Christmas Day cooking Christmas dinner for the soldiers. But he always made our Christmas cake. It was special as Christmas Eve was my mother's birthday and I can still picture the writing on top of the cake in red icing 'Merry Christmas and Happy Birthday'. About two weeks before Christmas a big hamper would arrive at our house; a lady my mother worked for always sent it. It was from a big store called Findlaters (long since gone). It would have all kinds of food in it: Christmas pudding, ham, Christmas crackers, tin of chocolate biscuits and fancy biscuits too, tea, jams, mince-meat, dates, fruit and the Big Red Christmas Candle, down at the end of the big box we would find a tin of sweets and our three Christmas stockings with our names on them. That night we would have a little party. We would put out the light in our kitchen and light the small candles on our wee Christmas tree; it stood in the centre of our table, it was not very high (by the way candles were in holders, I still have three of them). Visiting the crib in Inchicore Church was always a treat for us, it was really beautiful, as children we thought the figures were almost real. I suppose the best part of Christmas was sitting by the open fire with our Granny, she always came up from the country to spend her Christmas with us, she would tell us of her childhood Christmas.

CHRISTMAS — THEN AND NOW

Ernest M. A. Scott (b 1929)

Christmas Rhymers (Mummers), Ballynure, Ballyclare, County Antrim

Ah! Sweet shades of Christmas long ago
When Faith was Faith and not all show,
No tree, well lighted in corner there
But trusty lantern in kitchen bare,
The open fire with beech log hissing
No mistletoe used then for kissing,
The dresser sparkling with well-shone plate
While out in the loanin' beyond the gate
Footsteps are heard and the dogs start up
And sharpest of all is the wee collie pup,
The latch is lifted, a figure appears
In a slouch hat and coat right up to its ears,
In a loud voice demands room there to rhyme
And the children all rush to Mother's apron in time.
St George's broad sword turkey champion soon lays low
And eventually all come to the end of the show.
Soda farls and oatcake from the harning iron lifted
With country butter over all, leaves each player well gifted.
A box is produced and the good farmer then speaks
Thanking all for the show, puts his hand in his breeks
For some silver there sought, for the unfortunate plight
Of a labourer laid low with no income in sight.
For these were the days of no crime, just compassion
For the destitute poor in those days, before fashion
Highjacked the Spirit of Christmas, putting all behind bars
To wrestle with computers and Ronald Reagan's Star Wars.
Lord! give me the Christmas of childhood again
And thy praises I'll sing for ever. Amen.

Note: A harning iron – a hardening 'board' put on hearth to 'cool' oatcakes

A CRADLEBIRD

Nellie Ryan

Slievefinn, County Galway, 1928

It was December 1928, a very cold frosty evening. As the school was three miles from my home, my older sister took me to and from school. This was a very special evening as we got our Christmas holidays. We walked through the wood looking at the icicles on the trees and looking at the birds trying to get something to eat, twittering. We came from the wood to a garden in the neighbourhood. We saw a robin caught in a cradlebird. (A cradlebird was used to catch birds for people's dinners). My sister opened the cradlebird and let the bird go free. That made us both happy.

Our house looked so beautiful decorated with holly and berries. I felt so excited thinking of Christmas and wondering if Santa would come at all.

The following day was Christmas Eve. My mother had stuffed the goose. I helped her make the pudding. My father cut a turnip in half and put a red candle into it. We were all called and asked to bless ourselves and say the prayer we had said every night during the month of December.

My father asked my brother, 'did you give extra straw for the bedding of the cows and horses?'. My brother said yes and asked me if I would like to see how comfortable the animals were. Yes, indeed, they looked happy in all that extra straw.

Now it was bed time, my sister and I shared a room upstairs. We talked about Christmas and Santa. Suddenly we heard a quick step on the stair and then my Uncle Dinny appeared in the room and lo! he had a large Christmas stocking for me. Inside there were twelve candles every colour and a sconce for the candles to burn in.

Now my day was made. My sister and I had so much fun lighting one candle at a time for the twelve days of Christmas. It was the happiest day of my childhood, a memory I shall never forget.

GRANNY LOOKS BACK

Eileen Tansey (1903 – 85)

Ballitore, County Kildare, 1930 – 40s

The other day I watched one of my sons smuggling an assortment of wrapped-up toys of all shapes and sizes into the boot of his car. The sight brought back memories of Christmas thirty or forty years ago.

The children in bed at last on Christmas Eve, their stockings draped on chairs around the fireplace, with names laboriously printed by themselves pinned on, cakes and wine left by their instructions for Santa's refreshment, our own particular thrill as we laid out the toys, whispering in case an over-excited child might be awake in the room above us.

Then our awakening in the half-dark next morning by loud noises off stage, no lights for switching on that time, the burst into our bedroom, the jubilant cries 'Look what I got. Daddy, look at this ... Mammy look at that'.

And not least in their happiness was the exploration of the stockings, an apple, an orange, a small bottle of lemonade, a hankie perhaps for the girls and penknives for the boys, and tucked away in the toe, a few chocolates and a sixpenny bit.

And had Santa eaten the cake? Of course he had. 'But how did he know I wanted a doll?' How indeed, for how would anyone think she would when she had nine others in various stages of disintegration, but want it she did. God knows our children did not get all that much; but I believe they got as much pleasure from Santa's gifts as their own children do nowadays from toys costing ten or twenty times more.

I remember the pride of our eldest son on a clumsy old trike, bought secondhand and repainted by his father.

Among the toys there was always a Jack-in-a-box, a monkey on a stick, a game of Ludo or Snakes and Ladders, and above all — a bugle. A Christmas in which there would be no blowing of a bugle would somehow have lacked the final touch of magic. For when all is said and done, the real magic of Christmas is to be found in the homes where the children still believe in Santa.

As my son banged down the lid of the boot, and gave evasive answers to inquisitive little questioners in the back seat, I was Oh! so thankful that history of that kind was repeating itself, and I prayed that these same questions would be given the same answers in twenty years time.

ROWING TO CHRISTMAS MASS

Ann McGuire (b 1928)

County Galway, 1930s

Looking forward to the great feast of Christmas we were all happy and could not wait for the day. Everyone rallied around making sure everything was clean and in order. There were six children, five girls and one boy. The dad made sure the house was newly thatched and the older children got all the outer walls of the house and chimney top whitewashed. The lining of the chimney too was cleaned from all soot, in case Santa should get blackened. Even though he seldom brought more than oranges and sweets. Inside the house was painted, the wooden kitchen table scrubbed white and clean. All the bedrooms made neat and tidy and the curtains washed and starched and hung inside the sparkling window panes. Even the brass door knobs were not forgotten, they too were made shiny and bright.

The goose was killed, plucked and cleaned and left ready for cooking for Christmas Day dinner. All the shoes were polished and shone as they were left in a row according to the seniority of the person. On Christmas Eve everyone went to Confession making sure the soul too was fresh and clean for Mass and Holy Communion on Christmas Day.

All the animals got a special treat. The cows got a sheaf of oats as well as their usual stall of hay. Neither was the donkey forgotten (he was very special) as the cross on his back was the reminder to everyone of the Cross Jesus carried to Calvary. Also it was the donkey carried Mary to Bethlehem before Jesus was born. Therefore, he was given a very large sheaf of oats.

A light, but much deserved supper was relished by all, as Christmas Eve was a Fast Day. Seed cake was a special treat.

A lighted candle was placed on every window, and the front door was left open, just in case a stranger wanted shelter. The big open fire blazed as the father sat and enjoyed his well deserved bottle of stout. Mother would sit and read a story while we all sat round listening. We all knelt around the fire and said the Rosary before going to bed.

The biggest treat was still in store. Rising at 3 a.m. everyone dressed in their Sunday best. Making our way, guided by the reflection of light from the sea and moon, we rowed our boat to the mainland and happily walked the remaining three miles to Church. Making sure to arrive there before the last bell tolled for

Mass. We always stayed on for the three Masses on Christmas morning. The carol singing and the organ playing and the soft glow from the numerous candles lighting made all so heavenlike. Meeting all the people and exchanging greetings, will never be forgotten, as 'Happy Christmas' echoed along the road home.

SOULS AS WHITE AS SNOW

Anon.

North Cork rural area, early 1940s

Thoughts of childhood Christmases rekindle a warm glow
As I recall the magic of those days so long ago.
The atmosphere within our home of happy expectation –
Of all the joys that lay ahead, so filled me with elation.
Coming up to Christmas the shopping should be done,
Which meant the then rare pleasure of a journey into town
Where mother went from shop to shop buying Christmas treats
Fruit for the cakes and Christmas 'pud', some lemonade and sweets
Bread and herbs for stuffing, biscuits, chocolate and a 'Sup' –
To celebrate 'the Christmas' and cheer the adults up.
Next preparation was confession, which enabled us to go –
To receive Our Lord on Christmas morn, with souls as white as snow.
On Christmas Eve I'd sometimes ask would Santa really come,
But I never was forgotten, I'd find presents in my room.
The turkey filled with stuffing was placed in a large pot,
With glowing coals piled round it to keep it very hot.
Soon we'd hear it sizzle as the aroma filled the air,
It was that smell reminded me that Christmas was really there.
The house festooned with holly, the crib and candle bright
Were all there to remind us of that first Christmas night.
We did not then have tinsel, baubles, lights or Christmas trees.
We had warmth, security and love in my 'Christmas memories'.

The fruit for the cake mentioned here were raisins with the seeds still in them. We children had the sticky messy job of de-seeding them but it was all part of the excitement leading up to Christmas and was willingly done. The other Christmas treats were only available to us a few times during the year and never all together, so Christmas really was a special occasion. The trip to town was a once in a year journey for the younger children and a day much looked forward to. The mode of travel was pony and trap, which was the way we travelled to Mass, Confession, visiting etc. until we eventually got a bicycle to go to secondary school.

BURYING BABY JESUS

Philomena Hill (b 1933)

Killimor, Ballinasloe, County Galway, 1945

My dad, Guard John Murphy, Killimor, Ballinasloe, died in Our Lady's Hospice, Harold's Cross, Dublin, aged fourty-four, leaving my mother, aged thirty-nine, with ten children aged two and a half to eighteen years old.

On Christmas Eve of 1945, we spent most of the day playing outdoors in the snow while Mother stuffed a goose which had hung on a nail out in the back kitchen for several days. Mrs. O'Mara had sent the goose up to her with a basket of groceries. In the basket were sweets, biscuits and a bottle of raspberry wine, and a sweet cake for all of us. Before we went to bed that night we had a small party. We prayed and asked Santa not to forget us and we asked Baby Jesus to help Santa with our toys. Mother hung up our small stocking with big safety pins on a clothes line that hung over the fireplace.

Christmas morning we were all up bright and early. We tip-toed down the stairs and crept along the hallway so as not to awaken Mother. We took down our socks, and in it was a pair of knitted socks, a few sweets and a pencil. Not one toy for any of us, not even for the baby. After dinner we went to the church with the smaller children sitting up in the big pram. We looked into the manger crib. After all our praying Baby Jesus sent us nothing so we decided to hide Him under the straw. We climbed into the crib, pulled the straw up and hid the Baby Jesus under the straw as far down as we could. We then went home satisfied that Baby Jesus was hidden away. We told Bab Flood what we had done and she just smiled. She felt sorry for us and gave us some apples and oranges. The next day we went to the church only to see Baby Jesus back in his crib again. This time we buried the Baby Jesus again, but this time we used our shoe laces and tied him to the straw so that he couldn't get out. Mother was very cross and wanted to know what happened to our laces but we never told her.

The Garda Superintendent heard about our dilemma and a few days later a phone call came to the barrack to say Santa hadn't forgotten us and a large parcel was on its way from the Guards in the Depot Training Centre in Dublin. The parcel contained a beautiful doll, with a china face, drums, bugles, games of all kinds, a big fruit cake and socks for all of us. We were overjoyed.

Baby Jesus had loved us after all, even though he was a little late. We paraded up and down the street of Killimor to the delight of Mother and neighbours. No-one could ever imagine the joy and happiness that parcel brought to Mother and her orphans.

PENNY MEMORIES

Sara Whelan

Crumlin, Dublin, 1930s – 40s

Christmas is fast approaching. This festive season brings me many memories. Our stockings were filled with little things, all costing pennies or multiples of pennies — 'Sunny Stories'; a small paperback, two pennies, a bar of chocolate, a balloon, a few sticks of chalk, perhaps an apple and an orange, and one or two pencils. Such was our lot! I remember once, in the very early hours of morning, sitting in the bed eating a stick of chalk. You see the chalk resembled small sticks of candy and in the dark it was difficult to decipher whether it was candy or chalk. What a taste, try it — I don't think it would do you any great harm!

I once went on a rare school outing to Bettystown, and my mother placed a six penny piece into my right hand, and said, perhaps you may not need to spend it, and you could bring it back to me.

This sixpenny piece left a small ring impressed in the middle of my palm as I held on to it so tightly. This sixpenny piece would be to the value of about 2½p in today's financial world, but I brought it back to mother.

We had a very old aunt of my mother's who visited us a few times a year and when she came she brought eight pennies wrapped in the corner of her handkerchief. There were four of us at the time — 2d each, if my calculations are correct! We always bought 'Spinning Tops' the edible variety and they lasted us for hours on end and gave us endless pleasure.

In winter time my husband and his brothers loved winter and the snow. You see they swept the snow from outside neighbours' houses, for which they got a few pennies, and these pennies were given to mother to help her through the week, money being scarce.

My brother was a great picture fan, in fact he was in every

cinema in Dublin. On Saturday morning he made bundles of sticks to sell in order to make up the price of the Saturday afternoon matinee, four pennies or thereabouts. Sometimes he took logs to make the 'bundles' of sticks from mother's meagre stock, and oh, was she annoyed. That was a big crime for him. I nearly forgot another episode; he played cards for 'pennies' on the side of the footpath and once landed before Mr Justice McCarthy in the famous Children's Court — you see his winnings were 3½d. His second crime!

I once got a history book for 2d. It was literally 'in bits' but to please mother and to save her expense I suffered the history gladly. I really didn't like history, so having a nice new pricey book didn't appeal to me. Today I like nice new books.

Wool could be bought for a few pence per ball, but mother, who has passed to her reward, saved all odd balls of wool to knit infant clothes for the little babies in the Coombe Hospital. She did not seem to realise that the present day infants have 'grandeur' unlike the little infants of her day.

Do our children have such memories to pass on — I doubt it. We are not showing them the two sides of life and then when necessity comes they are unable to cope because everything was made too easy.

I do not mean to go on moaning. Thankfully I have every material thing I need. Having seen the two sides of life is a very worthwhile experience. It was all part of my childhood and I'm happy to be able to write about it to pass on to you.

X

TIMES OF SORROW, TIMES OF JOY

ST. MARTIN'S NIGHT

Violet Kearon (née Massey, b 1922)

November 3rd, 1930 Courtown Harbour, County Wexford

The greatest 'belief' or superstition I remember of my childhood in Courtown Harbour is that:

No fishing boat should put to sea on a St Martin's Night because on that night St Martin comes riding on his White Horses and claims the sea and its fish for himself.

This ritual was kept all down the years and all fishing boats were tied up in the harbour until the next day. There came a year which was very bad for fishing. The wind had held in the Nor-East, and this meant rough seas and the swell in the Bar, making it impossible for the boats to go out.

The Day of St Martin's dawned; a beautiful calm morning and afternoon with a glorious sun shining. The fishermen and the old sea-dogs collogued together and eventually around four o'clock, it was decided the boats would go fishing. 'God must mean them to with such favourable weather and money was so scarce.'

The wives and young ones saw them out to sea with some trepidation; but they waved them off from the pier-heads with the usual 'God be with you'. The men called back, 'Be there at eight with the ropes'.

There is a swell usually in Courtown Bar and most nights it was needed for the non-fishermen, women and children (over seven years) to be on the pier to pull the boats safely in.

The evening stayed lovely and the boats were on their way in, earlier than expected, as they were laden with fish, when from nowhere the wind rose and the sea turned from a calm pool into a fury and the white horses were on top of the waves. The call went quickly through the village 'run for the pier' and soon the street and harbour roads, which had been empty, barring the crowd of children playing, were alive with everyone running for the two piers. (The people on the street side of the small river Bug-o-Bee went to the North Pier and those on the south side went to the South Pier). The men with heavy ropes were ahead of everyone.

Some boats were nearly in with the men bent to the oars putting their utmost into the battle against the elements. These had lowered any sail. Out went the ropes to the first boat and then it was pull for all you were worth. The heavy men were at the back, women next and we children nearest to the boat. A man held the end of each rope and threw it out to the boat and they secured it and called, 'Pull'. Both teams did and brought that boat to safe waters.

Then it was back for the next one and so it went on until the six or so small boats were safely in. There were two larger boats and they had kept their sails up (they were not the experienced local men). One was driven onto the North strand but Thank God the men waded to safety. The other boat came to the mouth of the harbour but before they could catch the ropes, she struck her bow off the North Pier. The ropes were quickly hauled back in. There was a little bit of a panic on the boat.

'Catch the ropes', went up the cry, 'and we will bring you in.' And that is what we all did. The men from the first boats had raced to help and between well-given directions, the boat and crew were brought safely into calm waters. Shortly afterwards, as quickly as it had risen, the storm died down and the white horses on the waves disappeared. Everyone gathered together on the quay, beside the boats laden with fish, bowed their heads and gave, 'Thanks to God who had saved all'.

A vow was made, 'Never again will we go to sea on a St Martin's Night'.

A MEMORY OF MY GRANDMOTHER

Agnes Lynch (b 1914)

Ballyphilip, Whitescross, County Cork, c. 1900

It was a sweltering hot day in August in the very early years of this century. All day there had been movement of cattle through the cobbled farmyard. Huge horseflies buzzed among the stables and cattle stalls. The animals were restless. They shuffled and stirred uneasily in the hay. The sun fell relentlessly on the tired man as he manoeuvred the bull from the stall.

Brigid O'Shea (1840-1920), my grandmother, looked up in alarm as a different note arose from the lowing cattle, the raucous dreaded sound of an enraged bull, maddened by heat and flies. Hastily, she ran out the porchway to meet a horrific scene: the bloodstained bull pawed the ground on which lay the helpless farmhand, tossed like straw onto the mucky stones.

The redoubtable lady ran forward, loosening her striped apron. The angry bull charged and as it did so the woman threw her wide apron over the bull's head, blinding him for a minute or two. The bull thrashed right and left in a fury of rage. Seizing the unconscious man, my grandmother pulled him with a mighty effort towards the open bull stall. Dragging the unconscious body behind her, she reached the stable in frenzied haste and slammed and bolted the door.

Out on the farm the harvest continued under the sweltering sun. The hired help stopped mid-afternoon and swilled back their cans of sugary tea, until the low pounding registered with them. To a man they rushed back to the farmyard, seizing sticks and prods on the way. The bull conquered, they opened the stall door to find my grandmother valiantly staunching the flow of blood from the farmboy's gaping wound with a flat stone.

The pony and trap brought the injured man to the North Infirmary where he was given chloroform, operated on and recovered well from the brutal tossing. He worked for a further forty years on the farm whose mistress had saved him from certain death.

MY GOLDEN TRESSES

Christina O'Brien (b 1909)

Rathmines, Dublin, 1912

It was in the year 1912, July 20th to be exact. My mother picked me up, kissed me tenderly goodbye. Amid much confusion I heard her whisper she would not be coming back. I was four years old and of course did not understand the situation as I waved farewell. Later that day my sister was born. My beautiful mother died ten days later of toxaemia. My father was working down the country and could not cope so an aunt by marriage took five of us in.

We were aged between four and eleven years. The newborn baby of the family was adopted by two well-to-do ladies and had a very comfortable life. My two brothers, two sisters and myself were put to work immediately. This aunt ran a corner shop in Rathmines and was also a cab and car proprietor. I began early, tending to and feeding the cab horses of which I was terrified, I worked in the shop and house as well. As you can imagine there was no time for any personal attention. There was a business to be run and we were useful. My aunt however got continued praise for being so generous as to give five orphans a good home.

One day my sister was told to get me ready for an outing. I remember being really excited as this was a rare treat. She took a long time brushing my long golden curls that were admired by everyone. My mother I'm told, used to wash my hair in egg yolk and rinse it in vinegar.

We arrived at the barber's shop in Rathmines. I sat watching, fascinated as my sister had her already short hair trimmed. Then, to my horror, I was lifted into a high chair. My golden cascade of curls tumbled to the floor as the razor worked over my head leaving me shorn, like a boy. The pretty doll the barber gave me did little to console me, even he looked forlorn as he swept up my hair. My sister, Lill, dared not bring me home without the job completed as she would get such a beating. I cried and cried for days on end. I remember pulling up a stool to a high mirror, trying to see where my golden tresses had gone. This was the first of many tragedies in my life and one I vividly recall, as you can imagine growing up came pretty naturally to me after that.

A BIRTHDAY TREAT

Patricia Gibson (b 1926)

Bray, County Wicklow, about 1912

My mother used to relate that her parents promised to bring her on the train to Bray to celebrate her eighth birthday. It was a lovely sunny Sunday afternoon when they boarded the train at Amiens Street station. She had never been on a train before so this was going to be a very special treat and she was looking forward to it so much. My mother related how she used to wonder at the wild flowers jutting from the grass banks as the train chugged on and on; even the dirty black smoke coming from the engine never seemed to change the colour of the flowers.

Arriving safely in Bray she remembers walking along the promenade between her parents. Her father looked so dignified with his beard and wearing his gold watch chain, while her mother looked so elegant in her bonnet and beaded cape and skirt to her ankles. In retrospect she used to say what a handsome couple they were and looking now at my grandparents' photos I can wholeheartedly agree with her.

However, as she walked between them she could feel her ringlets bobbing up and down and occasionally they would all stand and watch the huge waves crashing down on the beautiful stones on the sea shore. It was lovely breathing in the sea air as they eventually came to the cliff walk. It was a narrow walk in those days; rough stones and a wooden stake in the ground with two strands of thin wire clipped to another stake — that was the protection one had from the railway line which was several hundred feet below. A few days before their visit to Bray there had been a heavy downpour of rain making the ground soft and dangerous.

They proceeded about fifty yards along the cliff walk when my mother spotted a flower she wanted to pick. Letting go the hands of her parents she ran back and reached to pick the flower when suddenly the soft ground gave way. She grabbed onto the wire and screamed as she swung over the railway tracks. She held onto the wire for her life; her parents tried to reach out without success. For what seemed like an eternity, her father used the crook of his umbrella and slowly pulled her to safety. My mother was naturally hysterical but her parents cuddled, kissed and consoled her. Eventually they made their way back down the perilous cliff path to the safety of the sea front and brought her in for tea and cake and ice cream.

Not one word was spoken coming home in the train. She could never forget the warm hands of both parents as they held their precious daughter between them. She believed they were thanking God for saving her and were saying a silent prayer in gratitude.

My mother often related how she went out full of the joys of her birthday and came home with her eyes stinging from her crying. For many and many a year my mother had visions of herself swinging over those railway tracks and thinking of what could have been a tragic birthday.

THE 1918 FLU

Mary Killeen (born 1909)

Slievefinn, County Galway

When I was about ten years of age a terrible flu spread all over Ireland, England and the USA. Thousands and thousands died from it, especially young mothers and their babies, young men and women.

I remember my own home. I lived with my parents, grandmother and my uncle, Martin. There were six of us at that time and my mother was expecting a baby when the flu struck. It was Christmas.

All flu victims got very high temperatures and mothers-to-be died, except for my mother. My father had a high temperature and the doctor ordered him to bed. He could not go because my mother was so very ill. Both she and my grandmother were extremely ill. My grandmother could not recognise anybody and was like that for weeks. Although we expected her to die, she lived on. My uncle got the flu and only lasted three days. My grandmother never knew he was dead until he was long since buried. She was devastated when she found out he was dead (he died on Christmas Eve) and she cried for months.

A nice young man used to visit our home. There was a family a few miles from our home, a man and wife and small children; the mother was expecting a baby. The young man I mentioned was walking home from our house. As he passed this house he heard someone calling for a drink of water. Nobody wanted to visit a house where the flu was but he was brave enough to go in and give her the drink. He went to the priest's house and the priest went to them. In the morning, the man, wife and baby were dead. The remaining children were sent away.

So many young men died in our parish. I was very sick myself and wasn't expected to live. In fact, I overheard the doctor tell my father that I wouldn't live (I am now eighty-five years old!). In the USA it was desperate. People died like flies, my uncle told me years after.

The coffins were left in rows all over the graveyard. Everybody who was able to work was helping to bury the dead.

It was a desperate fever and what doctors or people didn't know until long after it was over was that the patients should have been given a cold drink of water instead of whiskey or rum which was what everybody tried to give them although it was scarce and expensive. All during this flu there was a hard frost and snow.

A DOUBTFUL HONOUR

Eileen Brennan (b 1917)

Lee Fields, Cork City, 1930

I was madly envious of my best friend Mary because she was a member of the 'Blue' Girl Guides (BPs). She had me enthralled with stories of camp fires, hikes, sausages — and most of all 'Badges' — she had loads of them stitched on her sleeves. I wanted to join the Guides but my parents said to wait, as Irish Catholic Guides were to be formed. In a year or two after the 'incident' I recall, they were formed and I must have been one of the first to enrol. The Irish Guides became known as the 'Brown' Guides.

In my eagerness to catch up with Mary's badges, I studied very hard and my Dad said it was the first time I concentrated on learning anything !!

To go back to the 'incident' — Mary one Saturday told me she was to be examined that day for a 'Gardening Badge', and would I help her. I was delighted. I was to call to her house about 12 noon as the examiner was due at 2.30. When I arrived I noted Mary had raked the area of about 10 ft square. She had placed stakes all round the outside and was in the process of looping white tape around the stakes to enclose the 'garden'. It looked very pretty. However, there was nothing growing in the plot.

Mary caught me by the hand and we set off and climbed up a huge wall which bordered their garden and a public park and garden. Her plan began to dawn on me! We proceeded to pull up plants and flowers, terrified at the same time that we'd be caught. Back over the wall and quickly stuffed in all the material we had taken. The garden was now looking gorgeous!

Promptly at 2.30 the lady examiner arrived. Mary escorted her to the garden. I was hiding behind some bushes watching and noted the lady seemed all smiles. I felt things looked good!. Mary's Mom invited the examiner to join us for afternoon tea. We could hardly contain ourselves, waiting to hear the verdict. Before she left she told Mary she was very impressed with her garden and that she had attained the high standard to be awarded the 'Gardening Badge'. We were thrilled and then tore back up the garden to remove all the plants and flowers and to bury the evidence!! What a sight — the flowers had collapsed and were lying flat on the ground. We roared with laughter when we realised that had the examiner been delayed arriving Mary would not have received her Gardening Badge!!

A MEMORY OF 'THE TALKIES'

William Downey (b 1928)

Portarlington, County Laois, 1920s – 30s

Shown lately on television was the film 'The Black Eagle'. This silent film starred the famous Rudolf Valentino and brought back a period in my childhood which I thought I had forgotten. In bringing back these memories it also brought back what now seems to have been the most laughter-filled days of my life.

Those were the days of the first talking films and as often as not, the programme included an old silent film, usually starring Charlie Chaplin. Now and again a film like 'The Black Eagle' would be included. It was reflecting on this that brought Hannah to mind. Hannah was a big woman in many ways. She usually added to her small pension by selling rabbits from door to door. Those rabbits met their death at the hands of her son, Charlie. Now, at the time I am talking about, Charlie would have been about fifteen years of age and was skilled in most forms of hunting and indeed poaching. So, often Hannah would have a nice bit of salmon for sale due to the help of her son. She would wear a shawl under which she carried an enamel basin. This basin contained whatever she had to sell. Hannah was always spotlessly clean and wore a snow-white flour-bag apron which was ironed and cleaned to perfection. Charlie was another matter. He always wore a cap with the peak down over his eyes, rubber boots with the tops turned down and a dirty long mackintosh coat. Two or more dogs of doubtful parentage were always at the heels of the boy and he always carried an ash plant. He could use this 'weapon' too, should we snigger or such as we passed him.

Well, Hannah and Charlie were nearly always together, except when Charlie was away hunting or watching the river for salmon or the like. But whatever the week brought they were always at the matinee on Sunday. The picture-house was the CYMS Hall in Portarlington, and the seats were long wooden forms stretching from wall to wall. There was a balcony too with soft seats, but that was beyond our pockets. It cost 9d to go up there, whereas we were only charged 4d on the forms. Besides, we had Hannah and Charlie as well as the characters on the screen — even Charlie Chaplin could not have have given us as many laughs. There were films shown other nights as well as Sunday night, but Hannah never went then. She had gone one night when they started, but she found that she could not enjoy the show as the older people would not allow her to comment aloud on what was happening on the screen. So she decided on the matinees on a Sunday where we, the children, appreciated her running commentary and, indeed, encouraged her to shout and make loud comments.

Another explanation is needed here. Charlie could not smoke in front of his mother, although he was never seen without a butt hanging out of his mouth while walking the fields and countryside, so he was constantly going into the toilets during the film. This added to his mother's annoyance when she needed him to read something which came up on the screen. She could read some of the words but when she got stuck on one, we would hear 'Charlie! Charlie! Where are you? What's that word? Are you gone again, are you? You and that bloody lavatory. It must be a pump you have!' She would then ask whoever was near, 'Hey, what's written there? What's happening?'

Usually they would lie to her telling her something else was going to happen — something extraordinary and probably nothing to do with the story at all. Then the fun would start — to say that we were rolling in the aisles was not telling lies, I can tell you!

I am going ahead too quickly with my tale as I should tell you something else about Hannah. She was always in her seat at least fifteen minutes before anyone else with Charlie beside her, right in front of the screen, in the front seat. She would sit herself comfortably and make a well of her apron in which she would place her twenty Woodbines, box of matches and her two bags of sweets. The sweets came in packs made up in the shape of a cone made up by the person in the sweet shop by twirling them around his finger. He would count out the sweets in twelves — twelve sweets cost 1d. Hannah always had two packets, one of 'Bon Bons' and one of 'Bullseyes'.

Then, with everything to her satisfaction she would look around at every child as they entered, and had something to say to almost each one. Our matinees usually went as follows:

'Hello young Murphy, how's your mother? Did she get you a new baby? She did — a little girl, good, good.' 'Hello Whelan, got your hair cut? About time!' 'Hey, Doyle, can you read? Come in here beside me. Here, have a sweet.' Now she would have a second reader in case she would have need of him while Charlie would be out in the lavatory. She always addressed boys by their surnames, the girls were called by their first names. 'Hello Breda, isn't your dress grand. Did your mother make it? God bless her hands — ah, she was always good on the needle. God bless her, you're a credit to her.' 'Hold it, here we go.'

She always said the latter as the lights went out for the picture to start. But she would not be quiet for long! Rudolf Valentino did not impress her at all … 'Look at him — I wouldn't trust that fellow. I don't like his eyes. Isn't the horse lovely? That animal would get home the turf in a hurry, I tell you. Charlie, wouldn't he be lovely under the trap? Charlie, Charlie, where are you? Gone again and the picture only startin'. Bad sess to the same Charlie. Sure he could not be good. What did I send him to school for at all! Them Brothers, God bless them, they were wasting their time — I suppose he spent half the day in the lavatory then too.

'Hey, young Doyle, what's that writing? Do you hear me? What does it say? Ah, blast it, it's gone now. Oh, saints preserve us, will you look at the size of the bed! Begob, it's as big as a hurling field! Oh, Oh, does he blow a whistle to get things started? Oh, you're back again are you? Mind me auld corns will you? There now, sit still for a while till I look at this wan. Well I declare to God, will you look at her, hardly a stitch on her and the frost we had last night. Oh, here's your man! Will you look at him and the walk of him — sticking his chest out, like an auld turkey cock. Aha, he uses the Cherry Blossom polish I can tell you. Charlie, didn't I tell you you can't beat Cherry Blossom? Hold it, they're going to dance.' Then raising her voice: 'Give us a hornpipe love, 'tis you have legs for it.'

'Isn't her hair lovely? Terrible pity she hasn't herself covered and not have all them auld fellows gawking at her. Whisht! Whisht! He's lifting her up on the horse. Not a bother to him. Now that's good of him. Sure she'd ruin her good shoes on the road. Do you remember Charlie, what happened meself the day I wore my Sunday shoes up the bog! I'll never forget it, so I won't. Yes, well maybe I blemt him in the wrong, but may God forgive me, I don't like his eyes.' She spells out letters which have appeared on the screen 'I L-O-V-E Y-O-U. Oh, he says that he loves her. Watch out for him daughter, I would not trust him, I don't like his eyes. Just because he gave you a jaunt on the auld horse. Oh, sweet heart of Jesus, they're robbing the bank. Merciful Lord, they've shot the man!'

'Charlie, did you see that did you? They've left him lying on the ground, bleeding like a pig! Not one of them even saying an Act of Contrition in his ear. They're getting away. The Lord protect us all, what's the world coming to?

'Oh, look at your man getting out of bed, look at the knees of him and him in a nightshirt. Oh, merciful hour, I'd love to see your father in a getup like that. Ha, ha! Charlie, Charlie what does that writing say? Saint Anthony, he's gone again. Look! They're breaking down the door. Well God forgive them. Sure if it freezes tonight she'll get her death! They're crossing the river, aren't they lucky they didn't try it last week when we had all that rain and it was flooded, must have been the worst weather I can remember. The bloody County Council's no good either, you'd think they would dam it. Charlie, Charlie! Who'd believe it, he's gone again! Well, if I'm not to be pitied with that scamp. Pity he would not stay in the bloody lavatory and give me a bit of peace. Hey, young Downey, what does that say? Oh, never mind. Do you want a fag? No? Ah, maybe you're right. Where are me matches? Will you look at that street, must be the main street in New York. Look at them motor cars! There's a bus. Not one of them wearing a cap, would you believe it, all hats! The speed of them, see, the policeman has to tell them the way to go! God help us all this day, it must be a terrible place on a fair day. Blessed Mother, will you take a look at her hair, it's ruined. Oh, Saint Brigid help us, he's choking her. Will someone stop him? Charlie, Charlie, get your stick. God help me if he's not gone again. Hey you, if my Charlie was here he'd fix you! You're nothing but a guban to do that to the girl and she after doing a hornpipe for us and all. Anyway I knew nothing good would come out of her trotting around half naked.

'Hold on, here comes shiny shoes! He'll save her, good man yourself. Give it to him! Ha, ha. That's the stuff. Isn't that the pity, he's after tearing his shirt, a good shirt it was too. He'd pay a quare penny for that in Lee's I can tell you. Will you look at the lovely baby, a fine child God bless it! Must be six months old. Mary help us, will you look at that pram! I declare I never seen the like of that. Don't them women have it easy, when you think of us. God help us. Look, look, she's given it one of them bottles, well God forgive you. You hussy, why don't you feed the child right, there's enough of you in it, as anyone can see. Shut up, Malone! I'll tell your mother what you said! Here, do you want a bullseye, it's the last one left? It'll keep your dirty mouth full. You know more than your prayers, I'm telling you.

'Charlie, are you there? What's that you're eating? Oh, the best of beef, I'd bet. No rabbits for that lot. Will you look at what they're drinking, the size of the glasses. Sissies, you'd think that they would have a bottle of stout or a pint. Sure all the men I know do have a pint, but there's no minding that lot. The women going around stripped, shiny shoes on your man. You'd know he never done a day's work in his life. God forgive him. And the way she fed the baby, should be enough for anybody. God forgive her. That's all I can say. Charlie come on, it's over. Your father will be waiting. Where are you Charlie? God help me, he's gone again!'

Silent films, how are you? Hannah, I award you your well-deserved Oscar.

THE ARRANMORE DISASTER 1935

Jimmy 'Annie' O'Donnell (1924 – 94)

November 9th, 1935, County Donegal

You didn't forget your wireless — Paddy teases Eamon Ward, who is helping Mickie Gallagher make the sails ready.

'No, I did not forget, I have it up there in the bow, beside John Rodgers.' Under full sail they set off from Burtonport Pier, at half past five in a Nor-East wind.

They chatted happily of events in Scotland and at home and of people they knew. The young teased each other about the girls they had dated, or had not as the case was. Others talked about the high price of £1 5s they had paid for the suits they were wearing. They spoke of the latest styles in caps, which they all wore. Some liked the Mossend peak, which the wearer bent in half downwards, others liked the old style where you took newspapers and packed them into the crown of the cap to raise it higher. This style was called the Paisley crown.

The young girls sat huddled together, talking about the dresses they would wear to Neily Boyle's dance hall, and who they would dance and flirt with. They laughed as they discussed how all the young girls in Scotland wore make-up, powdering and painting their faces and using lipstick. They all thought that these changes would never come to Arranmore. It was all right for them to use a little powder on their faces whilst in Scotland, but never lipstick and no make-up while at home.

The older men talked nostalgically of those they had met in their youth, from Achill Island and the Rosses, of the fighting men and the great fights they had witnessed, of how the men of their youth were better, bigger, stronger and more handsome than the present. The women were also described glowingly as more attractive and beautiful. Everything was better, or so it seemed.

The small red sailboat set off with her cargo of twenty happy souls, all looking forward to being reunited with their loved ones on the island. They had spent their summer dreaming of them.

Their island home lay in the distance. An island of much beauty and gentleness, its people open and friendly. In the summer time, the calm surrounding sea is like a mirror and the waves lap gently on its strands. Small fields of corn and potatoes climb up the hillside and around them miles of stone walls dug from the land over the centuries. The white-washed cottages sat snug and warm that Sunday evening waiting for the returned emigrants.

They sailed into the South Channel between Duck Island and Rutland, heading towards the stream rocks. With eagerness in their eyes and laughter on their lips they anticipated their welcome.

The wind was getting stronger. Edward took his oilskin jacket and reached over to Hannah saying, 'There's a heavy hailstone shower coming, put this over your head.'

> The wind is fair and the sails are full
> The waves lap gently on the wooden hull
> You sit down low in that little boat
> Your curly head covered in your father's old coat
>
> Will you always be sixteen and never grow old
> Tonight will you sleep in a bed that is cold
> Hannah, have no fear of the danger ahead
> For tomorrow the island will be mourning its dead
>
> Last summer in June when you went away
> You cried that night and all the next day
> You wished and you prayed to be home again
> As you worked in the cold, the mud and the rain
>
> The hailstones crash on the wooden boat
> And hurt your hands as you hold your coat
> There's a crashing roar, a shout, a cry
> In the icy waters you must die
>
> Your mother is waiting to welcome you home
> But tonight you must sleep on the rocks and the foam
> Can you see in the distance your own Aphort shore
> On the isle of your dreams, your beloved Arranmore.

The wind increased and the hailstones were bigger. 'Mickie!' Edward shouted to his son, 'take the sprit out of the sail, we are travelling too fast in this hailstone shower. I can't see a thing from here. Someone call to John Rodgers on lookout in the bow there, if he can see any landmarks. We can't put about here and anchor until the shower is over, it's too dangerous in this northerly wind.

If the tide wasn't so high it would be breaking here.'

It grew darker and the heavy hailstones made a deafening noise against the sail and the side of the frail twenty-four foot boat.

'If only we were a little later, we could have sheltered at Rutland Island until the shower was over, or if we were earlier we would have passed those dangerous rocks and be in the safety of Illion Bay and on towards Aphort Pier,' Edward told Paddy who was sitting near him on the steer beam.

'Lower the sails, we are going on the rocks!' shouts John Rodgers from the bow.

Men shouted and cursed, women screamed and cried. Some tore frantically at the sails.

Edward turned the helm to put the boat about, as she slid over a large rock. The steer caught and was torn off. The following wave caught the boat broadside, capsizing her to port among the rocks. The loud screams, the desperate shouting of men and women for a few short moments were silenced quickly in the icy waters, where they struggled for their lives for a short time before disappearing below the surface of the sea, their lives lost for eternity. Some clung desperately to the upturned boat prolonging their lives for a little while longer.

Young and old, a happy bunch of carefree people had been looking forward to their homes on the island. They had dreams of richer lives and better days ahead but they ended on the 'Clutch Rocks' shortly before six o'clock that Saturday evening, the 9th of November 1935, only a short distance from their homes, where that night there were beds made but not slept in, meals cooked but never eaten. What should have been a joyous night would be one of sorrow and heartache by dawn when the living would search among the rocks for the remains of the dead.

From the author's book of the same name which he had published locally

NEW RUBBER BOOTS

Liam F. Derham (1927 – 92)

Skerries, County Dublin, early 1940s

The time was the early forties; the place a sea-side town. As a boy of eleven years of age, the abiding ambition in my life was a pair of Wellingtons. World War Two raged and rubber was

scarce but somehow or other I badgered my mother into buying
them for me even though money was also scarce. My father was
against rubber shoewear of any type, he would say 'they do not
allow children's feet to breathe'. He agreed rubber was fine for bicycle tyres! I was cunning enough to keep them out of his way
and my mother's strict instructions were that they should be
worn only when it was raining — somehow or other the logic was
that rain on the outside of rubber boots allowed a child's feet to
breathe. It did not rain for two whole weeks, unusual because it was
early spring.

In those years before chemical farming the toilers on the land
gathered seaweed from the strands and used it as a very effective
natural fertilizer. Three young farmers, against the advice of their
elders, ventured out to an island which at low tide was connected by
a very uneven causeway to the main shore. They travelled over this
rough terrain by way of horse and cart. The day was full of residual
winter tracery — a very bleak north-east wind blew strongly and
steadily and whilst the sky contained little heavy cloud, there was a
certain threatening greyness.

The afternoon of that day saw an end to my patience. I just had
to wear my rubber boots and despite the absence of rain I per-
suaded my mother that they must be tested as to whether they
were waterproof. She accepted my logic that to walk in water at
the sea edge was the obvious test. I proudly trundled my way up
and down on the sea edge daringly going right out to where there
was a grave danger that the very choppy sea might overspill into
the boots. Whether through fear or pure luck I avoided such a
ducking. I was absolutely elated and quite mesmerised by the
whole experience and indeed I felt very grown up. Glancing back
to the shore I was aware of the horse-shoe of houses looking out
on the sea. Some few looked very much lived-in but many had
that air of inactivity so characteristic of the tall bed and breakfast
abodes which come to life only when visitors arrive to swim in
the summer months. Nearby the low lying rocks were shrouded
in sombre brown seaweed with small patches of the slimy slippery snot-green type stitched in here and there. The southern side
of the bay was guarded by a rising headland which as yet did not
have the usual Spring patchwork of ploughed and unploughed
fields. The bare black cliff face contained no light and shade effects, however minimal, owing to the absence of sunlight.

Such was my absorption I failed to notice quite a lot of activity
further up the beach until the very stiff chilly breeze brought the
sound of distant voices to my ears. On looking in that direction I
saw several knots of people searching the seashore and one rowboat

bobbed up and down some small distance out in the sea. Slushing my way in their direction I met a friend of my father who told me that the three foolhardy young farmers had drowned and to my absolute horror, he there and then deputised me to become a searcher for the dead bodies. I was terrified. However, heaven spared me — others found them. The tragedy occurred because one of the cart wheels had slipped off the edge of the causeway thereby pitching the occupants into the cold waters. Their heavy winter clothing and rubber boots gave little chance of survival, more especially because 'locals' just did not know how to swim. In their struggles they did succeed in shedding their boots but to no avail. The horse somehow separated from the cart taking one broken shaft with it still attached to its harness and swam to a rocky formation where it perched somewhat precariously awaiting rescue.

On the world's stage the flower of youth wasted in battle in Europe and Asia. To an adolescent of tender years that great awareness which is the sentinel of sanity meant that I was untouched by such tragedy. Not so on the strand that day.

Poor boys, because that's all they were, their young corpses were gently lifted onto a farm cart, covered with rough sacking and then the cart bumped its rickety way up the stony forebeach to the nearest public house, which by law had to open its doors as a temporary morgue. I followed hesitatingly in my rubber boots and stared transfixed at the three pairs of bare blue feet protruding over the back of the cart. To this day in my mind's eye I can see ever so clearly the shuffling macabre dance of death of those poor feet.

THE STORY OF JOHNNY

Patricia Gibson (b 1926)

Dublin, 1950s

This is a true story which happened many years ago. I will begin by saying that the main characters were four elderly ladies who lived in the heart of Dublin and speaking about hearts they each had a heart of gold.

Also living with them was their widowed brother Johnny. They have all passed on now but I have very pleasant memories of their friendship. They were introduced to me by my late Dad,

God rest him. We used to make an annual visit to their home early in January. What wonderful friends they had and what talent. It would have been the greatest cabaret filmed if only videos were available then. Having had a lovely meal of turkey, ham, cake and plum pudding, etc. which tasted much nicer long after we had consumed ours at Christmas, we would adjourn to the drawing room and each of the guests would perform his or her party piece in turn. My Dad would sing 'Father O'Flynn' and 'Mother Machree'. A young girl would sing and play the harp and a young man called Jimmy would take a tin whistle from his pocket. It was a joy to listen to him, not forgetting a lady who sat playing the piano all night and entertained us with her beautiful soprano voice. Yours truly obliged with a recitation or two. I will always treasure those memories.

Before leaving their house we were proudly shown what the sisters described as 'their little pet', Johnny the budgie. Having admired him, much to their delight, we would each go our separate ways only to look forward to the following year when we would all be reunited again.

However, 'twas a cold November evening when I came home from the office. My dad, as usual, had my dinner prepared. Somehow I thought he was unusually quiet. Having finished my meal and looking forward to a read of the paper and ready to settle down to watch the telly, I looked at my Dad. His face was as long as a lemon. He produced a card which had come in that afternoon in the post — it read: 'Dear Mr. Gibson and Pat, I know you will both be sorry to hear poor Johnny passed away last night. Regards Bridie'. Now we both knew their brother Johnny was attending the doctor with his 'Oul Chest' as he used to say and he always seemed to have a perpetual 'bronchial' cough.

Dad looked at me and I read his thoughts. 'So you want me to take out the bike, call to the church near where they reside and get a Mass card for Johnny.' He nodded. I was tempted to refuse but they were such nice people, so sincere and genuine and I was pleasing Dad too.

So up on the bike and into the November fog. Then to the church, purchased the card and had Johnny's name enrolled. Arriving at the door I expected to see a card on it but then I thought they don't do things like that any more. The sisters greeted me with their usual charm, and remarked how good I was to visit them on such a cold evening. Where, I asked myself, were all the friends?, when from the upstairs room I heard ahu ahu ahu ahu ahu ahu ahu — it was Johnny coughing his lungs out. Now they weren't the type of people you could offend. I knew something was wrong but couldn't put my finger on it. All I knew was I had a card in my bag for a man who was truly alive in spite of his 'oul chest'. Supping the hot cup of tea Bridie finally said, 'You got our card?'. 'Yes', I cautiously said, 'Dad and I are so sorry'. 'I wouldn't mind', said another sister, 'Bridie had only given him fresh water and seed and when she looked in the cage about twenty minutes later, there was poor Johnny lying on his back, his two feet in the air, dead as a dodo.'

Naturally I sympathised with them. Johnny had been with them for nine years and he could perform for them, saying, 'Any water?' and 'Johnny Good Boy', and 'Hello Bridie'. He was part and parcel of their lives. The sisters were crying. I couldn't tell them why I had called so I left them and they thanked me profusely and I cycled home in the fog, totally confused and humbled.

Dad was waiting, anxious to know how I had got on and who was there. He kept going down the list of all the friends. When I could get a word in edgeways I said, 'Dad, I'm freezing cold, my journey was in vain, the deceased was Johnny the budgie. In future you'll just have to get your facts right'. Well he started to laugh convulsively, the more I pretended to be annoyed the louder he laughed. I can still hear his laughter in my ears.

'Dad, dad,' I said, 'I'd love a cup of tea and by the way you owe me ten bob for that Mass card'. And over the tea we reminisced about the four sisters and their child-like innocence.

A few months later the real Johnny died, God rest him. I couldn't find the card so up on the bike, into the Church, I called to the house. It was full of their loyal friends who were gathered round those four lovely ladies, and genuinely expressing their sympathy to them in their time of sorrow.

I quietly stood watching the scene when in a corner of the room I saw an old piece of curtain covering an empty bird cage.

The four elderly ladies were relations of Vera Lynn — 'We'll Meet Again'.

THE CLOUDBURST OF 1945

Jerry Nelius O'Connor (b 1920)

Macroom, County Cork, 1945

It was a very dark morning and the rain started to come down at about twelve o'clock as we were stacking up our turf in Paddy

O'Keefe's bog. We ran into a little hut that was nearby with other lads, as the rain came down in torrents with thunder and lightning. As time went by heavier and heavier the rain got and after about three hours we were forced to run for home under it all, just barely making the foot bridge that spanned the river Launey and as you would think, the whole place was lighting with flashes, and floods were roaring everywhere.

In the cemetery in Macroom a little iron cross marks a lonely grave. The inscription on the cross reads: 'In memory of Eileen Brock and her children Susan and James, drowned in the Launey River, on July 14th 1945.'

The following is an effort to reconstruct the events of that night of terror over fourty-eight years ago.

On Friday July 13th two caravans of travelling people arrived in Macroom, one was the Brock family, the other was the Lee family. They pitched their vans at a regular parking site on a piece of ground on the northern side of the bridge at Firville, off the Rusheen road. While the men organised the vans and horses, the women went into the town selling their wares and offering the 'services' of their profession of fortune-telling.

At about nine o'clock there was a real cloudburst along the Mushera and all the Boggeragh Mountains with thunder and lightning all night. In spite of the noise of the thunder storm and the rain, the wailing of the banshee was clearly heard in Macroom that night. In the fields, the hay was in cocks ready to be drawn home, but the floods from the hills swept these cocks before them, blocking the eyes of the bridge at Cappaleenbawn, causing the water to rise up and causing the bridge to fall. Eventually the force of the water uprooted boulders and carried them away down the valley to where the two fragile caravans stood.

In the report in the Cork Examiner, Mrs Lee said she heard the sound of gushing water at 1.00 am on Saturday morning. They thought at first it was the mill dam but soon realised the danger and called to the Brock family. The caravans were soon borne away on the crest of the flood, Mrs Lee went on to describe how James (senior) Brock swam through the river with his wife to bring her to safety but she lost hold, he swam the river several times trying to find her and the children — Susan aged three years and James aged two and a half weeks.

Other reports say that when Eileen Brock saw her baby son being swept away she left the safety of the bank in an effort to reach him in the flood. It is thought that Eileen's brother, who was also a member of the Brock household, made his way out of the caravan through the roof.

When the search for the bodies commenced the infant was the first to be found. The body was in a branch of a tree at Coolcower. The bodies of Susan and Eileen were not found until the following day. A church gate collection for the family was organised and the people of Macroom contributed £115. Members of St Vincent de Paul took care of the welfare of the family. They were housed until they were able to go back on the road again.

The cross on the grave was made in the foundry at Firville. The grave was visited for many years on the anniversary of the tragedy by Eileen's mother. Flowers regularly placed on the grave, would suggest that somebody still remembers.

A mission commenced in the parish of Aghinagh on Sunday July 15th 1945, those attending the mission had to travel in extremely difficult conditions as a result of the cloudburst.

HUNTING FOR FROGS

Jim O'Brien (b 1932)

Galbally, The Galtees, County Limerick, late 1940s

I grew up in a beautiful little village called Galbally which nestles at the foothills of The Galtees. The time is the forties, the backdrop is the aftermath of the War. Money was particularly scarce at all times and any means of raising some was as welcome as the flowers in May. I am reminded of one.

Although the country had suffered its fair share of deprivation and hardship it was taking off again. Education was to the fore and universities were filling up. We could read our daily newspaper again and one day I spotted an advertisement which read as follows: 'Male frogs required to aid research. Good prices paid for suitable specimens. Send to Biology Department, UCD.'

I had immediate visions of better times and submitted the scheme to my neighbours, the Dawson brothers. We were galvanised into action and a frog-hunt would take place next day weather permitting, in this case the wetter the better.

Our prayers were answered, and equipped with buckets we sallied forth after school. We somehow concluded that since it was raining heavily, the frogs would be leaping about in the fields which of course they were, but not to be discovered at will. Had we paused to think it through, we would have concluded that the best place to catch frogs is a pond, preferably overgrown with weeds. Had we not seen them at spawning time? Had we not marvelled at the stamina of the male as he straddled the female for seemingly hours on end, but I cannot remember now if it was the courtship season and I don't even know if our quest for money would extend to us pulling the males off!

Our odyssey has to be put in focus. There is a hill overlooking Galbally called the Black Hill. It is probably 600 feet above the village. For some strange reason, we concluded that our best chance lay in that fair hill and we sallied forth. With our buckets in hand we left our base in Carrickaroche and made our way to the summit. The best that can be said about our clothing is best left unsaid but our optimism never waned.

We had seen so many frogs in our lives. We had marvelled at their jumping ability, envied the male's libido, surveyed the thousands of tadpoles swimming about and even caught some, when younger, in jam-jars but there wasn't a frog to be found as we reached the top. There was nothing for it but to carry on so it was down the hill to Glenefy on the other side. We had hunted that hill and surrounding fields many times in our quest for rabbits, which fetched at least half a crown each. We knew every blade of grass, we knew the countryside but why hadn't it dawned on us about the ponds and streams?

We arrived home at nightfall. I can remember the scene as though 'twere yesterday. We were drenched through and through. I can see the Dawson brothers now as the boys they were — fifty years ago. I can see the buckets. I can recall the contents. Each bucket contained one frog and mine was but a tiddler. None were noble specimens but best of all I can remember their fate, their release in Hennessy's field before we changed and attacked our suppers!

AN EYE FULL OF MUSIC

Patricia Gibson (b 1926)

Olympia Theatre, Dublin, 1950s

This is a true story which happened to me and my late Dad in the fifties.

Coming home from work one evening he proudly told me he

had got two tickets for the performance of Handel's Messiah which was taking place the following week in the Olympia Theatre. Being a member of the local church choir, and the recipient of a Feis Ceoil Medal, you can fully understand my father's interest in music. He also was a very methodical person and insisted on being on time and not speaking during a performance whatsoever, unless it was *absolutely necessary.*

Well, we duly arrived on the night of the performance and Dad had booked centre seats, the idea being there would be no disturbance right or left if anyone wished to leave their seats for any reason. So at 7.45 p.m. we were seated; he had his coat folded on his lap and his gloves in his hat; the orchestra was tuning up and Dad was browsing over the programme and the artists' names who were about to perform. There was a great air of excitement, so finally when everyone was seated the heavy red curtain went up and the performance commenced.

Everything went smoothly, thank God. Then the Hallelujah Chorus was being sung with gusto by the choir. I felt, and still do, that Handel was inspired when writing that heavenly music. In the midst of all this I felt a tap on my shoulder and on looking around a lady quietly leaned towards me and asked me would I mind looking on the floor under my seat as she had lost her glass eye. Dear God, I thought, what can I do? I was thinking of Dad. He would notice any movement. However I felt I wanted to oblige the lady, so I decided to gently slide down as gracefully as I could and probe around for the object in question. Alas, no success. I then tapped the shoulder of the lady seated in front of me and requested her to look for the eye, which she did and thankfully she found it, and I handed it to its rightful owner.

All this was taking place as the choir were belting out the Hallelujah Chorus. My father put his hand to his mouth and said to me, 'In the name of God what was all that about?' When I told him he nearly burst with blood pressure. 'Out of all the audience it had to be you. You'll never accompany me again anywhere.'

I wanted to help him on with his coat after the performance but all I got was, 'I can manage thank you'. As we came home in the bus I tried to speak of the singing, etc. but I was met with stony silence.

However time eventually thawed him out. Dad had a great sense of humour and he related what happened to the members of the choir who could see the funny side of the story. As for myself, I then felt at liberty to have a jolly good laugh, which I had tried desperately to subdue in the Olympia Theatre on that never to be forgotten night nearly forty years ago.

WELCOME TO AUSTRALIA

Anne Carroll (b 1915)

Glasgow / Dublin / Sydney / Dublin 1982

A happy birthday and welcome to Australia —Hence my introduction to Australia November 1982 my 67th birthday. I felt so excited and a celebrity but I was soon deflated when my sister, who was meeting me, said, 'You dope. He saw the date on your passport'. I never thought I would see Australia but my sister who went there with her family in 1960 decided to give me my ticket as a retirement present on finishing work after twenty years. My sister Alice from Glasgow (where we were born and reared) met me in London en route. We walked off the plane into 30 degree heat. It was like that much of the time we were there. It was the first time for fourty-seven years that the three of us were together for Christmas. We are all widowed now so I don't think we will all be together again. It was wonderful. In spite of the heat we saw the Opera House and of course the harbour in Sydney. The QE2 was there at the time. It's such a cosmopolitan city. The Chinese quarter was really beautiful. We were known as the three sisters everywhere we went. We realised the connection when we visited the Blue Mountains. There is a monument there dedicated to three sisters. The legend is that their Maori warrior husbands went off to war and to make sure they would not be unfaithful had them encased in concrete. But they were killed in battle so to this day they remain so.

We also visited Surfers' Paradise, Canberra, and Bondi Beach which was a real eye opener. It hadn't rained for two or three months till Christmas Day, so much for dinner on the beach. It was a holiday I'll never forget and got us together. Marie is still there. Alice lives in Glasgow and I've been in Dublin since 1937. My own family are all scattered too, five in the USA, one in Scotland and one in Wales, all married. I have two daughters and one son here in Dublin. So no wonder my thoughts get confused.

XI

LOFTING THE VIADUCT

A contest of bowls in Cork in the 1920s

Michael Geaney (b 1913)

Mayfield, Cork City, c. 1920

In my young days, Baile na mBocht, better known as Mayfield, was an area of Cork famous for the success of its harrier club and the prowess of its hurling team. Back then, and I'll be eighty-one next birthday, Mayfield was only a little village on the edge of Cork City and the villagers were rightly proud of the achievements of their harriers and hurlers. But my earliest and fondest memory is the great road bowling contest between Timmy McCarthy Quirke and that great Mayfield bowl player, Jack 'Buck' McGrath.

Buck and his brother Matty were great friends and next door neighbours of ours, so on the particular Sunday afternoon that the great contest was to take place we were naturally invited to go with them in their pony and trap. The contest was to take place on the Bandon Road to see who could loft a 28 oz bowl over the Viaduct.

There was a mighty crowd assembled. Sidecars, waggonettes, traps of every colour, shape and form, from the farmer's cart, to the buggy of the local merchants, all bringing a great gathering of people eager to spend a Sunday afternoon watching this great trial of strength and skill between two great rival sportsmen. There was a hush of expectancy over the assembled crowd. McCarthy Quirke stripped first. He had the look of a man sure to win. He handed his coat to one of his supporters. A murmur, partly of admiration, partly of anxiety arose from the crowd as he bared his massive arms. Compared with Quirke, Buck McGrath appeared almost slight in build. 'I never saw the likes of him', someone was heard to exclaim in a low solemn tone. The crowd was silent. After a couple of lads, handy with a pen, collected the bets and recorded the names in a copy book, the two men were ready for the fray.

The organisers of the contest had provided the contestants with lighter 18 oz bowls for a trial run, to warm up and get the adrenalin flowing, so to speak, before the great test with the heavier 28 oz bowl.

At three o'clock the men were brought together. There was a brief meeting with the referee, a coin was thrown in the air. Buck McGrath won the toss and decided to let McCarthy Quirke go first.

Now that the preliminaries were over Quirke stepped onto the road, glanced up at the imposing height of the bridge and judged the angle from which he would deliver the bowl. Marking the spot with a sod of grass, he then walked back about twenty yards, rubbed his palms in the dust, felt the weight of the bowl, started his run, slowly at first, then accelerating as he neared the spot and when his foot touched the mark, the bowl went flying from his hand, like a missile from a catapult and went sailing through the air. It was within an inch of clearing the viaduct when it ricochetted off the handrail, failed to go over and came back down on the Bandon side again. 'Begor, Timmy,' said Buck surveying his adversary with admiration, 'You're good.'

Taking his place at the same spot, Buck contemplated the bridge. Anxious eyes were fixed on him, for all imagined he was beaten. He went through the same ritual of rubbing his palms in the dust. He turned to look at the disconsolate faces of his supporters, and in tones of deep fervour, he uttered the words, 'Ar son Baile na mBocht', grasped the bowl in his right hand, drew himself up to his full height, and racing down the road like an Olympic sprinter, he spun the bowl into the air, clearing the parapet by several inches to drop down safely on the city side.

A roar of exultation burst from the crowd. Hats were thrown in the air, and all Hell broke loose. He had done the little village of Mayfield proud.

Many years later a grandnephew of Buck McGrath, that is Matty McGrath's grandson, Frank O'Farrell, played for Manchester United, and when Matt Busby retired as manager of that team, Frank took over. But that is a story for another day. On that fine Sunday afternoon, back at the turn of the century, all we cared about was his granduncle, Buck McGrath, and the honour and glory he brought to Mayfield.

BALLYWILLIAM & OTHER PLACES

Mary Lefebvre (b 1933)

Ballywilliam, County Wexford, 1939 – 42

I was in Ireland for three years as a child from 1939 – 42. I consider them the happiest years of my life and often dream of life as it was lived in rural Ireland then. My Irish mother, because of the war, stayed with her family in Wexford, where I was surrounded with love, and had the freedom of the mountains to play on; what a gift of a childhood to any child!

DREAMS THAT HAVE FLED

Through the pink summer dawn, I walked with my mother
Cross ditches and fields, to Templeudigan's church.
Under tunnels of green, made from hawthorn and hazels,
By narrow old lanes, topped with young silver birch.

No hardship we had, for to walk, it was natural,
A fresh constant pleasure, each step of the way,
Past oats almost golden, and black grazing cattle,
In daisies were horses, a chestnut, and bay.

The bell ringing out from the mossy old steeple,
Menfolk stayed outside, in their blue Sunday best,
And talked of the races, the fair, and the hurling,
Till the Mass had started, and wives had been blest.

By the side of the road, some ponies were waiting,
Tied up to the ash plants, that grew in the ditch,
And each had a trap, or a gig, freshly painted,
Trotting home we'd be met by the old collie bitch.

But days have long gone, since the standing corn hid me,
The ears of the wheat, seemed as high as my head,
A miniature forest of straw, like the fairies,
Has vanished, with childhood, and dreams that have fled,

YOU MAY WEEP

Trotting down to Ballywilliam,
The old pony in the shafts,
To the Co-op grey stone building,
Full of food, and cloth, and crafts.

This is where we did our shopping,
Nine long miles to the next store,
Tea and sugar, Grandad's backy,
Sacks of dried peas by the door.

Sets of reins and webbing halters,
Blinkers, bridles, traces long,
Spares for every kind of tackle,
Chains and ropes and harness
    strong.

Farmers stood with dogs and
    cowsticks,
Clothes were rough and weather
    worn,
Talked of prices, corn, and root crops,
And of when the sheep were shorn.

Crocks and pots and jugs and dishes,
Bowls in earthenware or delft,
Cans for milk to stand in dairies,
On a stone slab or a shelf.

Tools that country people needed,
Smell of leather, smell of paint,
Stable lanterns, scythes and sickles,
Snares for rabbits, nothing quaint.

Standing on the wooden counter,
Tall glass jars were full of sweets,
Orange, lemon, cherry flavour,
Butter rums, my special treats.

This I found most fascinating,
Wires arranged all overhead,
Buzzing canister with money,
Bills were paid and off they sped.

What a wonderland for children,
Endless interest for the young,
Time to stop outside for gossip,
Hear a tale, or ballad sung.

Now it seems I must be dreaming,
Did a world like that exist?
People of computer games,
You may weep for what you've
    missed.

AWAY IN THE GUARDS

A Short Story by Joe McManus (b 1923)

County Cavan and other places, 1940s

It was mid-July 1940. A copy of the 'Irish Independent' lay folded on the teacher's desk. From his seat in a top storey room of the Vocational School young John McFadden peered at the banner headline. 'ANY ATTEMPT AT AGGRESSION MEANS BLOODSHED — Mr de Valera'.

A Class Debate — 'Should Ireland remain Neutral?' — was taking place. The Headmaster knocked on the door, entered, and announced School holidays. Debate turned into an impromptu concert. As one of the girls began singing 'The Hills of Donegal' a soothing breeze came through an opened window. A ray of sunshine dispelled the drowsiness. Soon John would make his dash for freedom.

Having completed the long, homeward cycling journey he was grateful for his mother's welcome. The roasted and mashed potatoes, gravied turnips, and sizzling rashers which awaited him in the pot oven on the griosach of the turf fire were transferred to the dinner table and soon devoured.

Rested, he heard the dreaded message: 'Daddy said you are to weed the potato stalks'. He crossed the hill above the house and went to the back field. He plucked and pulled at weeds until his back ached and his tender fingers were sore. The remaining ridges looked long and foreboding. He lay on his back in a furrow between the ridges and listened to the singing of the birds in nearby bushes. It was easy to distinguish between the lilting of the blackbird and the warbling of the thrush.

He fell asleep. When he awoke the sun had lowered and drifted further westwards. Sitting up, he saw little rabbits playing in Brady's field. Thinking of a line from one of Pearse's poems 'little rabbits in a field at evening lit by a slanting sun', he asked himself what other poets and writers he had read during the last term. Wasn't it Patrick Kavanagh who said that he would not let the stony grey soil burgle the bank of his youth? Neither would he. He made up his mind that when Garda McBrearty would call to take the return of Agricultural Statistics he would make enquiries as to the procedures for gaining admission to An Garda Siochana.

Startled by his father's call, 'What are you doing there?', he didn't wait to give an explanation but returned quickly to the house. Once he glanced over his shoulder to see his father carrying out an inspection of the weeded and unweeded ridges.

McBrearty paid one of his twice yearly visits. While mother boiled the kettle and spread the good table-cloth John gave him the returns for the whole townland. When the Garda removed his cap John picked it up and fondled its badge at the same time seeking his own required information. As the physical and educational requirements plus likely times of Garda Recruiting were noted, McBrearty spoke slowly:

'The best of luck to you John, but remember what I'm telling you. The first fifteen years will be the worst.'

Three jobs, lots of Army training, plus chest-expanding exercises and five years later, Recruit Garda McFadden passed out through the Depot Gates of Phoenix Park.

With so many essentials, such as pedal bicycle, watch, fountain pen, pencil, etc., he had found the Three Pounds Fifteen Shillings per week little better than the Army's commencing pay of Fourteen Shillings and Two Pence.

It was late on a grey November evening when he arrived in Ballyross, the town which housed the District Headquarters for the village of his destination — Ballypuka. His instructions were to collect a mattress at the Headquarters. As the bus conductor helped to unload his bicycle, trunk and police box he noticed an elderly postman wheeling a bicycle along the street.

'Excuse me. Can you tell me where the Garda Station is here?' The postman shook his hand.

'You're welcome. You must be the new Guard for Ballypuka.'

'Yes, How did you know that?'

'Sure, I'm from there myself. It came in the Chief's post three weeks ago.'

Belongings and mattress loaded, the hackney car moved off for Ballypuka.

When he went in, the Station Orderly was seated by an open turf fire building more turf against a protruding hob. He turned to welcome the new Recruit, enquired about the journey down and latest happenings in the Depot. Changing the subject to more pressing matters, he asked, 'Do you smoke?' 'No.' 'Have you your coupons with you?' 'I have.'

Searching his pockets the SO took out some coupons and money. 'Do me a favour. Go to the shop beside us. Hand in your coupons and ask for a packet of 'Kerry Blues'.

'When you get them say Guard McTiernan sent you for a packet of 'Woodbines' and hand in these coupons.'

John wasn't long back from the shop when the Sergeant came in, welcomed him and asked for his papers from the Depot. Taking the papers he went upstairs.

Guard McAlinden came in. He was due for patrol and asked the new man if he would like to come for a walk.

McAlinden was talkative. 'Were you long there when I came in?'

'About an hour.'

'Did McTiernan get you a cup of tea or anything?'

'Oh, yes, he did.'

'McTiernan is alright. On my solemn oath he is. He is a Mayo man. That's a Mayo man's oath. It's different to the legal one you learned in the Depot. Am an Antrim man meself. Did you meet thon fellow? Hard to know where he came from.'

There was no explanation as to who 'thon fellow' might be so John was left to figure it out for himself.

'I see you are a Pioneer. Come in and go out to time and there is little he can do to you. He will be on about "cases" but pass no heed. They are all poor, decent, hard-working people around here, never any crime in the place.'

'They kept telling us in the Depot about investigating traffic accidents. Do you have many?'

'Not at all. Only the Parish Priest, Curate, and Doctor have cars around here. If any of them have an accident it is just as likely to be in a field or bog as on a road — not a "public place" at all.'

Suddenly there was a swish of tyres. Coming around a bend was an unlighted bicycle. McAlinden took the rider's name and address, 'Andrew Buggy, Rinnaboley'. They were in the townland of Lurgan.

An aeroplane passed overhead. McAlinden explained that it was still necessary to record the movements of planes, so he noted the time and that the aeroplane was travelling in a South-Westerly direction.

They came to the end of the Sub-District and retraced their steps. The senior man felt the need for a couple of pints and entered a wayside tavern. On return to the Station he had some difficulty writing his Patrol Record. Notwithstanding his very junior status John ventured to offer advice. 'Don't forget about the aeroplane, Jim'. When the book was left open he read, 'At 9.35 p.m. found Andrew Buggy, Rinnaboley, using an unlighted aeroplane in Lurgan'. It was just as well thon fellow had retired to bed.

Time passed. Agricultural Statistics and a Special Census of Population ensured that the new man acquired a good local knowledge. In less than a month he had fallen in love and by the end of a year he had married. Months rolled into years.

Came a mid-September Sunday evening. Due to an urgent family matter his wife had left for Dublin that morning. He was Station Orderly. McAlinden, McTiernan and Michael O'Flaherty were out. Thon fellow had gone, too. There was silence save for the ticking of a clock. It was nearing 8 o'clock p.m. He paced up and down the narrow day-room. Three thousand miles away close friends of his now-shortened footballing days were ready to prove their strengths and skills on New York's hard-baked Polo Grounds.

For the first time he broke the 'Barrack Regulations', locked the doors, and headed for the nearest wireless set. All during the game he listened intently, at the back of his mind a nagging feeling that he might be caught out. Across the waves O'Hehir's voice pleaded with Radio Eireann or any other authorities who 'might be listening along the way' for five minutes more. Would he go or stay? He took his five minutes more.

Full-time Whistle. Cavan 2-11 Kerry 2-7.

Back at his post he checked the Diary. Everything seemed in order. Resting his elbows on the table he cupped his chin in his hands, said a wee prayer that his dear mother had been able to listen-in from her hospital bed, and that everything would go alright in Dublin. Allowing his thoughts to drift, he had a vision of the new Cathedral risen against the hill and imagined he could hear the pealing of St Felim's bell. He pictured the bands. Upper Lavey and Lower Lavey Fifes and Drums would vie for pride of place. He could see Drumcrow Warpipers, Oldcastle Brass and Reed forgetting the rivalry and crossing the divide somewhere near Castlerahan Chapel, Bunnoe Brass and Reed, Kingscourt, Drumaney, Cavan Labour honouring Bill Doonan by the banks of the Annalee.

The 'Sam Maguire' Cup would be carried back to old Virginia. Like the Hackler of old it would become well known in sweet Stradone, likewise in Lavey and Grousehall. John Joe would bring it to his beloved Cornafean. Hughie, in his new capacity, would bring it to Cootehill like he did under the Captaincy of the great Jimmy from Killinkere fourteen years previously and as Captain himself two years later. It would take the road to Doonaree and return to the Bridge of Finea. Tony would make sure it had come home to Ballyjamesduff.

But he would not be there.

He had to stagger the days now. Hadn't he used up last year's few days leave in February? Hadn't he to do three days SO in succession last June and hadn't Michael O'Flaherty to do likewise for him so that he could get a day and a half for his brother's Ordination and First Mass?

One transfer later John found himself in Glanbee. On a night cycling patrol with Michael McGeehan from Fermanagh they were protecting the fishing rights of some landlord. Pelted by driving rain, with more threatening from the black bosom of the clouds, they took shelter under a lone bush with a lake to their rear. Their carbide lamps spluttered and dimmed as the wet soaked through their so-called 'Waterproof' coats. John thought of his Father's recitation, 'The Calico Landlord lived bloated and puffed, a boycotted draper in Ballyjamesduff, under police protection he has got of late for evicting the tenants of his whole estate'. Were the books he had read at school wrong when they stated that Davitt and Parnell had rid the country of Landlords?

'What's happening at home now, John?'

'Funny, that is what I was thinking about.'

'I'll tell you. Your father is on his kailey and some neighbour is saying to him, "Where's John? I didn't see him this long time".

Your father is saying, "Ah, he has a great job. He is away in the Guards over in the West". The neighbour will say, "A nice clean job with a good pension".'

On the following morning the pair had changed into dry uniforms awaiting the Sergeant's inspection of their trouser creases, truncheons, handcuffs, haircuts, etc. Following this and an hour of law studies they were detailed to empty the contents of a dry toilet bucket located at the rear. Reluctantly, they obeyed.

McGeehan surveyed the scene. He took a shovel to lift up the handle. Accidentally, he hit and burst the side of the bucket. Contents spilled out. Mick stood back, 'Jaysus, I have a great job. I'm away in the Guards'.

John moved on to a bigger Station. He wrote to Mick describing his new Station and surroundings. In reply he received Mick's letter suggesting that he, John, should never cease praying for whoever had the pull to get him out of Glanbee. Mick had failed to work a transfer but as he put it: 'Thank God, I see a clearing in the wood. I will have twenty-five years service in June and I will be off to a wee farm the brother has left me at home.' John pictured him weeding potato stalks and listening to the birds.

The first fifteen years passed. As he looked at the newly-awarded chevrons on his sleeve Sgt. McFadden thought of McBrearty. The decision to promote himself might not have pleased some of the martinets he had encountered along the way. However, at the end of the remainder of his one and two score years' service he would have the satisfaction of repeating the line of a well-known song, 'I did it my way'.

With his bride of so many years ago ex-Sergeant John McFadden lives contentedly in retirement. Their family have grown up and scattered.

Strangely both parents feel happy that two of the younger ones are AWAY IN THE GUARDS.

POEMS

Thomas Harris (b 1922)

Belfast

THE ULSTER STORM, 1970

The wind and sea that pound and
　rage
Are but a breeze that blows
Compare the hate and venom spit
As the Ulster tempest grows.

The Protestants with faith avowed
The Catholic with his creed
Would be but the opposites
Had they been born mixed seed.

The door wherein religion locked
Will someone find the key
And mindful of God's children
　bred
Unlock the minds to see.

And see the children all as one
To have their faiths their own
And differ find there's much to
　learn
In the good seed to be sown.

A FALLEN FRIEND

Lift high this burden that you
　nobly bear
That all may know the plight of
　bitter strife
Walk not alone the road of my
　own kind
My field was of a wider view of
　life.

And slowly wind your weary way
　to see
My many friends of every faith
　and kin
Through streets I once did trudge
　and long since played
These were the happy hours the
　battles I did win.

Weep not for me as I am laid to rest
Make for my child and children
　everywhere
A happier land with cherished
　hopes to fill
'Midst pastures green — a life that
　all can share.

BECOMING A MAN

Michael Gilligan (b 1928)

County Limerick

It was a beautiful September evening. Dick Ryan sat outside his
fine two-storied house, reading his Sunday paper. A sixty-five
year-old farmer, tall, gaunt and hardy, bronzed by the many summers spent on the land. Should he raise his eyes from reading it
would be to gaze at, and admire the herd of Friesian cattle grazing contentedly in the aftergrass of the fields that stretched away
down to the river. This farm of 300 acres, situated in the Golden

Vale of Ireland, three miles outside Limerick City, had been built up by three generations of Ryan sweat. It was at peak production now, due to the enterprise of his eldest son Maurice. Old Dick did not now regret sending Maurice to the Agricultural College, even though it was his wife who had to insist that the lad get the best training possible. Were she alive today, she would be proud.

Still more would Old John Ryan the boy's grandfather, long since dead, be proud of his grandson and the changes he brought to the farm of Ard-na-Gréine, the new milking parlour, tractor and all such as made the place into a model farm. However it was long before the lad grew up that his grandfather had reason to be proud of his grandson.

The expansion cost had to be raised by Dick as owner but all of that was nearly cleared off now. Yes, the boy would inherit a fine farm. The work was done by the two of them and a hired man. There was a second son, Dick junior, but he was in Dublin, in the Civil Service. The father was proud of him also. He used to praise Dick junior, often within earshot of Maurice. This caused the farming son some unease. He, Maurice, was named after his mother's father, while young Dick was named after his Dad. This worried Maurice.

This evening, all is quiet. The whirr of the milking machine is silent after all the milking, tea is over and Maurice has driven off to return in the small hours of the morning. Old Dick didn't mind for wasn't the lad single and young lads of thirty-two have to have some enjoyment. The old man scanned the TV programmes to see what rubbish they were showing that night. The sound of a car coming up the long avenue from the main road to the house broke the silence and Dick wondered if Maurice was returning. He was surprised to see it was Canon Clarke, the local Parish Priest, who drove into the yard. The sheepdog which had been sleeping roused itself and gave a few barks of warning. 'Quiet, Shep', ordered Dick. 'I see the dog hasn't much time for the Clergy', said the Canon, as he emerged from the car. 'No then, but sure he's not used to seeing one here in Ard-na-Gréine. Are the Dues due?', joked back the farmer.

'My God, isn't it a terrible thing that when ye farmers see yer PP, ye think the worst. Couldn't it be a social visit that I'm on?', came back the Priest. 'Well, one thing I know, you are not on a sick call, thank God, but come in to the house, come in if it's a social call that brings you; I have something in a bottle that will make your nose shine.'

The priest followed the farmer into the house. 'Sit down there till I get glasses. You must excuse the cut of the place, but with only two men in it, it's not up to scratch.' 'It needs a woman's touch', said the Priest. The farmer ignored that remark. 'Say when', as he poured the whiskey. 'That's fine, I'm driving, and I can't be caught by the breathalyser', responded the Canon. 'Was there one of ye caught yet?', sounded Dick. 'Ah, stop that, you'll have the better of me whatever I say', said the Priest.

'I've said that this place needs a woman's touch and not to beat around the bush that's what I've come about,' said the pastor. 'And a good job too,' interrupted the farmer 'or that bush would become a hedge like some of your sermons, but surely you've not turned to marriage broker, and I've no intention of going off again tho' a new set of false teeth in my head, and a new hat with a little feather in it, and a pair of brown boots, I'd be anyone's fancy. I've often watched the young ones with their tight fitting jeans going up the church aisle, on a Sunday morning. Twould make one think all right, but what stops me thinking is seeing the old ones going up the aisle of a Sunday. What would my Nora think God rest her?'

The priest waited patiently. When he was sure that the farmer was finished he spoke. 'If you are finished with your flight of fancy, I'll continue. You know damn well it's Maruice I'm talking about and I'm no matchmaker either. Maurice has been going steady for some years with a lovely girl. He has proposed marriage.'

'Well, I'm delighted to hear it. It's the best news I've heard in a long time. I'm delighted but why didn't he tell me himself?', asked Old Dick. 'Well there's a snag', answered the Canon. 'You see', said he, continuing, 'I said Maurice proposed and was accepted, provisionally. She won't marry until the farm, lock, stock and barrel is signed over to Maurice. He has told her that doesn't matter, that there's no need for this and he wouldn't ask you. Eventually they came to me for help. I know your son's happiness is of paramount importance to you. Ard-na-Greine has been in the family for three generations already. I'm sure you want to see it continuing into the next . . . . Now what have you got to say?'

There was silence for a time. The priest felt a change in the atmosphere. The waning sun cast a gloomy shadow of the barn outside, across the kitchen. Old Dick, his jaunty spirit knocked out of him, all of his age showing in his face, sat wearily in the chair. It was if the doctor had told him he had a terminal illness. The silence was loud.

Eventually he sighed a weary sigh and then said, 'Your Reverence, you bring hard news. I thank you, for your job isn't easy, but then it never is. When bad news is to be broken, it's you who's asked to bring it, any one at all would be delighted to bring good news. Isn't it strange however that the news you bring is, or should be, good news, news of my son's marriage which I have hoped for, for years, yet I'm saddened beyond belief. I don't know the girl in question, nor do I think I want to know her, for I would wish Maurice's girl would marry him for himself and not for the farm. I would like if Maurice would look elsewhere for a wife, one who would be worthy of him, but that I suppose would be out of the question, and I'm not going to interfere in that. Now Father, I wonder if you believe in re-occurring history? Well, it's happening. I don't want to delay you but if you have time, I'll tell you a story, knowing that it will not pass your lips.' The Canon nodded in acquiescence and the farmer, in a slow unhurried voice, began his story.

'I was third in a family of three, John, Peg and myself. John, named after my father and for whom the farm was intended, was six years older than me. He was a wild, lovable chap, a great favourite in the Parish and beyond, but for farming he didn't have the interest. The upshot was he skipped off to England. It broke the mother's heart, he being her favourite, and it hastened her death. Peg joined the Nuns and only died two years ago in Africa. If all had gone well, and John had inherited, I suppose I'd have been shipped off to the Priesthood to keep up the tradition.

'So here we were, my father and me, working the farm. I was twenty-five when I made a trip to Lisdoonvarna and met Nora O'Gorman. It's strange to go all the way to County Clare to meet a girl, who lived ten miles from me here, but there it was. We started courting. I used to cycle every Sunday morning after the milking to Boora, half way to her place, from whence she'd cycle. We'd meet there. Eventually I cycled all the way and met her father, Maurice O'Gorman, a stronger minded man you wouldn't meet. When he heard that I was the younger son he wouldn't hear of us getting married until my father signed over Ard-na-Greine to me. Just like now, but with this difference, Maurice, inherits now, as Dick is well fixed in his fine job in Dublin.'

Here the Canon interrupted. 'Oh, I'm glad to hear that. You'll sign over the place then and they can be married?'

'Oh, not so fast', said the farmer. 'I won't be signing anything over. Just hear me out. What Maurice O'Gorman was afraid of was that John, my brother, might turn up, like "The Prodigal Son" of old and inherit. Do you know Father that's one parable I could never understand as long as I live. Well I could see sense in the argument but I would not broach the subject to my father. "Leave everything to me", said O'Gorman. He met my father. The thing was done, all signed over. I married Nora O'Gorman a month later.

'"When you marry a woman from the mountain you marry the mountain" — so the old saying goes. That's what I did. She brought a dowry with her but if she did she brought the O'Gorman clan with her. They were constant visitors, and Maurice O'Gorman was commander-in-chief. We couldn't do a hand's turn but he was there to give advice. My father was a patient man to endure it, but what could he do? He was only the boy now, his hands were tied. I know I should have done something then but you would have to know my wife to understand, and anything for a quiet life, so I remained silent.

'The baby was born the year after. Naturally, John should have been his name after my father or Dick after me but NO, Maurice was the chosen name. Still I never opened my mouth. Now hadn't we dropped low, or hadn't I dropped low? Worse was to come however, but not for a while. The birth of the baby seemed to give new life to my dad. The despondency which fell on him by the takeover by the O'Gormans seemed to lift as if by magic with the birth of the baby. He was content that Ard-na-Gréine was to remain in Ryan hands, come what may. He idolised the child, and with renewed vigour, dug into the work on the farm, putting up with the suggestions of Maurice O'Gorman, solid in the knowledge that his work would benefit the Ryans.

'The war was raging. We got word of an explosion in a munitions factory in England in which John was killed. The news shattered the father. John never married and with his death, my father knew that I was his only protection and he couldn't put any great reliance in me for I had proved that I wasn't worth much. His one joy was his grandson. The boy, now two, was walking and it was nice to see the old and the young walking down the avenue, hand in hand, and I swear that it was only the old man who understood the gibberish of the child. When Maurice started school, 'twas to his grandfather he told all of his news to and he was listened to with all the old man's attention. Then the accident happened.

'Never to be outdone in doing his share of work, although in his sixties, he was driving a horsedrawn rake in the meadow, when he was thrown. He broke his leg. 'Twas set in the hospital but it was not a great success. He walked with a stick after that, but needless to say his working days were over.

'Cordial relations between himself and my wife were never great, now they were non-existent. I would often be down the fields of a wet day and he would hobble down. I knew it would be to escape her tongue that made him venture out. Still I said nothing. He never complained. Eventually she, her father and her mother, convinced me he'd be better off in the County Home.

He'd have the best treatment for his leg, be with people his own age, and anyway his influence on the child wasn't natural.

'I'll never forget the morning I took him in. It was a miserable cold October morning. I had the horse tackled to the trap. He came out of the house in his long black coat, his black hat pulled down over his eyes, to conceal the tears he was shedding. He limped to the trap, behind him came my dear wife, followed by her bombastic father. He had come all the way over the ten miles to give moral support lest I should weaken at the last minute. I can still hear their platitudes "You'll be grand in the hospital. We'll be in to see you every Sunday". It was all lost on my father. Seated in the trap he took what was for him the last fond look at Ard-na-Gréine. Young Maurice came out of the house, ready for school. "Let Maurice come with us today", said my father. "I'd like to be chatting to him on the way in". My wife protested that the boy couldn't miss school. Well as it was my father's last request, and in spite of my wife's raised protest, and her father's insistences, I lifted the child up and placed him alongside his Grandfather. We set off for the County Home.

'During the journey, my father explained to the five-year old, how that Grandad had to go to hospital to have his leg cured from being sick, speaking to the lad in childish talk, which the boy understood. He told Maurice to "learn hard", to be a good boy for Mammy and Daddy. Then he tried to answer all the "Whys?" of the young lad.

'We reached the Home. The boy waited in the trap, whilst I COMMITTED my father.

'Driving away from the Home Maurice said, "What's the name of this road Daddy?" "It's called the Forge Road", I answered. "Why do you want to know?" "Caus", he lisped, "I want to know where to put you when you get old . . . " I turned the trap around, went back to the Home, and took my father back to his own Ard-na-Gréine.

'This was the day the Ryans took back Ard-na-Gréine from the O'Gorman clan. I won't go into detail on the reception we got from them when we arrived back. They started, but I cut in. "Sir", I said, "You are no longer welcome here. Please leave, and if it's your wish, you may take your daughter with you but my father and Maurice stay here". The father looked at the daughter. She looked at him, both had their mouths open, amazed, speechless. Old O'Gorman was about to say something, thought better of it, then turned on his heel and left. She ran to the door after him, calling "Dad". She waited a while. When she saw he was gone, she turned back in, saying, "I'll get the dinner ready. Ye must be hungry after yere journey".

'Now that's my story. I said to you not to tell anyone of it, but I will be obliged to you if you would tell Maurice and his lady friend the story. I would be a bit shy telling him of the service he did his grandfather long ago. I also know he'll be horrified to think, that I would think, that he would ever think, of putting his father into a Home. Well, Canon, marriage can change people, as I found out. I never thought of putting my father into a Home, until I married.'

The couple were married. Three years later, the Canon was driving past the avenue gate of Ard-na-Gréine. He saw Old Dick, still master, walking his grandson, John, their hands entwined, and Dick trying to understand the lisping of the child.

There was a good chance that Old Dick would never see the inside of a nursing home but would die at home in Ard-na-Gréine.

As for his own destiny, the Canon wasn't so certain.

PA-JOE & YALLAH PEG

Yvonne O'Connor (b 1925)

Cork City

PA-JOE

His parental birth certificate
Might have poetically described his kith and kin
As 'Romanys', 'Wandering Nomads', or 'Travelling People',
But chose instead, the colourless prose, for these
Poets of the Road
As merely 'No fixed abode' ...

And yet Pa-Joe, bereft of flaming hair,
Within his age group, would favourably compare
With the Honourable Patrick Joseph,
Son of Sir Snobbage from the Castle
But in the opinion of settled people
Castles were deemed to have their feet on the ground
While Nomad abodes have their shafts in the air ...

As Lady Snobbage was giving birth, on the refined couch
          of Chloroform
Her ladies waiting to hustle the male heir
To the wet nurse of his infant dependency,
Pa-Joe's mother birthscreamed the birds to silence

Ere swaddling him in the tail of her check apron,
She suckled him to the mead and honey of her wild
                    young breast ...

As she laid him in a moss cradle of spring-time violets
A screaming curlew wakened him from his birthsleep,
The first sound he ever heard and the last sound he would hear,
Breathing his end, beside the wind-swept road
That goes winding thru' the bogs of Ireland ...

Pa-Joe, your father had no house,
Your mother welcomed the warmth of the moon and stars,
For was not the world a cold place
To endure the birth-pangs of the baby destined to be scorned ...
Ah! But were you not born a poet
And was not your every day a poem
And did you not live to the full
The true poetry of Ireland.

YALLAH PEG

As of yore, I hob-nailed the hawthorn bend
And beheld Peg's Cottage
Straight as crow-flight, not twenty paces thence ...
Once as elegant as an Ash, now as bent as the Boss of a hurl,
She bee-busied hither and thither, eyes alert,
Compassing the country-side ... absorbing news ...
'Sacred and blessed hour, is id yerself that's in id', she greeted,
'Miracles will never cease 'til the hind leg of a dog is straightened'.

Vice-gripped was I ... in a woolly embrace ... Peg was
Swandowned in the comfort of a Baker's dozen of Cardigans,
'Wisha come in and sit down', says she,
'The hate iv the hob will aise yer bones.'
Her hawk-beak nose X-rayed this prodigal returned,
Morse-coding findings through beady eyes, to the Fort Knox of Knowledge,
Lurking through her eagle nest of greying hair ...
'Wisha Faith an' I'd pass yah on the road', said Peg,
'I never expected yah, not during sut an a Wattle!'
'I'll go bail, I often saw more mate on a Bicycle Pump!'

 It was great to be back on a visit to Peg
The kettle swinging on the Pot-hooks
Hissed its never-ending welcome ...

Heathered peat perfumed the 'Tay'
The new-laid brown eggs, exuded milk and honey.
I was back home again and sat absorbing the natural poetry
of Peg of the Bog,
The Will-o'-the-Wisp, whom they said was
'As odd as two left feet,
As Mad as a March hare
And ... As Yallah as the bake iv a Gander ...'

POEMS

Cyril Potter

Dublin

LILYPOND OIL PAINTING

A beautiful picture a sight to behold
Set in a garden naturally old
God-gift so beautiful ageless in time
Is a peace on earth with all mankind.

1927

O for the days that were so true
O for the days that I but knew
O for the peace on earth content
And the happiness I had, that
went.

But now it is that I'm grown up
And dreams are far away,
I'll cherish all the memories
That didn't come to stay.

RUNAGRY REVISITED

Rona Currey (b 1905)

Between Ballina and Foxford, County Mayo, 1915 and early 1960s

Back in the car we turned up the road towards the Big House. The Big House: I had never thought of it as big but in comparison with the one storey cabins, dotted around, I suppose it was. Cabins like the two we passed on the left, one of which had been occupied by my friend Mrs Reddington, the full time washerwomen, employed at The Big House. A special hut had been built for her in the stable yard, furnished with a stove for heating the flat irons, a copper for boiling sheets and towels, a tub or two for the soaking and a washboard. Overhead was a slatted drier with a pulley to lower or pull it up, for use on wet days or to air the ironing.

Mondays were for sorting: the coloured from the whites, the woollen from the cotton with one pile put to soak. Tuesdays and Wednesdays were set aside for the hot wash, with soap and rubbing on the washboard. If it were dry outside, which it seldom was, the washing would be spread out over bushes. Mrs Reddington taught me to iron. She also saved my life. In her simple way she thought Home Rule sounded comfortable and felt reassured when Uncle Charlie told her that it was coming on the next train.

A bump in the road brought me back to the present. Philip had drawn up at the entrance to Runagry, a rusty gate fastened with rope, dividing the drive and one time garden from the outside world. Dominating the scene stoood the house, like some old lady, doubtful of her balance, the Virginia Creeper-covered walls growing as they always had.

With the brightening of the sun I was reminded of the day of the Great Picnic that never was. We often took food with us when going down to the lough or off on fishing expeditions but we did not call them picnics. Sometimes there were magnificent tea parties outside the fishing hut when, on one occasion, it was said that Kenneth ate fourteen rock cakes. Sadly the sun seldom shone on these occasions. In fact, for us it seldom shone at all. One exceptional day stands out, with a dawn of brilliant sunshine; it was hot, it was summer. What a lovely day for a picnic we cried in unison — that is, apart form Aunt Ruth. Aunt Ruth's custom was to organise for the day ahead, regardless of what the weather might be and her plan for that day was not a picnic. 'No,' she said, 'we can't. We've got roast chicken for lunch. Besides Tuesday is bread-making day.' 'Won't it keep till tomorrow?', asked Uncle Charlie, always a child at heart. Aunt Ruth demurred. 'Please, Aunt Ruth, PLEASE', we had pleaded. Aunt Ruth, reluctantly , gave in , disappearing into the kitchen, with mutterings of not being ready before half past ten or eleven.

By noon excitement flagged. There was, too, a hint of change in the weather. By 12.45, with the ancient Ford waiting at the door, loaded with everything we might need, Aunt Ruth appeared. At the same moment the first fat drops of thundery rain fell splashing to the ground. By the time we were on our way the heavens had opened.

As I stood, immersed in memories, a cloud passed over the sun
and I shivered. Sensing the ghosts in the house I could see Delamore, the handsome aristocratic parlourmaid in the black dress,
starched apron and cap, uniform of the period. When I was older
it was explained to me that her name was a derivation of the
French, de l'amour, of love. In fact a lovechild, which set me wondering from which noble lord and kitchen maid or beautiful
young duchess and ghillie she might be descended? Which young
mother had been ostracised by her family for her indiscretion and
carnal sin? Where had Delamore gone after Runagry?

In the kitchen at the back of the house, a picture in my mind
conjured up Aunt Ruth pickling, bottling, or making jam or trout
paté, her trim figure neatly dressed in the already bygone fashion
of long, full, small-waisted skirt and blouse. Though she lived to
be over a hundred, she remained upright and slim, adhering to
the same picturesque way of dressing. As her ghost faded the
plum faced driver, Cassidy, replaced her, sitting at the scrubbed
kitchen table, before him a hill of potatoes, a daily routine. Cassidy, a bachelor, lived in a room over the stables. At regular intervals Uncle Charlie invaded the room, in order to recover any
misappropriated articles that cluttered it.

From the kitchen my mind drifted to the dark, damp drawing-
room, so seldom used, all of us preferred the cosier, smaller library where we would wind up the horned gramophone to play
the music that always inspired me to dance.

'Come on now,' said Philip, breaking into my far away
thoughts 'and stop day-dreaming. If you want to go down to the
lough we must go now. We haven't too much time.'

From being a ten year old I returned with a start to being a
grandmother of sixty plus, accompanied by a long suffering and
patient husband. At the risk of being caught as trespassers, we
climbed through the wire fence and made our way to the stable
yard at the back of the house. Amidst the weeds sprouting between the cobble stones stood a motionless donkey, or was it
Neddy's ghost? Nearby the pump rested, as if from the long
hours Cassidy and Anthony had worked with it, as it wheezed
and clanged, in order to supply the house with water.

A guilty feeling of trespassing urged me on though I longed to
linger, to explore every old familiar nook and cranny. 'The donkey of my day,' I said to my husband, 'nearly finished me off.'
'How do you mean?', he said. 'I was used to driving the donkey
at my other aunt's, aunt Con and I thought it would be fun to
drive this one. My younger cousin, Charles, Uncle Charlie's and
Aunt Ruth's grandson, thought so too. We went in search of An-

thony, the gentle cowman who always exuded a faint scent of new milk and found him and Cassidy gossiping, as they sorted out the messroom, where the feeds were kept. We asked if we might have Neddy harnessed. After a little persuasion, the two men glanced at each other and agreed but, with hindsight, I remember their hesitation.

Presently we were driving happily down the road towards the shop, when close to Mrs Reddington's cabin Neddy stopped and brayed. As you saw when we drove here, the road has a drop on each side of about 6ft to the bog below and it was from this lower land that a pretty little donkey returned his call. Neddy, in his excitement backed the trap towards the edge of the road. By now Charles and I were out of it and I was doing the stupidest thing in my life. I was behind the cart trying to push it from going backwards into the bog. At this moment Mrs Reddington came out took a firm grip on Neddy's headstall and told him sharply, to behave himself. Had I fallen into the bog with the trap on top of me well, I reckon I owe it to Mrs Reddington that I am here today.'

'I can hear her now, the way she said, 'Ach!', a look of disgust on her face. 'Whatever were they doing, letting children like you out with a rogue donkey?' The trouble is, even today, that Irishman like Anthony and Cassidy are incapable of saying 'No', especially to two pleading children.'

As I finished the story we turned away to the path leading down to Lough Conn, to Uncle Charlie's special little bay. It was exactly the same, mud between the rock like stones, mud that used to squelch between my toes when, out of sight of strict Aunt Ruth, I would take off my shoes and stockings and walk barefoot. Drawing level with Mrs Maguire's cabin I had a laughing memory of the day when, to my disbelief, I had seen a horse on the inside pressing its hind quarters against the window. Now from the cabin came a fair young woman with food for her chickens, not one of which, one knew, would be allowed inside. I asked her about Mrs Maguire. 'Ah, she was my granny,' she said in her soft lilting voice, while I could see through the open door that, like the village shop, the floor was no longer packed earth but carpeted.

As we walked on I remembered the evil smell of soaking flax, now there was no smell, flax was a dead industry. On reaching what I called Charlie's Bay, fresh memories came strong and fast. It was here that we children had spent most of our waking time. The hut was missing. The hut where the outboard engine was kept, the rods, the oars, the rowlocks, the teapots, cups and saucers, and other necessary and unnecessary items but the do-it-yourself stone pier was as firm as ever.

Uncle Charlie had three shooting dogs: a pair of glossy red set-
ters, Rex and Diana, and Tutu. Tutu was a black poodle bitch, de-
scendant of a long line of home-bred poodles, trained as
retrievers. On one occasion, as we chugged into the bay, at the
end of a days fishing, we took the waiting dogs by surprise. While
Tutu swam near the end of the pier, showing off to an admiring,
tail wagging Rex, Diana sat at the land end, ignored by the other
two, hunched in misery.

In those days Runagry was considered a long way form Ballina
and the shops, so the household had to be self supporting. Uncle
Charlie grew the vegetables and fruit for jam and he shot rooks or
rabbits for pies, also game when in season. Mostly we ate fish.
Stewed eels were a delicacy that Kenneth provided, getting up at
dawn to pull in his line. From him I learned to skin eels, skin and
degut rabbits, pluck and clean poultry. Occasionally I had a try at
milking the cows or churning the butter and sometimes I collected the eggs. We fed well and everything was fresh.

Philip took my hand. Dusk warned us it was time to go home. I
had one last look back.

'We fished most days,' I told him, as we walked back along the
path. Wet or fine, and there was an island on the other side with a
ruined castle. Cows used it for shelter and I smoked my first ex-
perimental cigarette in their company. I expected to feel sick and
was surprised to find I enjoyed my first smoke. I remember to this
day the picture on the packet, of a bearded sailor framed by a
wreath or garland, the word PLAYERS at the top.

A few miles along the shore, I told him, lived an old bachelor,
Freddy Peregrine Birch, in a large house with a billiard room and
a full sized table. Sometimes we would all go over for tea and cro-
quet. For those who sat and watched, peat smouldered in a bra-
zier to keep the midges at bay. Occasionally Kenneth and I would
stay behind for the night, to be fetched next day by boat. The
house keeper would lend me a pair of Freddy's pyjamas. He too
had a gramophone and, as usual, I was eager to dance as soon as
it was wound up and the needle in place. Once Kenneth was there
on his own but instead of waiting for the boat to collect him, he
'borrowed' a bicycle and rode miles round the lough, back to
Runagry. It was years before I understood why. Kenneth had
found Freddy too affectionate.

Philip laughed as I told him this story, opened the door of our
hired car and we were soon on our way to the hotel, back from
the past and into the present, to a glowing peat fire and a good
dinner.

XII

THE FOUR SEASONS

THE 'CRABBIT OLD WOMAN'S' POEM

Thomas P. White who submitted this thought-provoking poem writes: 'Since passing sixty, I'm never done telling young people that the worst part of growing old is that you only grow old on the outside, and I think this poem confirms that. I received it from a friend working in a hospital in Wigan, Lancs, only this week (October 1993). She did not tell me the name of the lady (RIP) who wrote it, but she did say there is a copy pinned up in every ward in the hospital.'

The 'Crabbit Old Woman's' Poem

What do you see nurses, what do you see?
Are you thinking when you look at me -
A crabbit old woman, not very wise,
Uncertain of habit, with faraway eyes,
Who dribbles her food and makes no reply
When you say in a loud voice — 'I do wish you'd try',
Who seems not to notice the things that you do
And forever is losing a stocking or shoe.
Who unresisting or not, lets you do as you will,
With bathing and feeding, the long day to fill.
Is that what you are thinking, is that what you see?
Then open your eyes nurse, you're not looking at me.

I'll tell you who I am as I sit here so still
As I use at your bidding, as I eat at your will.
I'm a small child of ten with a Father and Mother,
Brothers and sisters, who love one another.
A young girl of sixteen with wings on her feet,
Dreaming that soon now a lover she'll meet;
A bride soon at twenty — my heart gives a leap,
Remembering the vows that I promised to keep;
At twenty five now I have young of my own,
Who need me to build a secure happy home;

A woman of thirty, my young now grow fast,
Bound to each other with ties that should last;
At forty my young sons have grown and are gone,
But my man's beside me to see I don't mourn;
At fifty once more babies play round my knee,
Again we know children, my loved one and me.
Dark days are upon me, my husband is dead.
I look at the future, I shudder with dread,
For my young are still rearing young of their own,
And I think of the years and the love that I've known.

I'm an old woman now and nature is cruel
'Tis her jest to make old age look like a fool.
The body it crumbles, grace and vigour depart,
There is now a stone where I once had a heart;
But inside this old carcass a young girl still dwells,
And now and again my battered heart swells,
I remember the joys, I remember the pain,
And I'm loving and living life over again.
I think of the years all too few — gone too fast,
And accept the stark fact that nothing can last.

So open your eyes, nurses, open and see,
Not a crabbit old woman, look closer — see ME.

MY DREAM

Rachel Andrews (b 1926)

Shankill, County Dublin, on birth of granddaughter 1986

When my first grand-daughter was born, I was beside myself
with delight — she was so beautiful. But I had one regret
which caused a persistent little ache underneath the happiness, and
that was that my husband had not lived to see her.

Then I had this dream. One day, as I pushed the pram containing
my grand-daughter, I heard footsteps of someone running behind
us. I looked around but, at first, could not see anyone; then gradually, the face of my husband came into view — he was breathless
and excited. 'Let me see her — let me see her', he was saying. I
drew back the covers and lifted Baby into a sitting position while

her Grandad feasted his shining eyes upon her. The expression on his face I shall never forget — happiness, love, tenderness, awe, wonder, humility, holiness, gratitude — they were all there. From then on I never doubted that he had seen and loved his gorgeous little grand-daughter.

To date I have three lovely grand-daughters and I believe their Grandad knows and loves them all as his memory is kept fresh in them.

ANGEL-CHILD

Mairéad Bean Uí Dhúill (b 1929)

Munfin Wood, Ballycarney, Enniscorthy, County Wexford, 1940s

It was a bright sunny day in late autumn. The crispy golden leaves of the old oak trees made a crunching sound as they held fast to life, which by now was withering with the approach of winter. I looked up at the brilliant sky which did not threaten rain, despite the fact that the wind was from the south-west. 'What an ideal day for a country walk!', I mused as I patted my dog's shaggy head. That comfortable feeling of well-being, of health, of the realisation of no imminent major worries or sorrow enveloped me, adding zest to my footsteps, which led me to a wooded area, on the outskirts of which was a red chalet-type house abounding in memories. This had been the scene of my childhood, and at that time, the wood had been a maze of paths, big and small, the latter often inaccessible in summer, when briars and luxuriant undergrowth pushed their way across, impeding access.

Twenty or more years had passed since I had seen the place, and I was eager to see how it had stood up to the inevitable ravages of time and change. The main pathway stretched before me invitingly and I followed it. This led to three farmer's houses — houses which I had never visited despite their proximity, but the picture that flooded my mind was that of a thatched cottage with roses around its white door and a cobbled stone yard which contained a draw well. Many and many a visit I had paid to this house as a child and numerous were the times I had sat on the single bench warming my hands as I chatted with the woman of the house. Her husband was an old man, then well over seventy years old, although she was still in her fifties. They had a child —

an angel if you wish — a lad who couldn't speak or understand, yet who sensed affection or anger. No normal child ever received more loving and devoted care from mother or father. I remembered how his mother used to clasp him in her arms as she struggled with him to get on a garment, strongly resembling the Roman toga, over his abnormally large head while his hands hung listlessly, almost lifelessly; hands, waxen and to all appearances without use. At twelve years of age he was tall and ungainly, yet able to walk around the yard and enjoy the fresh air which blew through his long and sometimes unkempt hair. His name was Bartholemew but he was never referred to as any other than 'the child'.

A quarter of a century later as I approached the cottage, now a ruined wilderness, I felt sad — sad that the former occupants of the house were gone, sad at the metamorphosis of life and the inevitability of death. That was a nostalgic moment when I leaned over the tumbled wall still enhanced by autumn's glowing creeper. The draw well was covered in but the rusty remnants of the chain and bucket remained, not only to awaken memories, but to re-create the atmosphere of that day long ago when I had my first experience of fear and when I turned my thoughts heavenward as never before.

It was a bleak winter's morning when the frost glistened on the cobblestones outside the door, and the fire on the hearth threw its light around the rustic kitchen. It was about half-past-eleven and Molly was busy peeling vegetables for the mid-day meal. She worked quickly and efficiently concentrating completely on the work on hand. She was an industrious woman, almost a replica of Wordsworth's Isabel in his poem 'Michael', the shepherd of the Lake District. Thomas, her husband, was occupied out of doors chopping wood in a sheltered corner of the yard. He too was a hard worker who seldom was without something to do, and who lived only to provide for his helpmate and child. Both Molly and he were so busy that they did not check on the absence of the boy, who by now had reached the draw well. He must have stumbled against the cover, and as his weight pushed it aside, he fell feet first into the abyss, for such it was. The well was indeed twenty feet in depth and three to four in diameter. Stones, placed one on top of the other, paved its walls but there were a few that projected to help in descent or ascent. Thomas was first to the spot. He was crossing the yard for his whetstone when he was attracted by the uncovered well. As he was returning the cover, he heard a low moaning sound echoing from wall to wall. The truth of the reality struck him and jerking back the cover he began his dangerous descent holding tightly to the chain which chafed his roughened hands.

The rope that entwined the chain was rotten so his whole weight was borne by the chain. The man was seventy, hardly an active climber, but love gave him power and strength.

Just at that moment I entered the yard and as always went towards the well, which held a great attraction for me as it did for any child of nine. Imagine my amazement when I heard grunts and moans coming from the blackness below. I didn't delay. With a few bounds I was with Molly, gasping out my news. Without hesitation she too came running, calling down into chaos. She got a muffled answer and sensed immediately what had happened. We looked at each other in horror and disbelief, never dreaming that the child would be saved and hoping there would not be a double tragedy. 'Pray', she said, believing with her simple faith in the efficacy of a child's prayer. We waited, prayed and hoped. Eventually Thomas reached the top with his heavy and limp burden, to all appearances lifeless. We stretched down to receive the child and with difficulty managed to haul him over the brink. Molly held him to her heart and when her husband had joined us we all walked slowly and silently into the house. Bartholemew was stripped of his wet clothes, dried well and when wrapped in a cosy woollen blanket he had his first experience of the potency of brandy. Neither father nor son suffered any ill-effects and life continued for all three as before for many more years.

I vaguely remember being hustled home by our fussy housekeeper who warned me never to wander from home rambling through the wood or ... but this picture is dim in comparison with that other memory of an old man rescuing his angel-child and the joy of the woman at the happy escape of both.

GRATEFUL THOUGHTS

William Downey (b 1925)

Raheny, Dublin

My wife, sits in the lamplight, but busy as a bee.
Another garment knitted, for herself or maybe me.
Or maybe for a grandchild, there are some of them around,
She's keeping a watch on them, 'While their mother goes to town'.
For when this old house goes silent, now that we are on our own,
Things don't seem right, somehow, we don't like to be alone.

We miss the shouts and screeches, the whoops of kids at play,
So when they come to visit, that really makes our day.
Brings back to us, those days now passed, when from morning until
  night,
Our lives were filled with children's sounds, there was never peace
  and quiet.

'Oh.' The odd fight often broke out, but never lasted long,
My wife could always calm things, with a smile and verse of song.
She would sing to them the verses she had learned while still at school.
A quotation, from the Bible explaining how God rules.
How the world was full of wonders, if One took time to see.
Mistakes were always overlooked, except when made by me.

As I sit here and watch her, with her needles and her wool,
with her busy fingers moving,
I think, My God, she's good.
I thank Him for her presence for our health and family
For her children and their children are a sense of joy to me.

PROGRESS

Joseph Doyle (b 1935)

Dun Laoghaire, Dublin, 1990

He sat down in the his armchair thinking of the old times when he and his friends used to go fishing. The river that ran at the back of the cottages was a mecca for all his mates. Often they would go snaring rabbits or just have a nice chat while sitting on the parapet of the old stone bridge. The pub in the village with its open hearth fire held fond memories for him. Walking his dog through the fields were also happy times. The farm where he had worked for forty years, the little chapel and school were all part of his life.

He watched as they pulled down his world. The place he knew and where he had been born was all but gone. Bulldozers knocked down the old cottages as if they were made of paper. A new motorway ran through the farm where he had worked for so many years. Tall buildings rose up like monsters from the sea. New housing estates appeared like mushrooms in the early morning dew. Bridges spanned the new motorway like giant eagles' wings. Fast cars went by like the breeze. The old way of life was gone.

It was a new world for him. All his friends had moved away or were dead. He was staying in his cottage where he was born. They could build around him if they liked. He wasn't moving for anything or anybody. If they wanted his cottage they would have to knock it down on top of him. He rose from his chair and rubbed his eyes realising he had been dreaming. As he looked out the window he felt happy again. His little world was still there. The pub, school, chapel, river and the old bridge were intact. Everything was as it should be.

He knew it wouldn't be long before his dream was a reality. Maybe it was time for a change. Life had to go on. The old ways have to go sometimes. It seemed a pity that they should. He hoped it would be for the better.

MEMORIES OF FUNERALS AT NEWTOWN

Mamie McDermott (b 1916)

Cooley Peninsula, County Louth

Long ago, when a neighbour died all work stopped in the fields. People gathered at the home, to sympathise, to pray for the dead, to keep watch with the family until the funeral. Friends arrived from far-away places, for in our parish the word 'friend' apart from the usual meaning — meant a blood relation or marriage connection.

The following day men went to dig the grave at Newtown, always including one man who 'knew where the family buried'. They were usually fortified by a bottle of whiskey for, as there was no limit to the number of burials in any one plot, theirs was often a gruesome task.

The funeral took place the next day; the hearse, and the mourning coaches for the women, always drawn by black horses. The coffin was taken from the house, and placed on two chairs in the 'street'. The 'street' was the word for the space immediately in front of each house in our locality. When the coffin was placed in the hearse, the chairs were knocked over and left lying there — I don't know why.

The parish was divided by a lovely little stream, that rises in Mill's Bog and flows into the sea at Jemmy Smith's forge.

Offerings — a collection for Masses from the famine times were taken up at funerals on the Ravensdale side of this stream, not at those on the other side. Relatives contributed first, and gave the largest amount, then every one else present left an offering, the amount and the name was called by one of the men.

But we had 'one-up' on Lordship, for the priest thanked the congregation, sympathised again with the family and then spoke at length on the virtues of the Deceased. However, it was not in our parish that one widow whispered to her son after the sermon: 'Go up avic, and read the name on the coffin and see was it really your father he was talking about'.

The status of the family was judged by the total of the Offerings, the size of the gathering present, and the number of mourning coaches hired, but the local paper usually gave the same account for everybody: 'The Funeral was one of the largest seen in the district for years, showing the esteem in which the Deceased was held'.

If a poor neighbour died, who had no relatives left, some of the local men gathered money to pay the expenses of the funeral, including at least one Mourning Coach. I remember one such funeral when as children, May and Peggy McGee and myself — probably unknown to our mothers, got into the empty carriage and went part of the way for a ride. Then we got out and walked back stopping on our way home to watch the building of Dullaghan's new bungalow — a rare sight in Jenkinstown in those days.

It was a long hard walk to Newtown especially for the men, some of whom had been 'up' for the two night of the wake. The road is shorter now, as many corners have been cut off.

For centuries families have buried their dead at Newtown, long after the destruction of the chapel there. The surface was very uneven and it was a precarious job for the mourners to carry the coffin to its last resting place. There was a horrible sound of the first clods of mould falling, then the grave was quickly filled by many of the men present, changing places frequently, all wishing to show their respect for the family. Then long narrow rolls of grass, already cut, were unrolled and placed on the grave in the form of a cross. Whenall was finished one man would take out a penknife, and cut a nick in the shovels used, before placing them cross-wise on the ground. Again I don't know why.

Then everyone knelt and prayed silently. Many took the opportunity of going to graves of their own kin, and praying for them, for country people did not visit cemeteries as frequently as now-a-days. And as the mourners made their way home, I think the words of the Dublin poet Gogarty would express their thoughts:

> Our friends go with us as we go
> Down the long vale where all Beauty wends,
> Where all we love foregather, so . . .
> Why should we fear to join our friends?

The above contribution first appeared in the Lordship and Ballymascanlon Parish Yearbook 1988 - 89

BAWN FADA GRAVEYARD REVISITED

Nancy Power (b 1916)

Radestown, County Kilkenny

Have we left the lonely graves to badger, fox and hare?
Kinsfolk of the Dead no longer venture here.
Tall grass and weeds reach up to old mottled stone
Where once loved names by hands long still were hewn.

The path the mourners trod is now no more,
The lone pilgrim's way is marred by clods and crops and stone.
The rusty gate hangs loose where once the violets grew
That children plucked at Eastertide the lonely graves to strew.

This rugged place no longer fits the mould,
That calls for walks and marble smooth and cold.
No parish mass, no Council funds, this holy place befriends.
From marauders and despoilers Dear Lord I pray these graves defend.

I enclose a verse I wrote in sadness caused by the neglect of the old graveyard at Bawn Fada where my parents are buried. Repeated requests to the powers that be to look after this ancient place have fallen on deaf ears — so much for all this talk of 'Heritage'.

CURE FOR INSOMNIA

Eileen Tansey (1903 – 85)

Blackrock, County Dublin

Dedicated to Siobhán and Niamh

When they heard we were taking charge of two young grand-children while their parents were on a week's holiday, hitherto cheerful friends became prophets of doom. 'You don't know what you're letting yourselves in for', 'I wouldn't do it for a thousand pounds!', 'What! At your age? You must be mad!' I se-cretly considered that last remark in dubious taste. After all, I'm not THAT much of a dodderer — yet.

All the same, it was with mounting apprehension that we awaited the arrival of the little girls. The advent of the sixteen month old one didn't worry us so much, as she was still at the play-pen stage. But remote preparations for her three year old sister had to be made. These included the nailing on of wedges inside three kitchen cupboards that reached the floor. It meant that every time I wanted to get at cupboard number three, I had to begin at num-ber one and work forward, but at least it guaranteed the safety of my few bits of china, ornaments, carving knives, etc. After that a search had to be made for the door key of the room in which she was to sleep. We knew from previous experience that if she wasn't locked in she would be roaming around the house from dawn.

At six o'clock the first morning, I was awakened by a series of bangs on her door. These were followed by a silence which gradually grew ominous to my unpractised ear. What could she be doing? Was she strangling the other one? I was half way out of bed when the bangs began again, so I turned over for an uneasy doze. But it wasn't long until the thuds developed into a tattoo of kicks, accompanied by shouts of 'Let me out!' ... When I opened the door I found the culprit with two dresses half on, staggering around in a pair of stiletto-heeled shoes which her mother had left behind, and which had come in handy for waking us up. The younger one was placidly breakfasting on the insides of her teddy. They both greeted me with cries of joy and uplifted arms. It was the same every morning. And always made me forget that before the end of the day those cherubs would have turned into imps.

In the week's struggle to keep them intact, I had an average of half a dozen frights per day. The worst one was when I discovered the broken mirror of an old powder case in the young one's play pen. Feverishly, I picked up the pieces, fitted them back as in a jigsaw, and found one bit was missing. Up to that, her appetite for soap, paper and clay had seemed to do her no harm. But glass! My imagination had composed a telegram: 'Come back at once. Baby in Hospital', when the cat came to our aid by drinking the milk out of the saucer in which the missing splinter mysteriously lay!

Going to the shop was the highlight of the day. It took most of an hour to do the few hundred yards there and back. The younger one would make a beeline into every open gate along the way, and would sometimes stage a sit-down strike until coaxed to move by promises of ice-cream. Her sister would stare solemnly at any child we met, but would greet elderly men out exercising their dogs with smiling 'hellos'. The purpose of these, I found to my horror, was the extraction of pennies for lollipops. The only discordant note in our royal progress was the time she hailed the smart blonde from across the road as 'Other Grannie'.

My household chores piled up, neglected. Dressing, washing and feeding the two, soothing tantrums, bathing cut knees and bumps on heads, collecting toys from all over the place and bringing relays of drinks when they were finally safe in bed — a full- time job. I salute my young daughter-in-law and others like her who can do all those things as well as cook, bake, sew, mend, keep the house in order, entertain friends, and keep their sanity most of the time.

On the night after they had gone, I felt a pang as I reached for two things that had been forgotten for a week — my sleeping pill and the alarm clock.

A MOTHER'S DREAM

Belinda Downey (1907 – 88)

Ballina, CountyMayo

As I sit here by my window,
Dreaming of the past,
I think of my seven children,
Mary was the last.
The sad and happy moments
I spent here long ago,
They all come rushing back to me,
As I sit here in the glow.

I see the path around the door,
Where grass could never grow,
From the patter of seven pairs of
  feet,
Dear God I loved them so.
Some gave me joy,
Others gave me pain,

But even though through all their
  faults
I loved them just the same.

Some have married, some have
  gone
To lands across the sea,
I wonder do they ever sit
And think of home and me,
The moss is now on the path,
That once was kept so clear,
I think and grieve and pray for
  them,
and shed a silent tear.

POEMS

Teresa Dyas (b 1921)

Ballyfermot / Kimmage, Dublin

Enclosed please find two poems, one I wrote to console my family, when I thought I was going to die after I was told I had cancer, and the other poem I wrote a long time ago when I buried my first baby. This happened during the war when money was very scarce and the poem related to a lot of mothers who could not afford a grave for their babies.

TO ALL I LOVE

Remember me when you are
  glad,
Forget me if I make you sad,
All I wish is joy for you
Dying you know is nothing new.

Don't you cry when I'm not there
You know darn well I'm
  everywhere
Think of the tiny forget-me-not
Who struggles through that
  earthly plot

And greets the spring with bright
  blue eyes.
So lift your spirit to the skies

Don't be sad, I'll still be there
To help you with your every care.
All I want is to see you smile
For life is surely the shortest mile,
Don't waste a moment in despair
Find peace and hope in silent
  prayer.
(*Ballyfermot 1974*)

PATRICIA

It is often in the evening rush,
I see the robin and the thrush
Flying home to their warm nest,
it is then my conscience is put to
    test,
I wonder where my baby's lying,
once again I hear her crying,
And I again would all forsake,
if I could change a past mistake.
How many times I rue the day,
to think for her I couldn't pay
the ransom on a piece of clay.
Why didn't I my body take,
and sell it like a piece of cake
And place her in an ivory tower,
where I could spend a happy
    hour?
Then my reason starts debating,

think of what you'd have
    forsaken,
With whom would you have
    spent the hours,
with statue or perhaps with
    flowers?
Though her body lies in grave
    unknown,
her soul would have long since
    flown
And now in Heaven's golden
    tower,
where endless time knows no
    hour.
She has found eternal rest,
and smiles to know, you passed
    the test.
Kimmage, 1944

MY MA

Joseph Doyle (b 1933)

Dun Laoghaire, County Dublin

I could never understand her
And I had no da,
We lived for years together
Her name was my ma.

She was not a bad person
We just did not get along,
Everything I tried to do
She would say it was wrong.

As the years went on and on
We just seemed to drift away,
I do not know what happened
But we had nothing more to say.

If only she had said something
That would have drawn us
    together,
But she did not seem to give a
    damn
She was worse than the weather.

I never went to visit her
I had other things to do,
But when I went to see her
It was a case of having to.

It was too late when I saw her
She had already died,
I could have got to know her
If I had really tried.

MEMORIES

Larry Byrne (b 1928)

Aughavanagh, County Wicklow, May 1940

The Curlew's lonely cry I hear
Rain is drawing nigh I fear
And distant hills do now seem near
Across the brackish moorland mere.

While o'er the winding bogland stream
The silent crane its journey wends
In quest of trout and elvers sweet
To feed her young in their retreat.

The echoing call of the heather grouse
Does pierce the silence of her domain
As if in protest at the threatening rain
And to say to man. Go back. Go back.

While high above on yonder craggy
    ledge
The ever watchful stag surveys the glen
In fearful trepidation of the gunman's
    lust
To hunt his ilk into the dust.

The motherly hen along the lane does go
Hustling her brood through pip infested
    grass
Whilst overhead the hovering hawk
    awaits
The measured time to swoop and
    pounce.

Over underneath the ancient hawthorn
    tree
The forlorn donkey stands in silent
    melancholy
And shrouding hills that once seemed
    near
Now slowly slowly do disappear.

While most of life may be in gloom
At the thought of impending rain

Not so the ducks who view the rain
As a God-send to the dwindling drain.

That feeds the shrinking pond in yonder
    glade
They sally forth with quacks of ecstasy
And waddle off in sanguine style
Down towards the girdled wooded
    pond.

Of willow, sorrel, and cress and reed
They turn their heads from side to side
As if to harken thunder in the skies
From her covert the vixen observes all.

Unseen by all in the sheltered thicket
The wily vixen sniffs the downward
    wind
For she like all her young must feed
    today
If to fulfil her destiny in nature's way.

While o'er the pond the swallows skim
In quest of insects on the wing
For insects they must now fly low
In fear of Nimbus's impending show.

The farmer's wife hastily hurries forth
Her weekly washing to retrieve
From gorse bushes festooned in golden
    hue
That adorns the hidden rabbit warren.

She glances at the darking weather
Whilst muttering her female displeasure
At the unpredictable fickle weather
Blowing down from awful lovely
    Lugnaquilla

PEACE OF MIND

Theresa MacSweeney (b 1922)

Douglas Road, Cork, 1993

I am seventy-one years old and don't look on myself as elderly. It's all in the mind. I have very good health thanks be to God and a good sense of humour.

I reared a family of five boys and one girl. Most are married. I live alone. My late husband was very ill over ten years and I was glad to be able to look after him at home. My mother also lived with us and she lived to be eighty-seven. So maybe that is why I didn't get old. I hadn't time.

I learned to swim last year and play bridge a few years ago. This opened up a whole new circle of friends for me and we have a good time. I babysit for my grandchildren and accept all invitations to visit my three sons in England a few times a year. (They always send on the ticket). I have my widow's pension and peace of mind and contentment. I love my home and garden.

OLD PEOPLE IN SOCIETY TODAY

Bonnie Freyne (b 1925)

Ballyshannon, County Donegal 1940s / 1990s

Having had the experience of looking after old people over forty years ago it is interesting to compare the present-day care of our senior citizens to the late 40s.

Old people today are getting the care they deserve. Some are lucky to have their families to love and care for them and the State does its share. Free travel is a wonderful bonus and so many who would be lonely and housebound are free to travel and visit friends or go for a day's shopping to the town or city provided they live within a reasonable distance of bus or railway station. There is free electricity, TV licences and Senior Citizen parties and outings. The State pension for those eligible is quite good and Community Alert Areas in rural Ireland are very helpful and make us more thoughtful and concerned for each other — teenagers are encouraged to be aware of those living alone and asked to visit them which they do.

For those less fortunate who have to be admitted to geriatric homes, the treatment is excellent in Health Board homes. I have occasion to visit one quite often and even though they may be lonely and miss home they are well cared for, kept clean and neat, have occupational therapy, visits from hair dressers and chiropodists, good food, heat, library and TV if interested. For those who have to go to private homes it can be a big financial worry for the family as very few who have families have sufficient private means to maintain them indefinitely. Visits to the elderly are most important. The fact of feeling wanted and not forgotten means so much. A day out to visit friends or to go to a hotel for a meal for those who can appreciate it is essential. The fact of having to dress and put on something special, maybe a bit of jewellery or perfume for an elderly lady is a great uplift. Time to talk and more important to listen to any worries or anxieties they may have is so helpful to them.

There are Day Care centres where those who live alone or are in isolated areas are brought by bus once or twice a week to socialise with their own age group, enjoy a nice meal, bath, hair do (for women) do some crafts and a game of cards for both men and women.

Forty years ago as a young student nurse in Belfast — the nuns had a home for the elderly where we had to spend a certain period of our training — those poor old people had few comforts — there was more thought for the welfare of their souls than body or mind. They had daily Mass, Holy Communion, Devotions on Sundays. Radio only for Mass for those who could not go to the church in the home. They were kept clean and warm with very little variety of food, no community room to sit in or dining room, just sat by their bed sides and very often with not even a soft chair. Many of them never had a visitor or trip out, clothes were just old ones donated to the home, they were given snuff and tobacco once a week out of the pension money.

Thank God those days are GONE.

THE FORGOTTEN

Michael Gilligan (b 1928)

Limerick City

I sit here in this garden,
They say 'In sweet content'.
Under this chestnut tree,
Like a Gnome — an ornament.

There's no one comes to visit me,
My friends are gone, at Rest,
The few that's left, imprisoned,
In 'Homes', like me, depressed.

Thinking back to the 'Bad Old Days',
That we Old Folk called good,
When there were people, called
    Neighbours,
Who helped as Neighbours should.

When the sick, the old, the dying,
Had all at their beck and call
To sit with them, as they waited
For to hear Our Saviour's Call.

'Tis said, 'We have made 'Progress',
From those 'Bad Old Days',
No use looking back, 'tis over.
We now have better ways.

No one now is hungry.
We have come on a lot.'
Well, None in our Lane went hungry,
While there was a bit in a Neighbour's
    Pot.

Over half-Doors came a Greeting,
Every day of the week,
Where are those Greetings now,
From doors of Glass and Teak?

and half-Doors were seen all over
from 'The Pike', to 'Old John's Gate'.
From 'the Abbey', up to 'Vizes Fields',
'Careys Road' to 'Thomond Gate'

Over which they talked, and debated,
About every thing, 'This and that',
Old Woman, in Paisley shawl,
Old Man, in black felt hat.

But, those were the days of Honest
    people,
Who spoke without distortion,
Before 'Drunkards' became 'Alcoholics',
And Murder, mere, 'Abortion'.

So, it's time to lock Us away,
  We, who loved 'The Latin Mass'
And All, that was Good and Holy
For indeed, Our Day is past.

and, Our Children, that we so loved,
and gave education to,
Got on so well in Life,
Now look at what they do.

'You'll be grand out here, Such a lovely
    "Home"
Where "They", will look after You,
And have the very best of care,
Don't say we've got rid of you'.

They may come once a month,
  to pass an hour of 'Rain',
And talk of their Golf and 'Bridge', and
    such,
They add only to my pain.

They tell me about my Grandchildren,
'You'll be delighted for to hear,
Sailing and Tennis, Life's so Sweet,
They'll be out to see you Dear'.

And, the Young Ones, 'Boarding' in
    'College',
The 'Cost', so frightfully dear,

Glorified Orphanages, I call them,
When there's no one around to hear.

So, the Old and the Young are locked
    away,
In High Class Institutions.
To keep them at Home, t'would be a
    Bore.
A downright Bloody Nuisance.

Tho' rolling in Gold, would my children,
    if told
That the children they hold so dear,
Would one day grow cold, and when,
    their Parents are Old,
Would commit them, like me, in here.

And these 'Nursing Homes' are opening
All over the Country's face,
Where the Old are dumped and
    Forgotten
Don't you think it a horrid Disgrace?

So I sit here in this garden.
Under this chestnut tree.
Like a Gnome, a decoration.
'Please God, — COME-FOR-ME'.

Note: One line in the verse 'to spend an hour of rain' inspired the poem. A friend of mine was in the Hospice at Milford, here in Limerick (next door to the University). I was in the garden when the rain came, I thought to myself that this was an appropriate time to go and visit. I did, and asked in conversation to my sick friend, 'Do you have many visitors?' 'They come to pass an hour of rain', he said. I blushed as this is exactly what I did.

A 64 year-old, I was listening to your invitation to write to you (on the Gay Byrne Hour) this morning. I live with a brother and sister, none of us ever married and though very healthy Thank God, I, like the poet, can only 'Guess and Fear' for the future. My two relations are older than me. However, I keep lively, play bridge and chess, am a supervisor in our local Credit Union, attend all the rugby matches (we have three Limerick clubs in the top Division). Now though elderly I feel eighteen. I have submitted two short stories to RTE McManus short story competition.

Mícheál O Giollogáin

POEMS

Maureen Browne Mahony (b1901)

Glasnevin, Dublin

LIVE FOR TODAY

Wander along the bright path,
Not one that's dull and drear,
Think not of the aftermath,
You may have cause to fear.

This world can be a Heaven,
Let not each day slip by,
As if t'were something given
To contend with 'til you die.

Scheme not for the future
At the cost of present worth,
P'haps that planned out future,
May not be spent on earth.

Life is short — throw up the dice
And win just all you can,
E'en tho' sages give advice,
Plan your own salvation, man.
July 1926

AUTUMN

Dead leaves are falling softly
Summer's o'er
Bright days midst their foliage
Come no more.

'Tis said, trees revel in
Eternal youth
Not so mortals — years will
   prove
The painful truth.

Time rolls on — resembling trees
We do bloom
Then pathetically fade away
To the tomb.
October 1925

AT EIGHTY

'Tis hard to fancy that we'd be
At any Ball
And you and I
Jazzing and flirting alternately
At 80

'Tis hard to fancy that we'd join
In any sports
And you and I
Running and jumping alternately
At 80

'Tis hard to fancy that we'd ride
  By Pillion
And you and I
Bumping and screaming
   alternately
At 80

'Tis hard to fancy how our clothes
Would suit us
If you and I
Shortened and lengthened
   alternately
At 80

'Tis hard to fancy how our hair
Would hold out
If you and I
Bobbed and shingled alternately
At 80
May 1926

RETROSPECT

If I could look once more
Upon that calm sweet scene,
And linger there a little while
In peace serene
And see those things that
    brought me joy
So long ago,
The purple hills — the sheltered
    woods
With life aglow,
I feel all this would truly be
A wealth of happiness for me.

Yet were this wish of mine
    fulfilled
Of seeing again,
That dreamland of my younger
    hours,
Would it bring pain?
Time steals on — and the long
    years
Now gone between
Have changed perhaps the love I
    bore
For that fair scene,
Ah then 'tis best that I should be
Content within its memory.

PAULINE AND MICHAEL

Patricia Gibson (b 1926)

Dublin, 1992

They lay down to sleep,
The sky their roof,
Scanty clothes covering their
ill nourished bodies,
Slowly the cold claws of death
Crept silently over them,
They were found lying side by
    side,
Nobody wanted to know,
Let us hang our heads in shame.

Pauline and Michael were
    obvious in death,
Cameras clicked, their frozen
    bodies

Wheeled from the scene,
Appeared on our screens.
They did not want notoriety,
All they wanted was Love and
    Caring,
Let us hang our heads in shame.

A little Babe, born in a stable,
Under the stars,
2,000 years ago,
Pauline and Michael died
Under the same stars
2,000 years on.
Someone said 'Hypothermia',
No, we killed them.
Let us hang our heads in shame.

Dedicated to Pauline Leonard and Michael McNamara, whose bodies were found on waste ground in Benburb Street, Dublin. December 1992. R.I.P. I knew Pauline — I used to meet her on my way to the office, around the vicinity of Church Street. I attended her funeral.

THE FOUR SEASONS

Nancy Gray (b 1920)

I remember days in spring walking hand in hand with my beloved.
Dedicated to the memory of Paddy Gray (1901 – 81)

High above on every tree,
Branches filled with energy,
Fighting hard to burst out free,
Eager to display their finery,
While underneath in harmony,
Tiny tips of buds appeared,
To greet the golden rays of sun.

Summer days, when at last
their journey o'er nature showed
her glorious crown.
On every tree the leaves
  appeared,
To cover each with coats of
  varied hues.
While underneath on carpet
  green,
Caressed by the warm summer
  breeze,
Perfumed flowers danced to and
  fro.
And high above on every tree
Birds sing joyfully
In praise of God's unique
  tapestry.

Slowly on the Autumn breeze,

Each leaf from the trees gently
  floats away.
Some fall slowly to the ground,
To form a pattern of bronze and
  gold.
The flowers and birds have gone
  to sleep,
And await once more the Spring
  to greet.

Harsh the wind and cold the
  snow
The trees stretch up their arms.
Their icy fingers reaching high.
Now, stripped of all their finery,
Form skeleton figures against the
  wintry sky.

Now, each winter of my life,
As the seasons come and go
These sweet memories I recall.
Our love outlined in each
  summer rose
I know we'll meet again in
  'Paradise'
Where 'twill be Springtime
  evermore.

WOLFHOUND PRESS CLASSICS

FAMINE

Liam O'Flaherty

'The kind of truth that only a major writer of fiction is capable of portraying.' Anthony Burgess, *Irish Press*.

Famine is the story of three generations of the Kilmartin family set in the period of the Great Famine of the 1840s. A masterly historical novel.

THE IRISH FAMINE:
AN ILLUSTRATED HISTORY

Helen Litton

A concise history of the famine with quotes from first-hand accounts. Here are the people who tried to influence events — politicans like Peel, public servants like Trevelyan, Quaker relief workers, clergy and landlords, who wrestled with desperate need. This is the story of individuals — such as Denis McKennedy who died in Cork in 1848 because his wages were two weeks late.

FAMINE DIARY

Journey to a New World

Gerald Keegan

'Heartrending and powerful.' *Irish Times*

In 1847 Gerald Keegan was newly wed when he left County Sligo with his young bride to travel on a coffin ship to Canada. This is a fictionalised narrative by James Managan based on this nineteenth century diary.

These books are available from your local bookshop or from
WOLFHOUND PRESS
68 Mountjoy Square
Dublin 1 (Tel: 8740354 Fax: 8720207)